AF605894

AUSTERITY AND RESISTANCE

The Ontario Days of Action, 1995–1998

From December 1995 to summer 1998, Ontario witnessed eleven one-day general strikes and Days of Action across its major cities. These protests were sparked by the so-called 'Common Sense Revolution' associated with Conservative Premier Mike Harris, elected to office in 1995. Written during the twenty-fifth anniversary of this significant social movement, Austerity and Resistance aims to tell its story and draw lessons from it.

Paul Kellogg draws on his experiences as a former policy officer in the Government of Ontario and a journalist focused on social movements to offer a first-hand account of the challenges and contradictions of this era. He documents these tumultuous years, providing unique insights into how the social movement developed, shaped public consciousness, influenced policy, and impacted the lives of Ontario's political parties. The book explores how this understanding informs perceptions of neoliberalism in Ontario, arguing that Harris was wrong in his cuts to services, attacks on unions, and reductions in the public sector during the 1990s, a path that Conservative Premier Doug Ford appears to be repeating in the twenty-first century. Vividly illustrated, Austerity and Resistance tells the story of a significant social movement while drawing crucial lessons for today's political landscape.

PAUL KELLOGG is a professor in the Centre for Interdisciplinary Studies at Athabasca University.

Austerity and Resistance

The Ontario Days of Action, 1995–1998

PAUL KELLOGG

Original Illustrations by Markus Neal Humby

UNIVERSITY OF TORONTO PRESS
Toronto Buffalo London

Toronto Buffalo London
utppublishing.com
Printed in Canada

ISBN 978-1-4875-5662-4 (cloth) ISBN 978-1-4875-5665-5 (EPUB)
ISBN 978-1-4875-5663-1 (paper) ISBN 978-1-4875-5664-8 (PDF)

Library and Archives Canada Cataloguing in Publication
Names: Kellogg, Paul, 1955– author
Title: Austerity and resistance : the Ontario Days of Action, 1995–1998 / Paul Kellogg ; original illustrations by Markus Neal Humby.
Description: Includes bibliographical references and index.
Identifiers: Canadiana (print) 20250276011 | Canadiana (ebook) 20250276054 | ISBN 9781487556624 (cloth) | ISBN 9781487556631 (paper) | ISBN 9781487556648 (PDF) | ISBN 9781487556655 (EPUB)
Subjects: LCSH: Harris, Mike, 1945– | LCSH: Social movements – Ontario. | LCSH: Strikes and lockouts – Ontario. | LCSH: Neoliberalism – Ontario. | CSH: Ontario – Politics and government – 1995–2003.
Classification: LCC FC3078.2 .K45 2025 | DDC 971.3/04 – dc23

Cover design: Val Cooke
Front cover illustration by Markus Neal Humby

We wish to acknowledge the land on which the University of Toronto Press operates. This land is the traditional territory of the Wendat, the Anishnaabeg, the Haudenosaunee, the Métis, and the Mississaugas of the Credit First Nation.

University of Toronto Press acknowledges the financial support of the Government of Canada, the Canada Council for the Arts, and the Ontario Arts Council, an agency of the Government of Ontario, for its publishing activities.

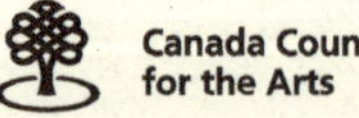

Funded by the Government of Canada | Financé par le gouvernement du Canada | Canada

Contents

Figures and Tables

Figures

Tables

Preface

From December 11, 1995, through all of 1996 and 1997, until coming to an end in the summer of 1998, 11 one-day general strikes and "Days of Action" were mounted in major cities throughout Ontario – Canada's biggest province and heart of its manufacturing sector. These protests were sparked by the so-called Common Sense Revolution (CSR) associated with Conservative Premier Mike Harris, elected to office in 1995. This book, written during the twenty-fifth anniversary of this great social movement, aims to tell its story and draw some lessons. Harris has long since passed from the political scene. But in 2018, the very conservative Doug Ford became premier of Ontario, was re-elected in 2022 and again in 2025, and he is reading from the same playbook as Harris, feeding the illusion that cuts to services, attacks on unions, and reductions in the public sector will be "good" for the people of the province. Harris was wrong about this in the 1990s, and Ford is equally wrong in the twenty-first century.

We do not have, as of this writing, a movement on the scale of the Days of Action to contest Ford's policies. But – there are echoes reminiscent of the earlier era. The struggles to defend health care and education were a central part of the Harris-era social movement. September 25, 2023, the Ontario Health Coalition (OHC) brought at least 5,000 people to Queen's Park to protest Ford policies leading to increased reliance on the private delivery of health care. OHC executive director Natalie Mehra said: "We want to send a very strong message … The Ford government has no mandate to privatize."[1] In December 2022, "Hundreds of teens from York Memorial Collegiate Institute staged a mass walkout to protest what they say is an unsafe learning environment, over-policing and a lack of teachers."[2] The biggest struggles in the Harris era were around labour rights. In November 2022, the Ford government was forced to repeal Bill 28, which had imposed a contract on 55,000 education workers "and banned them from walking off the job, while using the Charter's notwithstanding clause to shield the legislation from legal challenges."[3] According to Martin Regg Cohn, Ford had to back down because he "wasn't banking on labour leaders coming together from both private and public-sector unions to threaten a massive general strike over his suspension of collective bargaining rights."[4] Until the Days of Action, the phrase "general strike" was really not part of the political discourse in Ontario. Its presence in the Ford era is very much evidence of the collective memory of struggles from the Harris era.

A 2011 article I wrote on the origins of the Days of Action sketched out the original frame for this book.[5] The Canadian Association for Work and Labour Studies, the Canadian Political Science Association, Historical Materialism, Athabasca University's Arts and Science Research Speakers Series, and the British Sociological Association all provided me with opportunities over several years to workshop presentations of early versions of several of its chapters.[6] The bulk of the manuscript was completed in 2021 while on sabbatical from my teaching position at Athabasca University, and it relies on a mixed methodology, with four components.

Participant observation – After defending my doctoral thesis at Queen's University in 1990, I was hired as a policy officer in the Government of Ontario under New Democratic Party (NDP) Premier Bob Rae. From my position in the Cabinet Office, working on the NDP signature policy of delivering public auto insurance, I witnessed both the euphoria of enthusiastic young policymakers striving to make a difference in the lives of Ontario's citizens and the deep disillusion which took hold as the NDP slowly capitulated to heavy neoliberal pressures and abandoned this important reform. In a real sense, the climbdown from public auto insurance in 1991 was the direct precursor to the attack on public-sector unions in 1993, both playing a key role in demoralizing the electoral base of the NDP and laying the basis for the election of the Harris Tories. Following the defeat of the Rae government by the Harris Conservatives, and during the 1995 to 1998 Days of Action, I was a full-time journalist covering the movement against the Tories. Putting out a small newspaper every two weeks was an enormous effort for our very small staff (never more than three of us, sometimes only one), and we relied heavily on volunteer activist-journalists. From the "dress rehearsal" student strike in January 1995 until the calling off of the Days of Action in July of 1998, our little team produced eighty-four issues of the newspaper – 1,008 pages, roughly 1.2 million words – much of it focussed on the struggle against Mike Harris. My notes and original drafts for the articles printed in edited versions in those years exist in print form (367 of them for the period in question) in my personal archive. Where relevant, cited articles from this print archive have been posted to my website, *PolEconJournal*.[7]

Archival research – Two other archival collections proved to be important. First, the Canadian Auto Workers (CAW, today UNIFOR) produced a weekly newsletter, *Contact*. In 1995 the newsletter had been published for twenty-five years, and in the four years of the Days of Action, from 1995 until 1998, it published 170 issues, all of which I was able to locate and read. Given the CAW's central role in the Days of Action, this proved to be an invaluable resource, and unfortunately, copies of this newsletter are today quite difficult to obtain. I have relied extensively on *Contact* archives throughout. Second, while preparing for a 2012 presentation sponsored by my university, "Social Movements and Trade Unions in an Age of Austerity," I discovered an archive – the transcripts of testimonials delivered to a hearing on a controversial bill of the era – that became, as I read through it, more and more compelling. Here were the voices of Ontario – some in support of the Tories, the vast majority in angry opposition – articulating their concerns, fears, hopes, and dreams. These voices needed to be dusted off, pulled from the archives, and allowed to speak to a new generation confronting twenty-first-century versions of Mike Harris – which I tried to do in chapter 5 and in appendix 1.

Media coverage – In addition to the sources listed above and coverage in the major dailies, local newspapers were a rich source of material. In the years since, that source has become much less robust. September 2023 gave us a window into why that is the case. That month, Metroland Media Group announced it would seek bankruptcy protection. "The move means large swaths of Ontario are poised to lose their local papers and more than 600 employees are set to lose their jobs." Just days later in Quebec, Métro Média declared bankruptcy "permanently ending its coverage of local government in parts of the province's two largest cities."[8] It is twenty-five years since the Days of Action, and it is shocking to see just how much more extensive local coverage was in that period, compared to local coverage in daily newspapers in the internet era. That coverage of the Days of Action movement was indispensable.

Statistical discourse analysis – Statistics presented in a cursory way can sometimes hide more than they reveal. The modern reader will be aware of the "politics of numbers" after the years-long controversy over how many turned up to Donald Trump's first inauguration, and the even more bizarre and dangerous refusal to agree with the counting of ballots that elected Joe Biden as president. These number games were very much part of the politics around the Days of Action. In *Escape from the Staple Trap*, I introduced the term "Statistical Discourse Analysis" to describe a method of the careful and critical use of detailed tables and figures to "make visible the actual, not the imagined contours" of "facts" as they present themselves.[9] Throughout, I deploy Statistical Discourse Analysis to try and "look behind" statistics as they are generally given, to give new or more subtle insight into the issues at stake. After the chapters on the two biggest mobilizations of the movement – the Hamilton Days of Action in February 1996 and the Metro Toronto Days of Action in October of that year – I provide a "politics of numbers" sidebar with a detailed exploration of the manner with which the size of those events was misleadingly minimized.

One curious technical issue had to be addressed while researching this book. Some of my notes from the era were in paper form. But a good portion had been saved as computer files in the 1990s. I quickly discovered, when I returned to the research, that those files were, in the second decade of the twenty-first century, completely unreadable. However, up at our cabin at the United Jewish People's Order's Camp Naivelt, my old 1990s-era laptop was on loan to the Camp's children, who found it endlessly fascinating to use a relic from another century as a tool for composing poetry, screenplays, and other creative works. What had now become a children's toy still had loaded into its little hard drive the software required to read those old computer files, and with a little work, old files written in legacy versions of Word, Excel, Pagemaker (Adobe *and* Aldus) and Quark Express, slowly came back to life.

The outmoded technology which confronted my research can serve as a metaphor for the outmoded ideology that confronted Ontario in the 1990s, an outmoded ideology trying to force a modern society into frameworks from a mythical past. Every generation confronts politicians imprisoned by these kinds of outmoded ideologies – in our era Ford, but also Trump, Erdoğan, Putin – the list is long. Every generation also builds movements to resist those outmoded ideologies. Sometimes the activities of the activists who are the core of these movements seem a bit otherworldly. Gathering after work in small committee meetings that go on for hours. Writing leaflets (or nowadays, social media posts). Printing placards and organizing pickets. Sometimes it is not clear what the connection is between this often intense and sometimes fraught activity and the social and economic issues at stake.

In the chapter on Peterborough's Day of Action, I quote from an article by autoworkers' union leader Sam Gindin, where he describes a middle-aged observer articulating a sentiment often directed towards activists engaged in these "otherworldly" activities. Looking at that city's Day of Action demonstrators, the man asks: "What are they all doing here?" His middle-aged wife has a profound and quiet response. "They're here for us, George."[10] Her sentiment captured exactly the motivation of all genuine social movements, passionate campaigns for our generation and the next, and the social assistance, public health care, education, and childcare all of us require. The reason any of us write these books and participate in and try to understand movements such as the Days of Action is because of the generations which have gone before, as well as the generations to come. So, on that basis, I would like to dedicate this work to all of the next generation in my universe – whether nieces, nephews, children, or grandchildren, and all the partners thereof. I'll name just two – the one we tragically lost in 2019, my nephew Noah, and the little one who was born in April 2023, on what would have been Noah's birthday, my grandson Elijah. The rest of you know who you are. This book's for you.

– Mackenzie Paul Kellogg, Toronto, March 2024
Member, Athabasca University Faculty Association,
Canadian Freelance Union (Unifor) and
the Writers' Union of Canada

Acknowledgments

During the very big set of experiences which comprised the Days of Action social movement, I knew that a book on the subject was called for. However, it was only when I was hired to teach in the graduate program at Athabasca University in 2010 that I had the resources and support to bring the project to fruition. Financial assistance from an Athabasca University Research Incentive Grant made travel to archives possible, and several grants from Athabasca's Academic and Professional Research Fund supported presentation of this research at scholarly conferences. I used the resources at Athabasca's library extensively and received excellent professional assistance from the library's staff. A research affiliation with the University of Toronto allowed access to that university's unparalleled research facilities. The careful guidance of Daniel Quinlan at University of Toronto Press, the superb copy-editing of Perrin Lindelauf, and the detailed and professional work of Michel Pharand in preparing the index were indispensable. Working with Markus Neal Humby on the illustrations that accompany the book represented the renewal of an old partnership from our student days, when he illustrated the cover for the student handbook I edited. Then as now, his work is first-rate, and I look forward to many more collaborations in the future. As always, long conversations with Abbie Bakan helped shape much of the analysis. I had two children in school during the Days of Action, and I hope both Adam and Rachel recognize something of their experience in this text. Responsibility for the final product is, of course, mine alone.

AUSTERITY AND RESISTANCE

Introduction

From Coronation Park to Queen's Park

It was just before midnight, October 24, 1996. None of us were quite sure what was going to happen. Piling out of our cars, we approached trade unionists who were picketing Canada Post's South Central Letter Plant in Toronto, Ontario. The pickets were illegal, and most on the line wore some sort of disguise. A general strike to shut down Toronto – part of the "Days of Action" movement – had been called for Friday, October 25, a one-day strike to protest the austerity policies of the Mike Harris Conservatives. It was to be followed by a mass demonstration on Saturday. We had already seen some magnificent actions against the Conservatives. The first Day of Action, on a bitterly cold December 11, 1995, in London, Ontario, exceeded all our expectations. Thousands struck or stayed off the job. The movement had stopped next in Hamilton with a mass stay-away and an enormous demonstration, then travelled to Kitchener-Waterloo and Peterborough, all with large mobilizations, all with illegal one-day strikes.

But October 25 was different. This was Toronto, a city at the time of some three million people, the heart of the province, the capital. What would be the response to the call for a strike on Friday, October 25? What would be the response to the call for a mass demonstration on Saturday, October 26? Few had doubted the possibility of action in the old union stronghold of Hamilton, but Toronto? We got our answer just before midnight, October 24. A Toronto Transit Commission (TTC) driver – member of the Amalgamated Transit Union Local 113 – sat in his streetcar watching the pickets at the postal station. We went up to him and asked him what he was going to do. Would the TTC shut down? "I can't speak for everybody, but I tell you one thing. I'm not going to work, and the people I work with aren't going to work." We knew then there would be a general strike. Toronto would be shut down in the biggest one-day mass action in Canadian history.

The next day, at 8 a.m. on a sunny morning, a few friends and I made our way down to Coronation Park on Lake Ontario in downtown Toronto, preparing to join others in a march and rally on the second day of Toronto's Days of Action. There were many I expected to meet in the park – union and social movement activists who had put their backs into building an anti-Tory movement, what became the three-year-long "Days of Action."

I didn't expect to meet my teenage niece. But there she was, waving to me as she got off a bus from her home in Northumberland County, arriving in Toronto to join the demonstration. I ran up and gave her a hug; she went off to carry placards and demonstrate with her friends. I then realized that we were going to see something magnificent in Toronto on that day. When a call for action from the megacity is answered by young people from the county, then we have a mass movement on our hands. And on those two days in 1996 – the Metro Toronto Days of Action – the movement *really* was mass, a movement challenging what was euphemistically called the "Common Sense Revolution." On Friday as many as one million stayed away from work. The streets of Toronto were silent – except for the chants of picketers and protesters. On Saturday a massive crowd of at least a quarter of a million wound its way through the streets of Toronto, past the Convention Centre where the Conservatives were holding (another) policy convention, a sea of humanity – workers, students, the unemployed – expressing their outrage against the Conservative attacks, flexing their muscles, feeling their power. That day, everything seemed possible. Many expected Toronto to be a springboard from which to launch a province-wide strike against the Common Sense Revolution. But Thursday, November 7, 1996 – just days after the magnificent Toronto protest – the heads of thirteen unions – led by the so-called pink paper group – announced they were pulling out of the protests.[1] Instead of using the Toronto strike as a springboard to build momentum on the ground, they chose to put all their eggs in the basket of working to re-elect the NDP.

Despite this divide in the union movement, there would be six more Days of Action – none, however, with the numbers and militancy of London, Hamilton, or Toronto. The resulting disorientation in the Ontario Federation of Labour (OFL) left it unprepared when a new front emerged in the fall of 1997: the massive, angry, and enormously popular two-week illegal strike by Ontario teachers. That strike reignited calls for a province-wide general strike, inspiring delegates to the OFL biennial convention to vote overwhelmingly in November 1997 to mandate their leaders to set a date for such a strike within the year.[2]

But the call never came. July 27, 1998, at a meeting of heads of unions at OFL headquarters in Toronto, Ontario's labour leaders called the movement off.[3] The issue of a province-wide strike wasn't even put on the table. Not one leader of one major union – not of the left or the right – was willing to put forward a motion to set a date for a province-wide strike.[4] The anti-Tory movement continued, but a bitter taste was left in the mouths of many activists, whose expectations had been raised so high. The great, generalized actions of the general strike movement were replaced by more fragmented, local struggles. In calling off the Days of Action, the OFL heads of unions argued that this would better prepare them to challenge the Tories electorally. But in the wake of their decision, support for the Tories slowly increased, resulting in the party's re-election in 1999.

More than a decade ago, I suggested that there were three moments when an alternative was possible – three watershed moments, where the Days of Action movement could have been the springboard for a breakthrough in the fight against the Tories, perhaps even to a wider, province-wide general strike[5] – and that analysis still seems accurate. The first such moment was the Hamilton Days of Action, February 23 and 24, 1996, which occurred just hours before the launch of a massive strike against the Tories under the banner of the Ontario Public Service Employees Union (OPSEU). Simply because of its enormous scale, the Toronto outpouring in October 1996 was the second. Finally, the third and most significant moment was without question the two-week illegal teachers' strike, from October 27 to November 7, 1997 – extremely popular with students and parents. That strike posed in thousands of activists' minds the need for and possibility of mounting solidarity strikes to (a) ensure victory for the teachers and (b) bring wider layers into the struggle against austerity and against the Tories.

We got an insight into why such a step was not taken, and why these three opportunities were missed, in a revealing end-of-term interview with OFL head Gord Wilson. In November 1997 – after the return to work of the teachers, and towards the end of the Days of Action – Wilson, about to step down after eleven years as president, spoke with the *Toronto Star*'s Ian Urquhart.

> Gord Wilson believes strikes may have outlived their usefulness. "In most cases, the picket line doesn't work any more, except as a morale booster," said Wilson ... He was quick to add a qualifier ... He believes *political* strikes designed to force changes in government policy, such as the one just engaged in by the teachers, can be effective ... although he doubts most Ontario workers are ready for such collective action. But in most *industrial*

disputes, Wilson thinks strikes no longer produce the desired result and labour must look for new ways to achieve its aims.[6]

I would suggest that the contrast to be painted should not be the one Wilson draws, between "industrial" and "political" strikes, but rather one drawn more than a century ago by the great socialist theorist Rosa Luxemburg. In her magnificent analysis of the Polish, Russian, and German workers' movement during the 1905 revolution, she, like Wilson, contrasted different types of strikes. But for Luxemburg, the contrast was between "demonstration strikes" and "fighting strikes." The former we had in quantity from 1995 to 1998 – the formal, mass protests "begun and ended after a cut and dried plan, a short single act of one variety."[7] She argued that the great mistake of social democracy (the official movement leaders in her day) at the time was to assume that this form of mass strike was the highest possible achievement of the movement because it was "carried out by the decision of the highest committees and furnished with a plan and panorama."[8] The truth, she argued, was just the opposite. These "demonstration strikes" were the beginning of the movement, not the end of it. The most profound expressions of the movement "were not demonstration strikes but fighting strikes, and as such they originated, for the most part, spontaneously, in every case from specific local accidental causes, without plan or design, and grew with elemental power into great movements."[9] The OPSEU strike of 1996 and the teachers' strike of 1997 don't exactly fit the picture being painted here by Luxemburg. But if not precisely the same, they both contained elements of the "fighting strike" she describes. The teachers' strike in particular, exhibited the "elemental power" of an angry section of the mobilized working class, and both clearly posed the possibility of a strike action by one section of the working class developing into a great movement of the class as a whole. The importance of these kinds of fighting strikes was precisely what Ontario union leaders could not or would not see.

In April 2011, while presenting an early version of this research at the annual meeting of the British Sociological Association, I took advantage of being at the London School of Economics to arrange a meeting with respected industrial relations scholar Richard Hyman, a professor at that university. I brought with me a tattered copy of his 1971 pamphlet, *Marxism and the Sociology of Trade Unionism.*[10] The analysis of the trade union bureaucracy developed in that work, and the exploration of alternatives to bureaucratism, whether in the British shop stewards' committees or the Italian "internal commissions," had deeply influenced my research into the workers' movement. After I made these observations, Hyman gave me a quizzical look and said, "Have you read my 1979 follow-up article?" I had not, but soon did. In it, he argues: "It has long been common to discuss internal political relations within unions in terms of a dichotomy between 'bureaucracy' and 'rank and file' ... Not infrequently, such a perspective has involved a somewhat idealised and romanticised conception of shopfloor organisation and action."[11] He pointed out that it was "the Red International of Labour Unions, which in the 1920s turned the three words 'trade union bureaucracy' into an incantatory epithet."[12] That is a cautionary tale for those who know the history of the RILU – an ill-conceived attempt to establish "Red" unions, organized separately from the mainstream workers' movement – an attempt which inevitably ended badly.[13] With this cautionary tale in mind, I have tried to avoid painting a too simplistic binary of "bureaucracy" versus "rank and file" and let a theoretical frame emerge from a careful recounting of the events as they happened.

After sketching the social, economic, and political stage of Ontario from the mid-1980s to the mid-1990s, the book will trace the origins of the Days of Action movement – an understanding of which cannot be arrived at simply from the standpoint of the institutional history of trade unions, but which must take the more difficult road that follows the evolution of mass consciousness, and the impact of grassroots organizing by some well-known, and some not-so-well-known individuals and groups. Second, the book will give an insight into the deep roots of the anti-Tory movement through an in-depth examination of the extraordinary hearings held across Ontario to what some called the "Bully Bill" – an omnibus bill that codified many of the key cutbacks and deregulation policies of the Common Sense Revolution. Third, the book will tell the story of the three high points and three lost opportunities – Hamilton in February of 1996, Toronto in October of 1996, and the great illegal teachers' strike of 1997. Throughout, the book will examine the tensions at the top of the movement, including the special role of the CAW and the Canadian Union of Public Employees (CUPE) in encouraging the movement, as well as the "pink paper" pessimism that divided the movement. Finally, the book will conclude with an attempt to draw some lessons for the future (and perhaps the present). In the spirit of Rosa Luxemburg, who ascribed importance to both elections and mass strike movements, the Days of Action movement can be seen as an example of "social movement electoralism" – a movement on the streets in a symbiotic relationship with parties and politics. In the spirit of E.P. Thompson and G.E.M. de Ste. Croix, who both insisted that "classes make themselves," the Days of Action were without question an important marker in class formation in the province of Ontario.

Chapter One

Contours of Politics, 1985–1995

In the twenty-first century, Alberta has become the centre of conservatism in Canada. For most of the twentieth century, it was the province of Ontario that played that role. From the election of George Drew as premier in 1943, to the defeat of Frank Miller in 1985, Conservatives controlled the Ontario Legislative Assembly – an unbroken forty-two years of one-party rule in the province. Frequently, the Conservatives ruled with not just majorities, but crushing majorities. In 1981, Premier Bill Davis had a seventy-member caucus, facing thirty-three Liberals and twenty-one members of the NDP. In 1971, John Robarts's caucus had seventy-eight members as opposed to twenty for the Liberals and nineteen for the NDP. Go back to 1951, and the seventy-nine Conservative members faced just seven Liberals and two members of the Cooperative Commonwealth Federation (CCF – predecessor to the NDP).[1]

The monolith cracked in 1985. After winning four consecutive majorities, Bill Davis stepped aside, replaced by Frank Miller as premier. In the general election, Miller's Conservatives won a plurality, but not a majority. Together, the Liberals' forty-eight seats and the NDP's twenty-five could out-vote the fifty-two Conservatives. David Peterson's Liberals and the NDP – led by Bob Rae – signed an accord, whereby the twenty-five NDP members agreed to support the forty-eight Liberals, provided an agreed-upon legislative agenda was adhered to. The accord lasted two years, and suddenly Conservative Ontario was confronted with an activist and very non-Conservative government. Over a two-year period, the accord resulted in 117 bills including:

- protection for renters through new rent control provisions
- protection for access to health care by ending extra billing by the province's doctors
- protection for women in the workforce through pay equity legislation[2]

When Peterson called a snap election in 1987, he was rewarded for this activist agenda with 95 seats in the 130-seat legislature, the humiliated Conservatives seeing their popular vote drop by 400,000, relegated to third place with just sixteen seats. When Peterson set an early date for a general election after just three years, looking to consolidate that majority, he saw little threat from the much-reduced Conservatives – now led by an obscure former golf course manager named Mike Harris – not to speak of the social democratic NDP. Steve Paikin relates a conversation with then attorney general Ian Scott as the campaign got underway. "He assured me that while the voters might be cranky at the moment, they ultimately would hold their noses and re-elect the Liberals. After all, he added, 'They're not going to vote for Mike Harris, and what are they going to do – vote NDP?'"[3]

But that is precisely what "they" did. Bob Rae's NDP won 1.5 million votes, 200,000 more than Peterson's Liberals, half a million more than Mike Harris's Conservatives, and with seventy-four seats to the Liberals' thirty-six and the Conservatives' twenty, Ontario had its first social democratic government. In 1985, when David Peterson was sworn into office, ending more than three decades of unbroken Tory rule, he held the ceremony "on the front steps of the Legislature at noon. The party had taken out newspaper ads inviting the public to attend the ceremony in an effort to show how open the new government intends to be."[4] The swearing-in of Bob Rae's NDP government was on a whole different scale. It was held in the cavernous Convocation Hall at the University of Toronto. Rae and his new cabinet were met by two thousand cheering trade unionists and social activists, "many weeping unashamedly, too choked up to utter a word if [their] lives depended on it."[5]

However, majority in the legislature did not mean majority support from the population. Ontario, like the rest of Canada, uses a first-past-the-post system, and Rae's majority came from just 37.6 per cent of the vote, considerably ahead of the Conservatives' 23.5 per cent, but just 5 per cent in front of the Liberals' 32.4 per cent. It was in 1971 that eighteen-year-olds were first able to cast a vote in an Ontario provincial election, and in that year, 73 per cent of registered voters in Ontario cast a ballot. That figure has been declining ever since, to a shocking low of just 43.8 per cent in the 2022 provincial election, increasing only slightly to 45.4% in 2025. A majority victory based on declining electoral participation indicates a shallower base of support for the governing party. Figure 1 tries to capture this, showing the depth of support for the victorious party at the time of each general election from 1971 to 2025, the depth being calculated by representing their popular vote as a percentage of registered voters in the province.

Figure 1.1. Depth of Support for Governing Party, Ontario, 1971–2022.

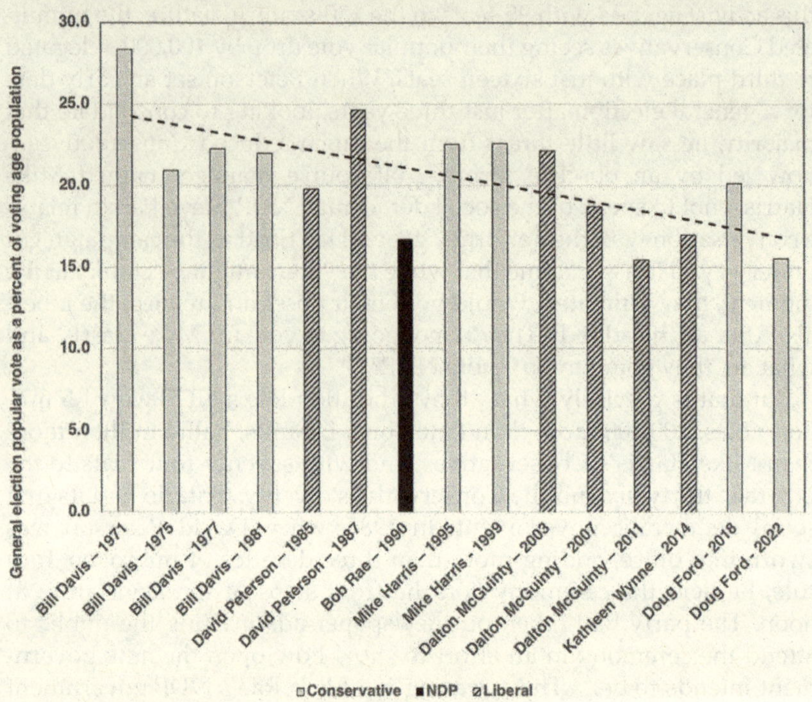

Author's calculations, based on data from Elections Ontario.[6]

Each premier is listed for every election year in the half-century of elections represented here, the eight Conservative victories shown in grey, the one NDP victory in black, and the six Liberal victories with stripes. The trendline, superimposed on the results, clearly reveals a half-century slide in the depth of support for winners of election in Ontario. Bill Davis in 1971 recorded votes on election day representing 32.5 per cent of registered voters. Of note for contemporary readers: the shallowest level of support for any victorious party in any election, is the 17.9 per cent registered by Doug Ford's Conservatives in 2022. David Peterson in his landslide of 1987 came closest to the 1971 figure, his vote representing 29.5 per cent of registered voters. But the fragility of Bob Rae's majority stands out sharply, with the NDP vote in 1990 representing 23.9 per cent of registered voters, a much shallower base of support than Bill Davis had in 1971, and an early warning sign of potential instability to come.

Image 1.1. Bob Rae, NDP premier of Ontario, 1990–5.

Rae and Recession

The surprise NDP victory in 1990 coincided with what many called the worst recession since the 1930s.[7] This was a bit hyperbolic. The recession of the early 1980s had been very similar, both in its depth and duration, with unemployment jumping into double digits in July 1982, peaking at 12.9 per cent in January 1983, and staying around 10 per cent until March 1984.[8] However, the recession which began in 1990 *was* severe – and sudden. Before the election, Liberal Finance Minister Bob Nixon had boasted that his government had achieved the first balanced budget in twenty years. But when the election rolled around in September 1990, "there were 107,000 fewer Ontarians employed than at the beginning of the year. By the spring of 1992, a total of more than 330,000 jobs would disappear."[9] The surplus of which Nixon had boasted turned out in reality to be a $2 billion deficit, and much larger deficits were inevitable, as tax receipts for the government collapsed in the wake of growing unemployment,[10] unemployment driven by tens of thousands of layoffs in Ontario's manufacturing sector.

The Rae government's first response was an "Anti-Recession Program" – deploying a cautious quasi-Keynesian approach to the economic downturn – refusing to cut spending, letting spending increase by close to $1 billion, and letting the budget deficit drift upward to $9.7 billion.[11] The latter – the increasing deficit – gave fuel to the NDP's Conservative Party critics. The former – the cautious "anti-recession" measures – could not prevent the recession deepening and unemployment increasing at a sickening pace. In September, the month of the NDP victory, unemployment in the province had drifted upward to 5.9 per cent, from 4.3 per cent one year previous. By March 1991, it had soared to 11 per cent and stayed in double digits until May 1994.[12] This catastrophe for the unemployed in search of work was simultaneously a catastrophe for governments in search of revenues, dependent as they were on income tax.

In the shadow of this ominous economic and fiscal crisis, the NDP proceeded to unroll its reform agenda, including the strengthening of pay equity, improvements to employment standards, improvements to parental leave, and raising the minimum wage.[13] Preceding all of these was the attempt to implement a promise made in the 1990 election – to replace private delivery of automobile insurance with a public auto insurance company. In many important ways, the fate of that reform set the tone for the entire Rae administration.

In the mid-1980s, an insurance crisis had arisen throughout North America. In Ontario, "municipalities, school boards, day care centers, taverns and even the national ski team were told that their premiums would go up by 500 percent ... At the same time, motorists saw their premiums double and triple."[14] The David Peterson Liberals said during the election campaign of 1987 – a campaign which gave them a majority government – that they had a plan to hold down premiums by implementing a partial "no-fault" approach to auto insurance, considerably restricting the right to sue in exchange for greater certainty when it came to compensation by insurance for damages, injuries, and lost income. The controversial new law, which came into effect June 22, 1990, saw more than 90 per cent of drivers lose their right to sue in the event of an accident. "Instead, they will receive compensation for lost income up to a maximum of $600 a week. Those requiring rehabilitation and long-term care are also eligible for supplementary benefits."[15] According to the Liberals, without this reform, premiums were slated to rise by 30 to 35 per cent a year. With their "partial no-fault" approach, premium increases could be limited to 8 per cent.[16] What the Liberals wouldn't address was the waste and inefficiency built into private delivery of insurance of any kind, not to speak of the extra costs pushed onto consumers by the profit motive typical of any business in the private sector. Bob Rae's new majority government, elected September 6, 1990, promised to address this by implementing a driver-owned public auto insurance company.[17]

However, the contradictions of the NDP approach were evident from the person Rae chose to oversee the proposed public automobile insurance reforms, Welland Member of Provincial Parliament (MPP) Peter Kormos. While an eloquent critic of the private auto insurance industry and a strong advocate of public auto, Kormos was also a former criminal lawyer and was committed to expanding the "right to sue," which he saw as being taken away from Ontario drivers by the Peterson Liberals. When the Liberals put forward their plan to limit the right to sue, Kormos said "I'm not happy at all," arguing "that the conditions placed on the ability of accident victims to sue are vague and would rob people of their right to seek full compensation through litigation."[18] Kormos was committed to a hybrid approach – public auto insurance with an expanded right to sue beyond that allowed by the Liberal government. The other policy officers and I, working for the Rae government's "Automobile Insurance Review" (AIR) team, were confronted from day one with the difficulties this posed in attempting to outline the contours of the new public automobile insurance corporation. On the one hand, it was quite easy to demonstrate the efficiencies and cost-savings possible by eliminating the profit motive and duplication of effort endemic to the private delivery of insurance. However, those cost-savings were considerably lessened by the commitment to expanding access to the courts – an always time-consuming and expensive proposition. This contradiction muted the promised cost-savings the NDP had touted in the election campaigns of 1987 and 1990. The resulting compromise approach left the Rae government vulnerable to a campaign from the Insurance Bureau of Canada arguing that moving to public auto and eliminating private delivery of insurance would lead to the loss of four thousand jobs.[19] That campaign moved from rhetoric to action in August 1991, when five thousand mostly women clerical workers, "carrying signs reading 'No pink slips, please' and 'Don't take my job,'" demonstrated at Speakers' Corner, Nathan Phillips Square in Toronto. Most labour demonstrations feature speakers from the union movement. This demonstration featured speakers from business – including "Judy Maddocks, a manager at Royal Insurance Canada" and "Kathleen Smith, a data security executive at State Farm." Speakers at the rally highlighted new research that indicated that the potential job losses involved in the shift from private to public auto would be not four thousand but as high as ten thousand.[20] The NDP blinked, public auto insurance was shelved, and business opposition to the Rae agenda was emboldened.

While the hybrid approach of Kormos did not help the cause of public auto, it was by no means the principal reason for the NDP climb-down on public auto. The 1991 "pro-labour" stance of the insurance industry in its opposition to public auto insurance might have been gaslighting, but it was also the first salvo of a "social movement from the right," which the NDP was simply unprepared to challenge. The year 1992 revealed the real contours of this social movement from the right – business fear of pro-labour legislation. A business lobby cohered around the Ontario Chamber of Commerce, the Canadian Federation of Independent Business, large auto, insurance, and other corporations. Far from positioning themselves as defenders of jobs, they felt threatened by what Rachlis and Wolfe labelled "the most advanced labour-relations regime in North America."[21] In 1992, the NDP government tabled Bill 40. Nicknamed fondly by many in the labour movement as the anti-scab bill because of its most prominent provision – outlawing, during a labour dispute, the use of replacement workers (otherwise called strike-breakers or scabs), the bill also allowed for, among other things: the continuation of benefits for workers on strike, automatic access to first-contract arbitration, and the right to picket on private property where the public normally has access (i.e., shopping malls).[22]

Not only was the NDP government unprepared to challenge this opposition from the right, but they were also unprepared to maintain their opposition to the neoliberal discourse on deficits, cutbacks, and austerity. The year 1992 was not just a year in which the NDP rolled out pro-labour reforms, it was also the year in which the deficit soared to $10 billion. Rae and his finance minister, Floyd Laughren, were committed to capping it there and then bringing it down. They feared that continued high deficits would worsen Ontario's credit rating, discourage foreign investment, and worsen an already bad economy.[23] Rae and Laughren led a pivot away from the mild Keynesianism of their first year in office and towards a kind of fiscal conservatism, proposing a mix of tax increases and spending cuts totalling $8 billion. Thomas Walkom called the plan "the largest single cut-back made by any Canadian government up to that point. Even the deficit-conscious Mulroney Conservatives had never taken that much out of the Canadian economy."[24] It was clear to everyone that public-sector jobs were on the line – and that there would be harsh implications for public-sector wages.

This new reality expressed itself first in negotiations with OPSEU in 1991, continuing into early 1992. In the context of the soaring deficit, government negotiators wanted to link pay increases to staffing levels – any increase in wages to be accompanied by a reduction in jobs. OPSEU president Fred Upshaw compared the NDP bargaining position to that of Mulroney, who had similarly argued that any 1 per cent gain in wages for federal civil servants, members of the Public Service Alliance of Canada, had to be accompanied by two thousand layoffs.[25] The issue came to a head on November 26, 1991, at the biennial convention of the OFL. Rae and his entire caucus came to meet with an organization that had, arguably, been the NDP's closest ally in its election victory the year before. As Rae made his way to the podium for a scheduled speech, between 200 and 300 delegates pointedly walked out – 170 OPSEU delegates, joined by "a sizable number" of PSAC [Public Service Alliance of Canada] members and some members of the Canadian Union of Postal Workers.[26] Virginia Galt characterizes the walkout as being led by Upshaw.[27] David Rapaport paints a different picture. He says that the opposition to Rae appearing at the convention came from OPSEU delegates "who raised the question about 'our boss' coming to a labour convention." Rapaport says that "Upshaw managed to cool them down, but he was not prepared for a motion urging the OPSEU delegation to protest ... by walking out when the NDP leadership appeared. We walked."[28] If Upshaw was at the front of the walkout, he was running to the front of a movement he did not control.

As the 300 walked out, they were booed by some of the remaining 1,200 delegates – and Rae when he appeared at the podium received a standing ovation to chants of "Bob, Bob, Bob."[29] Militant postal union leader Jean Claude Parrot, while defending the right of OPSEU and its allies to engage in a protest action and criticizing those who booed them, himself stayed in the convention hall with the majority.[30]

A Movement Divided

The internal politics of OPSEU were one aspect of a confused, bitter divide that had begun to split the labour movement, a divide with multiple dimensions. The biggest, most visible divide was the tension between the public-sector workers who had led the walkout versus the largely private-sector union delegates who stayed to give Rae a standing ovation, a tension which was openly expressed by some[31] and "simmered throughout other convention debates – occasionally erupting into open hostility."[32] Private-sector union delegates – whose industries were bearing the brunt of the hundreds of thousands of layoffs – were resentful towards what they saw as a public sector that was relatively insulated from the pain of the recession. This was a harbinger of divides to come in the years ahead – think Doug Ford's "gold-plated pensions" argument in our era.[33]

In the end, the OPSEU negotiations came to a successful conclusion just two months later, where, in fact, wages were traded for job security, "a conscious trade" according to Ron Elliot, chair of the negotiating team.[34] This too, was to be a harbinger of future developments, the direct precursor to the huge controversy over the Social Contract. Health care workers in British Columbia – a province also facing high unemployment and a fiscal crisis – "had been negotiating what they called a 'social contract' to preserve jobs and wages." In 1992, CUPE representatives in Ontario had suggested a similar approach – which Health Minister Frances Lankin supported, but who was, according to Thomas Walkom, "unwilling to bring it to cabinet for fear of interfering in collective bargaining."[35] One year later, there was no such trepidation. With a goal of saving $2 billion a year for three years from public-sector wages as part of their war on the deficit, the NDP advanced a Social Contract similar to BC's, which traded wages for job security. There was one, enormous difference – Rae and the NDP were doing this outside the regular collective bargaining process. The Social Contract legislation, Bill 48, passed into law in 1993, gave the province the authority to, in Sid Ryan's words, "rip open signed collective agreements."[36] In passing that legislation, Rae also accelerated the ripping apart of the Ontario labour movement. The contracts in question were public-sector contracts, and understandably the unions most infuriated by the legislation were the public-sector unions, including Sid Ryan's CUPE as well as the provincial workers organized in OPSEU. They were joined in their opposition to the legislation by one very important private-sector union, Buzz Hargrove's CAW.

And in fact, the promise of the Social Contract, to protect jobs at the expense of wages, was a promise unfulfilled. Rae's successor, Mike Harris, became known as the person who massively cut employment in the Ontario public sector. However, the downsizing of the public sector very much began under Rae with the Social Contract. Between 1990 (the first year of the Bob Rae NDP government) and 2002 (the last year of the Mike Harris Conservative government), employment in the Ontario Public Service (OPS) declined from 106,873 to 88,102, representing public-sector job losses of 18,771.[37]

However, left there, the picture is misleading. Table 1.1 breaks the figures down into annual totals and then divides the results into two portions – one for the Bob Rae years (October 1, 1990, to June 26, 1995),

Table 1.1. Provincial Government Employment, Ontario, 1990–2002

Premier Bob Rae			Premier Mike Harris		
	Average Employment Level	Year on Year Change		Average Employment Level	Year on Year Change
1990 (Oct.–Dec.)	104,965		**1995 (Jul.–Dec.)**	101,842	
1991	108,762	3,797	**1996**	95,366	(6,475)
1992	108,231	(531)	**1997**	91,730	(3,636)
1993	104,617	(3,614)	**1998**	87,836	(3,894)
1994	101,796	(2,821)	**1999**	88,550	715
1995 (Jan.-Jun.)	99,777	(2019)	**2000**	88,926	376
			2001	87,194	(1,732)
			2002 (Jan.–May)	85,362	(1,832)
Total job losses under Rae		(5,189)	**Total job losses under Harris**		(16,480)

Author's compilation from data in Statistics Canada.[38] Averages exclude months where there were strikes.

and the other for the Mike Harris years (June 26, 1995 to April 14, 2002). The results are revealing. While Mike Harris did oversee a steep reduction in public-sector employment – reducing the size of the OPS by 16,480 during his time in office – earlier, Bob Rae's government had seen a reduction in the OPS of 5,189.

Years after the Social Contract controversy, it is difficult to convey just how deep the divide in the movement was at the time – between unions and the NDP, and within the union movement itself. In June 1993, after two months of negotiations, OPSEU and other public-sector unions walked out of negotiations with the NDP. The day before, "rank and file unionists invaded the Social Contract talks at the Royal York Hotel in Toronto." One of those involved in that protest called it "a moment in history."

> It was so emotional. We were singing "Solidarity Forever" and "We Shall Overcome." People were hugging each other – even old enemies. It was crucial that the rank and file was in the room, to put pressure on our leadership. I kept standing up to catch the president's (Fred Upshaw) eye, to remind him that the rank and file were there. I thought all along that [they] shouldn't have been at the table in the first place. They should have just freaked right off![39]

In protest against the ripping of collective agreements and the imposition of the Social Contract, Ryan and Hargrove resigned from Rae's Labour/Management Advisory Council. Julie Davis, at the time secretary-treasurer of the OFL, resigned as president of the Ontario NDP. According to Ryan: "Her resignation must have been a huge personal blow to Bob Rae because she co-chaired his victorious 1990 election campaign."[40] The divide which had appeared first at the OFL in November 1991 was now to deepen – on one side a section of the union movement, public sector plus the CAW, furious with the NDP; on the other, most of the private-sector unions and a handful in the public sector remaining loyal to the NDP. The divide was so big that someone as prominent as the late Jack Layton announced from a public podium in November of 1993 that he would never again run as a member of the NDP,[41] an extraordinary statement from someone who would years later go on to become the enormously popular leader of the federal NDP, leading it to its greatest ever success at the polls.

At the November 1993 OFL convention, the executive board put on the floor a motion to withdraw support from the NDP in the next election unless Rae and his government repealed Bill 48. In support were 1,000 delegates – public-sector unions and the CAW. But 500 mainly private-sector delegates stormed from the meeting and distributed their own position paper reaffirming support for the NDP.[42] Just before the walkout, the pro-NDP union delegates circulated a statement to the 1,500 delegates, printed on pink paper – and from that point on the unions represented were labelled the "pink paper" unions. "Political Action and Ontario Labour" argued the case for sticking with the NDP.

> While all of us share the anger of our union brothers and sisters in the public sector over this legislation and call on the Rae government to repeal the bill, we cannot support a policy which we believe will be disastrous for the future of the Ontario labour movement.
>
> The fracturing of the labour-NDP alliance and the likely electoral result will be deeply appreciated by our real enemies on the right. It is our conviction that public-sector workers, indeed all working people, will be the losers if the Rae government is replaced by one of the business-financed parties.[43]

But perhaps more important than this strategic argument was an underlying political economy. As Jason Ziedenberg has argued, "the Pink leaders depict their workers as 'wealth creators,' distinct from the public-sector workers, who seemed merely to be spending the hard-earned tax dollars of the Steelworkers. Liz Barkley, then president of the Ontario Secondary School Teachers Federation, remembers hearing as much from a Pink union head: 'We took our hit during NAFTA [North American Free Trade Agreement],' she was told. 'It's time you people took your hit.'"[44]

Importantly, the pink paper walkout in 1993 was not simply a moment, but the cohering of what was to become an organized faction within the Ontario labour movement. In 1994, in the run-up to the Canadian Labour Congress convention, the pink paper group gathered together to prepare for convention debates, looking to rebuild the relationship between the economic organizing of the labour movement and the parliamentary wing represented by the NDP[45] to "turn the tide and bring the rest of the labour movement back on side."[46]

The argument of the pink paper unions was put succinctly in a document entitled, "Rethinking Our Mission in Ontario: A Discussion Paper for Union Leaders," which was submitted to the NDP renewal conference in 1994. It argued that to overly focus on the Social Contract was to miss the chief enemies confronting labour – free trade and unemployment. The latter were threats to private-sector unions in particular, as the "steep decline" in employment in manufacturing industries was paralleled by a "steep decline in the position and strength of industrial unions." To some extent, the focus on the public-sector attacks was becoming a distraction.

> The noise that can be generated over relatively-recent public spending cutbacks and job reductions far exceeds what labour has been able to sustain over the more catastrophic and economically-debilitating losses in mines, paper mills, appliance plants, and clothing manufacturers over the past decade and a half.[47]

The Rae government was up for re-election in 1995, and the election campaign had a completely different feel to the one in 1990. The electoral base of the NDP was angry and demoralized. That the NDP was in trouble was clear to everyone. Lisa Wright pointedly noted that "after the Social Contract negotiations in the summer of 1993, thousands of NDP members tore up their cards and quit the party" and that by 1995 membership in the Ontario NDP had "fallen by about one-third to about 22,000."[48] What was less clear was who would defeat them. I was not alone in asserting that "Lyn McLeod's Liberals will be by far the biggest beneficiary of the NDP decline." In the same article where I made this (incorrect) prediction, there were clear warning signs of the anti-NDP vote taking another direction. "Members of the Ontario Public Service Employees' Union demonstrated against Rae in

Image 1.2. Mike Harris, Conservative Premier of Ontario, 1995–2002.

the first days of the election. Several in the few dozen or so at the picket announced they would 'support the Reform Party,'" which obviously made no sense because Reform was not on the ballot in the provincial election of 1995. But Mike Harris was on the ballot, and Harris had already "campaigned aggressively amongst autoworkers in Oshawa. Many in the former NDP stronghold said they would back Harris."[49] We will see in the next chapter the tight relationship between the rise of Reform federally, and the rise of Harris provincially.

When the votes were counted, the NDP had lost decisively. Its popular vote plunged by 700,000, while the Conservative vote soared by more than 1 million. From the halls of government, the NDP's seventeen seats did not even qualify them as the official opposition, a post filled instead by the Liberals whose popular vote remained above 1 million, allowing it to win thirty seats. The Conservatives, with eighty-two seats, had a clear majority, and they set out to deal with the debt burden through an austerity program far more extreme than any envisaged by the NDP, an austerity program euphemistically called the "Common Sense Revolution."

Chapter Two

Contours of a Backlash

Who were these Common Sense Revolutionaries replacing Bob Rae's social democrats? The actual Common Sense Revolution document was drafted by the Bradgate Group, named after the Bradgate Arms, a Toronto hotel where what was to become the Mike Harris team often met.[1] At the centre of that team was former golf course manager, Mike Harris himself, "with his North Bay mistrust of taxes"; former Bay Street executive William Farlinger, "with his faith in private enterprise"; and former Ontario Conservative Party president Tom Long, "an admirer of former British Prime Minister Margaret Thatcher." The descriptions of these three come from Thomas Walkom's important 1997 analysis of the Tories' rule in office. According to Walkom, the Common Sense Revolution that these three crafted "took Harris's brand of instinctive anti-tax, antigovernment conservatism and located it in the context of the more generalized and intellectually consistent conservative revival that was sweeping the Western world."[2]

The document forged at the Bradgate Arms became the campaign platform for the Tories during the 1995 election. The document promised to balance the budget but at the same time cut provincial income taxes by 30 per cent. How would a balanced budget mesh with these kinds of reductions in revenue? In part through drastic reductions in expenditure. They promised to "cut overall government spending by 11 per cent without taking money from health, classroom education, and law enforcement." A significant portion of the savings would be found through an attack on the poorest of the province: "Welfare rates would be rolled back to a level set at '10 percent above the national average of all other provinces.'"[3] Embedded in the document was suspicion of the poor and a belief that "cheating" was endemic in the province. Hence, it argued for workfare. "All able-bodied welfare recipients under the age of sixty-five, including single mothers with children over the age of three would be required to work for their cheques." All of this was dependent on economic growth so that despite a reduction in tax rates, overall taxes would increase. The CSR revolutionaries argued that if they removed obstacles to business, they could kick-start that growth – and one of the main obstacles they identified was the NDP's Bill 40. This bill was designed, as we have seen, to remove barriers to forming trade unions and placing barriers to the practice of strike-breaking. The bold promise of the CSR was that through these measures 725,000 net new jobs would be created over five years.[4]

At the time, perhaps the most commonly accepted analysis of the Harris Tories was to see them as a radical expression of "fiscal conservatism." Yonatan Reshef and Sandra Rastin position Harris as part of a trend driven by the desire to balance budgets and eliminate government debt, linking him domestically to Alberta's Ralph Klein. "The need for fiscal restraint was obvious to Ralph Klein and Mike Harris."[5] A core aspect of this view, clearly outlined by Walkom, was an ideology which saw "too-much-government" as a barrier to economic growth. "High taxes and other unspecified barriers to growth" were seen by Harris and his allies as the problem. Hence, "a tax cut is the answer. To pay for this tax cut, government spending must be cut – but that should not cause undue hardship since government spending is out of control anyway."[6] In the immediate aftermath of the Harris victory, I emphasized a corollary to this viewpoint, saying that the Tories had been elected "in the context of a declining economy which will make Harris attack with a vengeance the living standards and social services of Ontario's workers."[7] Three factors are then closely interrelated: anti-deficit fiscal conservatism, anti-government tax aversion, both exacerbated by recession conditions, which push everything in the direction of an attack on workers' rights and social services.

But Reshef and Rastin immediately added another dimension to the fiscal conservatism approach. They linked both Klein and Harris to Margaret Thatcher, prime minister of Great Britain throughout the 1980s, who was "determined to reform British government by reducing the autonomy of the civil service from the political arm of the government, making government operations more economical and efficient." There is quite a large literature that sees Thatcher as much more than a fiscal conservative – someone who presided over a "counter-revolution" against gains made by the left and the labour movement in the militant 1960s and early 1970s.[8] David Camfield applies this perspective explicitly, taking the term "class war conservatism" coined by Ralph Miliband,[9] and applying it to Ontario in the mid-1990s. Mike Harris,

Image 2.1. Ralph Klein, Conservative Premier of Alberta, 1992–2006.

Camfield writes, "embraced, even welcomed the political polarization of the province and confrontation with the organized working class."[10] Douglas Nesbitt sees it in much the same light, calling the Harris agenda a program "designed to renovate the state, rationalize the social safety net, repeal barriers to capital accumulation, and decisively weaken the strength of organized labour."[11]

There is something to all these approaches – seeing Harris as a fiscal conservative, bent on slashing the deficit, in combination with a Thatcher-like determination to oppose and – through confrontation – weaken organized labour, all in pursuit of what has come to be known as a neoliberal agenda. But with the benefit of hindsight, and with the "benefit" of witnessing a new wave of right-wing conservative governments this century, it is clear that something more needs to be added. We have to incorporate the concept of "backlash," defined by Abigail Bakan and Audrey Kobayashi as "an ideological current or policy platform that is based on conservative premises but is distinct from conservatism generally because of its specifically reactive character."[12]

In the United States, Donald Trump's successful first run for the presidency in 2016 represented in large part a racist backlash against eight years of an African American family residing in the White House.[13] In Ontario, several commentators have argued that Doug Ford came to office in the province of Ontario in part as a backlash against the presence in the premier's office of an openly lesbian grandmother.[14] Kathleen Wynne served as Liberal premier of Ontario from 2013 to 2018. By March 2017, Wynne had the distinction of being the most unpopular premier in Canada, with her approval rating at just 12 per cent.[15] One year later, Wynne had pushed that number up to 19 per cent, but that still put her dead last among all premiers.[16] When the votes were counted in June, that is exactly where Liberal Party support sat – just over 19 per cent, far behind the now official opposition NDP (34 per cent) and Doug Ford's victorious Conservatives (41 per cent).[17]

It is extremely difficult, without the concept of backlash, to explain what can only be called the hatred that became directed towards Wynne. Some charged her with corruption, but this was completely spurious. There had been a gas plant scandal, but it had unfolded under the watch, not of Wynne, but of Dalton McGuinty – and was one which the voters in the province completely discounted when they handed Wynne a majority in 2013. During her tenure, there was one court case alleging bribery during a by-election, but it was dismissed for lack of evidence.[18] And Doug Ford – the man who swept her out of office – has been haunted his entire political career by repeated charges of corruption and influence-peddling.[19] Wynne's government did privatize Ontario Hydro and did legislate striking college workers back to work. But could that account for her extremely low poll numbers? Much of the rest of her record was extremely progressive, as we will see later in the book.

Similarly, I would argue that backlash was an important factor in the rise of the Harris Tories. Peter Graefe and Carol-Anne Hudson have documented the "anti-welfare backlash that helped elect Harris,"[20] a backlash which would be codified when in office through some of the most punitive cuts to social assistance ever implemented by a Canadian government. In addition, the rise of the Harris Tories embodied a backlash against other aspects of NDP governance, particularly NDP policies seeking to target systemic oppression. In particular, employment equity legislation – designed to redress generations of discrimination against women and people of colour, codified in Bill 79 and passed in 1993 – became, according to Brian Tanguay, "the target of most of the criticism and generated more controversy than almost any other NDP initiative."[21] Grace-Edward Galabuzi says that while "the government regulation was meant to combat discrimination in employment, the discourse around the legislation became highly racialized and precipitated a backlash."[22] Proclaimed by the NDP in 1994, the legislation "ignited a backlash in the 1995 election campaign" according to Rand Dyck[23] and was "repealed by the Tories one year later in an atmosphere of extreme backlash, upon the election of Mike Harris and the Ontario Progressive Conservatives in1995."[24] Before being withdrawn, it was viciously mischaracterized and denigrated as being a "quota law"[25] even though, as Bakan and Kobayashi[26] point out, the legislation "did not include quotas or statistical standards, instead calling upon employers to develop appropriate goals and flexible plans."

Walkom says that Harris's opposition to employment equity "went beyond his Common Sense Revolution platform."[27] But whether or not it was embedded visibly within the CSR is not the point. The real question is the role this attack on employment equity played in mobilizing an anti-NDP pro-Tory base. In fact, a case can be made that a backlash against employment equity was at the very core of the Harris project.

Employment equity became an issue at both the federal and provincial levels. Bakan and Kobayashi write that the then new Reform Party (later Canadian Alliance, ultimately to be absorbed into the Conservative Party of Canada) "adopted an anti-employment equity position as one of the major planks in its platform." The Reform Party was "playing to a public among whom, according to polls at the time, only about 20 percent favoured employment equity. The rhetoric of the opponents at the time shows a well-established political tactic: to focus narrowly on one putative aspect of the new law, namely job quotas, which ironically were not and had never been a part of the legislation, and then to focus on that issue ignoring all others."[28]

That mischaracterization came not only from the right but also from the left wing of the political spectrum. Reg Whitaker – Distinguished Research Professor at York University[29] and frequent contributor to *Socialist Register* – was scathing in his attack on the legislation. He quoted from the act, which mandated that "every employer's work force, in all occupational categories and at all levels of employment, shall reflect the representation of Aboriginal people, people with disabilities, members of racial minorities and women in the community,"[30] and called the proposition "palpable nonsense."

> Why should all occupational categories be mirror reflections of the exact demographic proportion of these groups in the society? Might it not be that even in the absence of discrimination, women would not choose to pursue certain occupations in numbers equivalent to their 51 percent of the population?[31]

He argued that the impact of such legislation would be to discriminate against young white men.

> Young, white, able-bodied males will find themselves placed at the back of employment queues and at the bottom of promotional ladders. Not the architects of discrimination themselves, they will become objects of discrimination in order to pay for other people's historical injustice.[32]

Importantly, there were other voices on the left and in the workers' movement who took a diametrically opposed view. After the election of the Harris Tories, when the new government put forward Bill 8, the misleadingly titled "Job Quotas Repeal Act," whose intent was to eliminate employment equity, Peggy Nash, then assistant to the president of the CAW, announced that her union would not participate in what she called the "façade of consultation" on the new bill. She drew a direct parallel between the attack on employment equity and the simultaneous attack on labour rights being carried out by the Tories. The CAW clearly indicated the likely impact of repealing employment equity legislation, giving "greater power to employers to use favouritism in promoting employees."[33]

In the run-up to the 2018 Ontario provincial election that was to see Doug Ford elevated to the premiership, Anthony Morgan wrote a comparative analysis of the Harris and Ford Tories, adding other important dimensions to this backlash perspective. He sees the Harris backlash reflected in three attacks. The first was the one discussed here, the repeal of the Employment Equity Act. The other two had their roots in responses to racism and police violence. In May 1992 there were angry protests against racism and police violence – including the Toronto police killings of twenty-two-year-old African Canadian Raymond Lawrence, and the acquittal of two Peel Region police officers in the killing of African Canadian teenager Michael Wade Lawson. These protests have become known, misleadingly, as the "Yonge Street Riot." In response, the NDP government tasked Stephen Lewis with "investigating its underlying causes." The former ONDP leader recommended strengthening the Ontario Anti-Racism Secretariat. Harris disbanded that secretariat shortly after taking office. Lewis also recommended an inquiry, the Commission on Systemic Racism in the Ontario Criminal Justice System (CSROCJS). Its report[34] came out six months after Harris took office and "was discarded into the dustbin of history."[35]

Morgan says that all three attacks – on employment equity, the CSROCJS, and the Ontario Anti-Racism Secretariat – were examples of "white rage," which he defines as "a form of resentment-fueled social, political and legal backlash against actual and perceived advances made

Image 2.2. Dudley Laws (1934–2011), one of the leaders of the 1992 protests against police racism.

Image 2.3. Preston Manning, founder, first and only leader of the Reform Party, 1987–2000.

by racialized citizens through racial justice law and policy reforms."[36] The term, Morgan indicates, was coined by Carol Anderson, who says that this is "not only about visible violence" but rather an attempt to capture something which "wreaks havoc subtly, almost imperceptibly" as it "works its way through the courts, the legislatures, and a range of government bureaucracies."[37] This subtle havoc was documented by Bakan and Kobayashi. The factionally misnamed "Job Quotas Repeal Act" "not only eliminated all measures in place to advance employment equity, but it required that all information gathered in connection with the previous law be destroyed, occasioning a massive paper shredding exercise."[38] Not only was the law to go, so too was all the research that went into its creation. For those familiar with episodic moments of book burning in the twentieth century, such an approach should give one chills.

Reform Party's Shadow

Return for a moment to the phenomenon of the Reform Party. The Reform Party incubated both Stephen Harper and Jason Kenney – leading the former to become prime minister of Canada (2006–15), and the other to become premier of Alberta (2019–22). The Reform Party's shadow also fell over the political career of Mike Harris. From early on in his tenure as leader of the Conservatives, Mike Harris openly courted Reform Party voters. In a June 1991 visit to Kingston, Ontario, he delivered a speech whose main points struck the *Whig-Standard* journalist who covered it as "very similar to many being made recently by Reform party leader Preston Manning." He quoted Harris's appeal to Manning supporters. "I ask those who think of joining the Reform Party to join with us, and continue the reforms in our party."[39] His election in 1995 was widely seen by many as a populist "lurch to the right" that had his party "following a Reform agenda."[40] Early on in his tenure, he travelled to Ottawa for an hour-long meeting with Manning, where they declared "their common cause on issues near and dear to them: tax relief, spending cuts, immigration, social policy and gun control."[41]

Opposition to so-called quotas, as Bakan and Kobayashi pointed out above, was certainly a factor for both Harris and Reform. There was another unstated issue. For Reform, more than anything else, the politics of backlash centred on Quebec. Manning's movement emerged as a split from the Progressive Conservatives, driven by what Manning and others saw as "concessions" to Quebec nationalism being made by both the Liberals and the Conservatives. In the 1997 election campaign for instance – the campaign which introduced us to Jason Kenney – the

Table 2.1. Federal Election Results, Per Cent of Vote by Party, Oshawa, 1984–2021 (Winning total for each election shaded grey)

Election Year	NDP	Liberal	Conservative	Reform Party / Canadian Alliance
1984	42.3	18.1	38.8	
1988	44.3	20.5	33.8	
1990 (By-Election)	47.6	34.4	6.4	
1993	14.9	38.3	15.0	28.9
1997	17.4	37.7	16.5	28.4
2000	11.1	42.9	15.1	28.8
2004	32.2	30.5	33.2	
2006	33.5	24.0	38.6	
2008	34.7	16.0	41.4	
2011	37.9	7.0	51.3	
2015	31.9	27.3	38.2	
2019	28.5	25.4	38.9	
2021	28.5	23.1	39.7	

Author's calculations based on data from the Parliament of Canada.[42]

Reform Party broadcast television ads calling for "a voice for all Canadians, not just Quebec politicians." It featured a "large red circle with a slash through images of Jean Chrétien, Jean Charest, Gilles Duceppe and Lucien Bouchard."[43] This anti-Quebec politics – a story buried with the passage of time – was central to the education of the Reform Party's early cadre. Quebec never loomed large as an ideological issue for Harris. But in courting the Reform Party base, Harris was courting a base shaped by this anti-Quebec politics.[44]

Reform Party backlash politics were a key factor in pulling politics to the right in Ontario, laying a foundation for Harris. A snapshot of the impact of this backlash politics can be gleaned through an examination of the federal electoral history in the riding of Oshawa. For generations at the centre of Ontario's auto industry, Oshawa has been a historic union city, and in the 1980s was an NDP stronghold, the federal seat of then-leader Ed Broadbent. Table 2.1 shows that in the general elections of 1984 and 1988, Broadbent easily captured the riding, winning more than 40 per cent of the vote in each election. In the by-election of 1990, his successor, Michael Breaugh, similarly won handily, winning almost 50 per cent of the vote.

In 1993, Breaugh's and the NDP's vote collapsed, losing the seat to the Liberals. In that election, and the two subsequent ones, the NDP vote stayed below 20 per cent – dropping to just 11.1 per cent in 2000 – while the Liberals took in around 40 per cent of the vote. However, it is misleading to see the key political dynamic as a shift from the NDP to the Liberal Party. The real change in the riding was the explosive arrival of the Reform Party/Canadian Alliance, capturing almost 30 per cent of the vote in 1993, 1997, and 2000. With the election of 2004, when the Reform Party/Canadian Alliance became a (or *the*) part of a new united Conservative Party, and in every election since, Oshawa has been held by the Conservatives. In 2004 and 2006, the NDP banner was carried by Sid Ryan – whose name will play a prominent role in this book – and in 2008 by Mike Shields, former president of Oshawa's CAW Local 222. These high-profile candidates led to a considerably improved performance for the NDP, but not enough to dislodge the Conservatives. This one-riding sketch shows how right-wing backlash politics were able to pull one riding – even one with a long working class and social democratic tradition – from the column of the political left to that of the political right.

Nowhere was the shift from social democracy to political conservatism more exemplified than the provincial shift from the Bob Rae NDP to the Mike Harris Tories. Certainly, the Harris Tories were part anti-government fiscal conservatives as analysed by Reshef, Rastin, Walkom, and others – and part neoliberal "class war conservatives" as analysed by Camfield, Nesbitt, and others. But to a much greater extent than many commentators – including myself – saw at the time, they represented a politics of backlash, precursors to the even more furious unrestrained backlash that has become so defining of politics in the twenty-first century.

Perhaps the key to seeing this is to differentiate between the issue of political rule and that of political mobilization. Without question, the rule of the Harris Tories – with their predilection for minimal state regulation, low taxes, and barriers to unionization – was one that pleased big business. In 1997, OFL president Gord Wilson wittily characterized the former golf course manager Harris as "simply the biggest caddie business in Ontario has ever had."[45] This relationship between business and the Tories was impossible to hide. During the 1995 election, when Harris released his list of endorsements, it included "Peter Munk, chairman of Horsham Corp., a gold-mining and real-estate conglomerate; John C. Eaton, chairman of Eaton's of Canada Ltd., the department-store chain; and Trevor Eyton, chairman of Brascan Ltd., a diversified holding company."[46] Once in office, his policies received what Jim Turk characterized as "delighted praise" from key pro-corporate institutions including "the Business Council on National Issues, the Fraser Institute,

Figure 2.1. Change in Vote, Total, and By Major Party, Ontario, 1990–5.

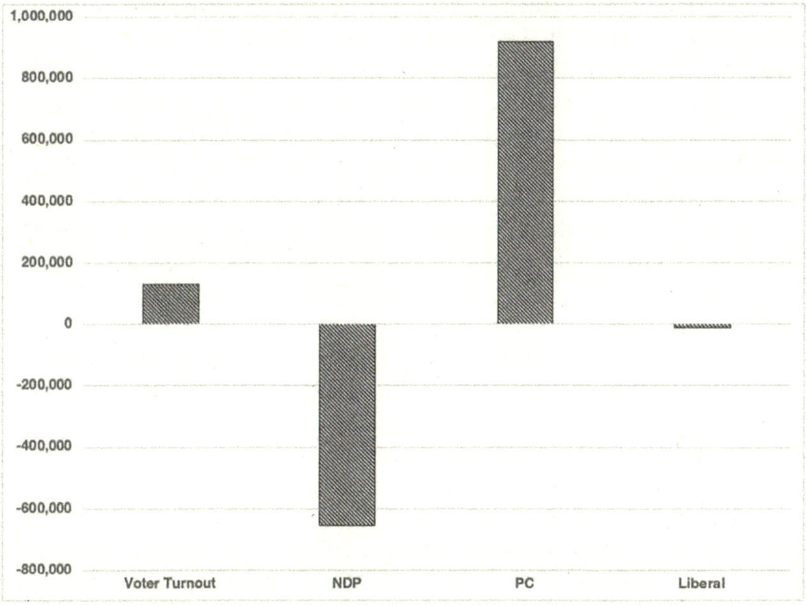

Author's compilation from data in Elections Ontario.[47]

the Canadian Federation of Independent Business and the C.D. Howe Institute."[48]

But political mobilization requires more than an articulation of the needs of the wealthiest of the electorate. Harris had to win votes to implement these policies, and he gathered those votes by the hundreds of thousands. Figure 2.1 shows the change in vote for the three major parties as well as in voter turnout between the 1990 election of Bob Rae's social democratic government and the 1995 election of Mike Harris's Tory government. Votes for the Liberal Party were almost identical in the two elections. By contrast, the NDP received 600,000 fewer votes in 1995 than in 1990, while the Tory vote soared by almost 1 million. It is possible that hundreds of thousands of NDP voters stayed home – disillusioned after the Social Contract fiasco – and that Tory supporters, who had stayed home in 1990, returned to the polling stations in the hundreds of thousands. But it is also possible that hundreds of thousands of voters switched from the NDP to the Tories. The federal riding experience of Oshawa, examined in detail above, indicates that even in a working class social democratic town such as Oshawa, backlash politics had an appeal.

Jason Ziedenberg's eyewitness account of Tory *affect* during a tense moment early in their rule gives an insight into the passions driving the Harris Tories. Saturday, February 24, 1996, while 100,000 were on the streets of Hamilton demonstrating against the Common Sense Revolution, 1,100 delegates were behind closed doors in the same city at a Conservative policy convention, listening to their leader, Mike Harris. Ziedenberg is an interesting witness to the Days of Action. He was very much an advocate of the protests, but not an uncritical one. Commenting on the crowd of demonstrators outside on the streets, he quotes a friend remarking, "what a white wash," and says: "True enough: the march, like the union movement in general, wasn't much a reflection of Canadian diversity." However, inside the room in which the Tories were meeting "was a sea of blue and black suits. If the demonstration outside was 'a whitewash,' then I had just walked into a loaf of Wonderbread."[49] The "loaf of Wonderbread" gave Harris a standing ovation when he announced the "'success' of cutting the provincial welfare rate by 22 percent" – an attack from which the poorest of the poor in the province have yet to recover. Before that standing ovation, "the loudest applause came when he celebrated the end of employment equity 'quotas,' and the elimination of Bill 40, the NDP's labour law."[50] The repeal of such a pro-union bill fits very well with a "neoliberal" or "class war conservatism" analysis of the Harris Tories. But the repeal of employment equity? The full name of the legislation in question was the "Act to Provide for Employment Equity for Aboriginal People, People with Disabilities, Members of Racial Minorities and Women." Thinking of that "loaf of Wonderbread" lustily celebrating the demise of this attempt to level the playing field for these systemically oppressed groups is strong evidence of the angry backlash motivating the Harris Tories.

Backlash Within

Ziedenberg highlights another disturbing undercurrent in the debate within the workers' movement, which underlines the extent to which the politics of backlash existed within the workers' movement itself. Ziedenberg calls David Mackenzie, a staffer for the Steelworkers, the "ring leader of the Pink Paper Group"[51] and cites confidential memos in which Mackenzie "describes a working-class membership that couldn't care less about the equality concerns that drove those lesbian, gay, native and women activists." Ziedenberg quotes a 1993 memo co-written by Mackenzie saying: "The dirty secret that many choose to evade ... is just how distant the political, social, and equality views of union leadership are from those of the 'members.' This is true even in the most self-righteous organizations that have hammered away at the NDP and the Rae government."[52] In another memo, Ziedenberg says that "Mackenzie targeted affirmative action and social programs as policies that his members find wasteful and unjust."[53]

Whitaker's opinion piece (above) and Mackenzie's private memos were articulating the "silent voice" that few would go public with – the anger of a section of the "traditional" workers' movement towards the concerns of oppressed groups. Ziedenberg made an analogy with the "Reagan Democrats" in the United States, who were "predominately white, working-class, or downwardly mobile middleclass Americans, often from union households, who veered toward supporting the Republican critique of the evils of the welfare state, affirmative action, and other equity policies. This section of the electorate helped keep Reagan in power, even as he dismantled workers' rights. In 1994, 45 percent of union members voted for Republican 'Contract with America' candidates who promised to make the U.S. a union-busting country."[54] Reagan is long gone, but when Trump swept the old rust-belt stronghold of the Democratic Party in 2016, and again in 2024, it was clear that this aspect of working class consciousness – this reactionary aspect – was still a factor with which to contend in the twenty-first century. A similar kind of backlash was seen in the election of Harris – an uncomfortable aspect of working class culture and consciousness that Ziedenberg suggests was part of what became an enormous backlash against activism.

These kinds of backlash politics were not, of course, confined to the pink paper unions. In the CAW stronghold of Oshawa – epicentre of the Reform Party's electoral surge in Ontario – those backlash politics were in part behind one of the first moves to separate from the NDP: a 1993 vote by CAW Local 222 to pull its funding from the party, a move which spread to the CAW in Windsor. The arguments for the split were not because it was too right-wing, but rather that it was too *left*-wing, a party that "supported only 'special interests.'" Ziedenberg says that the unionists who led the disaffiliation move, "appealed to union members as 'property owners,' 'whites,' 'males,' and 'taxpayers.'"[55]

The Oshawa campaign was led by Doug Gammie, part of a seven-person "Canadian Auto Workers Members Committee Against Political Affiliation" that gathered 8,400 signatures on a petition to disaffiliate from the NDP. Gammie claimed to be "not anti-labour" but rather "pro-jobs." But he put his argument in a manner that in fact, did feel anti-labour. "At a time when Ontario needs growth in its economy, the NDP government policies are pro-labor and they're discouraging investment in Ontario."[56] In Windsor, the campaign to disaffiliate was led by Wayne

Manley, former president of the Windsor West Reform Party Riding Association. He insisted that his was "not a political cause – it's an anti-politics crusade."[57] But in the case of Oshawa, at least, there were politics behind the "apolitical stance" – and some of those politics were *very* right-wing. According to Gammie, in addition to economic concerns, his Oshawa committee "is also angry with CAW support of an NDP push to restore native fishing rights on the Bruce Peninsula."[58] For workers in Oshawa to be energized by an Indigenous rights issue some three hundred kilometres and a four-hour drive away clearly reveals the backlash content in at least this moment of anti-NDP organizing. When the Oshawa local did vote overwhelmingly to sever its ties with the NDP, Preston Manning himself did his best to fish in these troubled waters. "I hope the Reform Party replaces the NDP in the hearts and minds of CAW members," he said to about one hundred supporters in May in Oshawa, where he provocatively opened a Reform Party office "in a building that once housed offices for both the union and the New Democrats."[59]

OPSEU – in 1991 the first to articulate labour opposition to Rae – was also not immune to these backlash politics. Return to the story of the walkout at the 1991 OFL convention led by OPSEU. Future OPSEU president Leah Casselman – at the time a vice-president of the union – defended the walkout saying: "Don't slap us in the face by bringing in an employer when we are in the middle of negotiations." OPSEU's Mike Oliver, at the time president of the Cornwall and District Labour Council, challenged the critics of the walkout. "When my brothers and sisters are criticizing us for exercising our democratic rights, then there is a problem in the labor movement."[60] A prominent steelworker leader, Carolyn Egan – who bucked the trend inside her union and remained a consistent supporter of the Days of Action – was speaking for many of us when she saw the walkout as a sign of a radicalization to the left, a "display of militancy" that demonstrated that "the unofficial truce between the Ontario labour movement and the NDP government is now over."[61] It is clear with the benefit of hindsight that the reality was more complex. In the political context of late 1991, an anti-NDP walkout by OPSEU represented quite contradictory consciousness within the union, quite in keeping with the very contradictory nature of the union itself.

Included in the ranks of OPSEU are social service workers, such as Upshaw, with a background as a nurse in a Whitby psychiatric hospital.[62] However, Casselman and Oliver – the two OPSEU leaders cited above defending the 1991 walkout – have very different backgrounds. Both were corrections officers: Casselman worked at the Syl

Apps Youth Centre in Oakville and Oliver worked at the Cornwall Jail, which was, until its closing, the province's oldest.[63] It is a straightforward issue to place a nurse such as Upshaw within the public-sector union movements that emerged in the late twentieth century at the core of some of the most important labour struggles of that era, in Ontario and elsewhere. It is a quite different matter with corrections officers working in the jails and prisons – and at a federal level in the penitentiary system. Corrections officers are embedded into institutions with internal cultures steeped in violence and racism. Oliver's experience was a jail in Cornwall, my hometown, and I, for one, would regard critically any militancy emerging from the Cornwall jail.

Corrections officers exist in the universe of law enforcement, and in Ontario during the Rae years, there was militant opposition to the NDP government coming from another section of law enforcement – the police associations. In the summer of 1992, delegates to the Ontario Police Association were "poised to declare a political war against Bob Rae's New Democrat government" according to a report on their meeting published in the *Toronto Star*. Central to their anger were issues of race and racism, "what they perceived as the anti-police tenor of Stephen Lewis's report on racism, and proposed employment equity legislation."[64] By 1994, police opposition to Rae led William McCormack, then head of police services in Toronto to urge, in the words of conservative commentator Alan Fotheringham, "civil disobedience." Again, employment equity and the fight against racism were front and centre, including Rae's "promises to promote women and racial minorities," culminating in him picking Susan Eng to lead the Police Services Board. Fotheringham went on to say, "police naturally object to what they regard as interference by do-gooders, especially when the new head monitor is a female who is, shall we mention it, of Chinese extraction."[65] No one saw *this* opposition to Rae as a "move to the left." The point is, not all militancy emerging from the working class is a sign of a move left, and in the Rae years, there was a sea of quite conservative opposition to the NDP that might at times have "looked" left and militant but had very right-wing content.

Remember how the final report of the CSROCJS, commissioned by the Rae administration, was not published until Mike Harris had been elected and "was discarded into the dustbin of history."[66] However, the interim report of that same commission *was* published while Rae was still premier. *Racism Behind Bars* is a devastatingly persuasive exposé of the violence and racism permeating the corrections system in Ontario, with a particular focus on the role of corrections officers. The report's authors said they were "told repeatedly during our initial consultations" that Ontario prisons were "very hostile for black prisoners and staff. It was said that in some places overtly racist language is used constantly, racial stereotyping is common practice, and correctional officers (COs) use excessive force against black prisoners."[67] Some of what is described in summary form makes for difficult reading. "Black female and male prisoners also reported that COs used 'Jamaican' constantly, both as a term of abuse and as a way of describing the 'worst' prisoners in their facilities. According to many black women, for example, COs who treat them fairly courteously say 'You're OK, you're not like the Jamaicans.'"[68] The report compiled a list of the racist names "used for units that house black and other racial minority prisoners. Some white and black COs said that they dislike these terms but emphasized that the names are well-known and commonly used. The examples provided were all shocking, offensive, and deeply racist."[69]

The point is not to suggest that every corrections officer adhered to these views. The point is to highlight the uniquely violent and openly racist environment that exists within the jail and prison system in Ontario. With this understanding, we have to nuance any analysis that sees militancy coming from corrections officers within OPSEU as a sign of consciousness moving to the left.

These contradictory currents impact the whole history of OPSEU. On the one hand, it was a huge step for the union to elect Upshaw to the presidency in 1991, "the first black person to be elected president of a major Canadian union."[70] Known as a "strong advocate of employment equity," Upshaw recounted the day before his successful election that in an earlier union election campaign, some of his backers had been asked "why they would support a n***** for the board."[71] Two years later, he was narrowly re-elected, defeating Casselman 523 to 438.[72] But in 1995, it would be a different story. Upshaw came last on the first ballot in an election that would elevate Casselman to the leadership.[73] There was a candidate on the ballot – David Rapaport – who articulated deep concern with the NDP and was widely seen as a candidate of the left. But it was not Rapaport, but the former corrections officer Casselman who in the end would win and succeed Upshaw.

The backlash within was also inside the NDP itself. In 1994, the Rae government set out to extend rights for same-sex couples within the province – tabling Bill 167, "The Equality Rights Amendment Act." If implemented, it would have equalized financial rights and adoption rights for same-sex couples.[74] There was some anticipation that this bill might well pass. A 1993 by-election in Toronto's St. George-St. David riding had attracted candidates from all three major parties who supported the principle of same-sex benefits. Liberal leader Lyn McLeod articulated her support for the eventual winner Tim Murphy by "challenging Premier Rae to end discrimination against lesbians and gays."[75] If the Liberals were onside on same-sex benefits, then the legislation would pass easily.

However, this is a tale of two by-elections. If in the context of downtown Toronto, support for same-sex benefits could find a hearing, that was much less the case in rural and small-town Ontario. In 1994 a by-election was held to fill the Victoria-Haliburton seat left vacant by the resignation of NDP MPP Dennis Drainville. In the 1990 election, Drainville had surprised everyone and taken the largely rural seat handily – winning more than 15,000 votes compared to less than 9,000 for the Conservative candidate and 8,000 for the Liberal. With McLeod's Liberals doing well in the polls and the NDP sagging, it looked likely that the seat would change hands, moving from the NDP to the Liberals.

No one reckoned with the power of backlash. On March 9, the Conservatives took a new tack in their campaign, launching a newspaper ad in the local paper – the *Lindsay Daily Post* with a coded homophobic message. "The NDP and the Liberals have their priorities all mixed up. The NDP Government's new priority is to introduce a law that would provide gay and lesbian couples with the same family benefits as married couples." In this ad, the Conservatives didn't oppose the bill on an openly homophobic basis, but said they would pivot away from "new spending schemes that will increase the cost of doing business in Ontario" and instead focus on "job creation"[76] – as if same-sex benefits would impede job creation!

The result surprised everyone. The NDP vote completely collapsed, their candidate Art Field polling just over 1,000 votes. The Liberal vote increased slightly to almost 10,000. But the victor was Tory Chris Hodgson, polling 12,000 votes.[77] Suddenly, it became clear to the Tories that backlash politics might be a game changer, and the Liberals had considerably less enthusiasm for same-sex benefit legislation. When the vote on Bill 167 happened, McLeod and all but three Liberals voted against it. For the NDP, there were two scandals. The first was that the bill was defeated because twelve NDP MPPs sided with the Tory and Liberal positions and voted "No." The second scandal was with Rae himself, who did not impose caucus discipline, but instead allowed for a "free vote." When grilled as to why he would let this happen, and why these twelve faced no consequences for their actions, Rae's only response was: "Some people have a deep emotional response to this issue,"[78] which is of course no response at all.

If the twelve faced no consequences for their actions from Rae, they also received no benefits from the electorate. All twelve men (and yes, all twelve were men – Mike Farnan, Anthony Perruzza, Gord Mills, Pat Hayes, Fred Wilson, Mike Cooper, Ron Hansen, Dan Waters, Tony Rizzo, Allan Pilkey, Don Abel, and George Mammoliti)[79] lost their seats in the 1995 provincial election, some by astonishingly high margins (by 10,000 votes for Farnan, 8,000 for Pilkey, Cooper, and Hayes). Waters and Rizzo would re-emerge a few years later as Liberals, as would the omnipresent Mammoliti, until he found a home with the Conservatives, and a new career in municipal politics, failing in a bid to become mayor, but reconciling himself to being a supporter of the conservative mayor of Toronto, Rob Ford.[80]

The same-sex controversy calls into question an underlying assumption of the pink paper unions, that workers had to be elevated to an understanding of the policies of social democracy. What happens when backward politics are embedded, not at the base of the movement, but at the top, within the very "political alternative" that is supposed to be inculcating the workers with "social democratic values"?

Chapter Three

Contours of a Movement

In the first months of the Harris government, little was heard from the official labour movement. The Social Contract had split the labour movement down the middle. Most public-sector unions, along with the Canadian Auto Workers in the private sector, bitterly opposing the Social Contract, had turned their back on the NDP. The United Steel Workers (USWA) and most private-sector unions tried to stay loyal to the NDP despite the Social Contract. This divided labour movement was in no shape to lead a response in the first months of the Harris government.

Remarkably, the divided and demoralized labour movement of the spring had become united, angry, and mobilized by the autumn. One foundational moment in that re-energization of the labour movement was the opening day of the fall session of the Ontario legislature on September 27, 1995, where between 5,000 and 10,000 marched on Queen's Park in a demonstration jointly organized by the Embarrass Harris Campaign and the Labour Council of Metro Toronto and York Region,[1] (today, the Toronto and York Region Labour Council). At a different register, the re-energization of the labour movement was reflected a few weeks later, when the OFL met in session. The 2,000 delegates – much closer to the anger of the rank and file than the often cautious and sometimes demoralized central union leadership – voted to launch a series of one-day, one-city general strikes to oppose the Harris cuts, general strikes which came to be known as "Days of Action."[2]

To understand the shift from demoralization to confidence and militancy, the analysis must depart from the plane of institutions and engage in the much more complex work of assessing social movement activism. The re-energization of the labour movement was built on a foundation created by forces *outside* the institutions of labour. Immediately upon the electoral victory of the Harris Tories – while the official labour movement remained disoriented and demoralized – a series of small community coalitions sprang up, hounding the Conservatives at every turn. Through the spring and summer, these small coalitions operated in isolation from the union movement. The September 27 demonstration outside the legislature – the first big action in which social movement activists were joined by significant numbers of labour activists – made visible the fact that a change was happening. It is this interaction between social movements and organized labour that will provide the frame for this chapter.

Dress Rehearsal – January 25, 1995

Turn the clock back to January 1995, just before the election of the Harris Tories. In the social movements, there was real confusion. The NDP government, greeted with euphoria in 1990, was now isolated and increasingly desperate. Its policies had alienated the NDP from the very people who had put the party in office – organized labour, students, and the poor.

Above we examined the NDP attack on public-sector wages – euphemistically called a "Social Contract" – which had split the labour movement and turned thousands of once enthusiastic NDP supporters into indifferent bystanders. There were other policies with which the NDP was alienating its base. On March 28, 1994, NDP Social Service Minister Tony Silipo announced that the government would hire 270 special investigators at a cost of $20 million, to investigate every social assistance file in the province, and in addition, give municipalities an additional $20 million to "fight welfare fraud."[3] Many identified this as a straightforward mimicking of the scapegoating policies of the right wing. "It's political opportunism," said Ernie Lightman from the University of Toronto. "It's good to beat up on welfare recipients heading into an election."[4] The NDP government eliminated student grants for university and college students, presided over a significant increase in tuition fees, and laid the groundwork for Ontario post-secondary students to become some of the most indebted in North America. Waiting in the wings were the Liberals and the Conservatives – both jockeying to take advantage of the disillusion at the base of the NDP, to ride into office.

However, the threads which were to combine to create the Days of Action movement were visible if you looked for them. Politics is not just a story of the official parties. Deep forces were at work, pulling people from passivity and into mass action. Forces outside the ranks of organized labour went into action, and in turn, had an impact on the confidence and combativity of unionized workers. The first sign of this was not in the workers' movement, but in the student movement, arguably, the prelude to the Days of Action movement.

The Canadian Federation of Students (CFS) had called a Day of Action for January 25, 1995. This was not unusual. CFS had frequently called demonstrations against government education policies. But this time, the issue was more serious than usual. The federal Liberals were proposing policies which would lead to serious cuts to funding for universities and colleges, policies which, if implemented, would see tuition fees double in just three years. These cuts were part of an overhaul of federal financing, unprecedented in its scope.

The Liberals had taken office federally in November 1993. The early 1990s recession had sent budget deficits to record levels – $40 billion for the federal government, more than $60 billion if the provincial government deficits were added in.[5] The Liberals announced that these deficits had to come down, and they systematically set out to try to bring this about. Liberal Prime Minister Jean Chrétien and his finance minister, Paul Martin, began a process of cutbacks whose effects were devastating to health care, education, and social assistance across the country. In a very short time, federal government spending had been slashed by 20 per cent. Close to 50,000 public-sector workers, employed by Ottawa, were let go.[6]

One of the principal mechanisms used by the Liberals to slash spending was to change the rules by which tax money was transferred to the provinces. The central components of the "welfare state" – health care, education, and social assistance – while delivered provincially, are extremely dependent on "transfer payments" from the senior level of government. It is the federal government that has the greatest taxation power in Canada. Figure 3.1 illustrates changes in those transfer payments from 1966 to 1998, annual health, education, and social assistance transfer payments from the federal government to the provinces, adjusted for inflation (i.e., converted into 2025 dollars), and then divided by the population to provide a "per capita" transfer figure.

The steep rise in per capita transfer payments from budget year 1966–7 to budget year 1976–7 tracks the expansion of the welfare state marked most significantly by the passing of the Medical Care Act in 1966 – made possible by the support of the Tommy Douglas-led NDP for the minority government of Liberal Lester Pearson.[7] In that act, the federal government committed to providing half the costs for the delivery of health care in the provinces. But from that point until 1995–6, there was essentially stagnation, reflecting the shift in 1977 by the Pierre Trudeau-led Liberals from fifty-fifty cost-sharing to annual

Figure 3.1. Major Transfers to Other Levels of Government, 1966–98 (per capita, 2025 dollars).

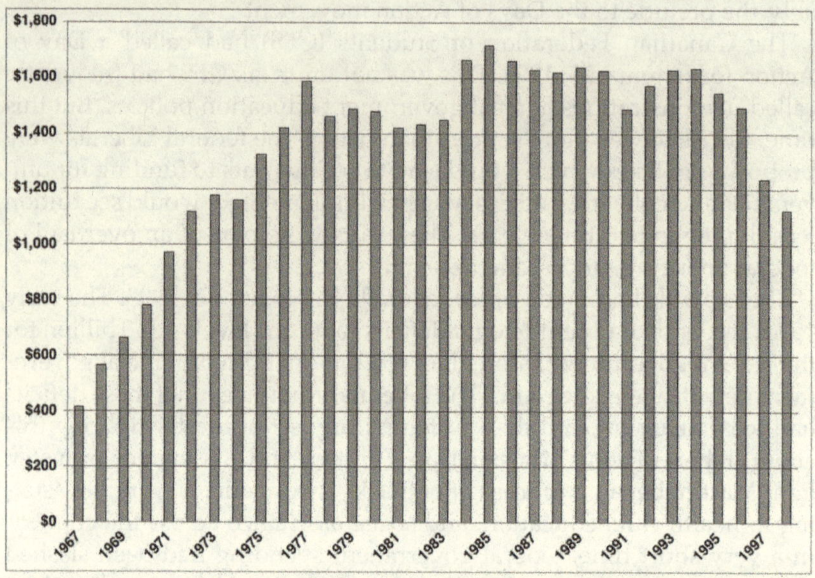

Author's compilation from Government of Canada and Statistics Canada.[8]

block payments. "Marc Lalonde, a former federal Minister of Health and Minister of Finance, stated that since federal transfers to provinces were tied to provincial health care spending initiatives, shared-cost programs were proving to be expensive for the federal government, and these costs were unpredictable."[9] In the next three budget years, stagnation turned to a slow decline, and then in 1996–7 and 1997–8 to a very steep decline: in the latter year per capita transfer payments retreated to where they had been a quarter century before. These changes coincided with the shift to a new formula for transfers, implemented in the budget year 1996–7 as the Canada Health and Social Transfer, governed by the Federal-Provincial Fiscal Arrangements Act, an act modified on several occasions in the years following.[10] The net effect of these modifications was to completely alter the profile of social spending in Canada, pushing more and more of the responsibility towards the provinces. From 1984 to 1994, transfer payments increased slightly in absolute terms (from $47.9 billion to $48.9 billion in 2025 dollars), decreasing slightly in per capita terms (from $1,811 to $1,634). But from 1995 to 1998, they were cut dramatically so that by 1998 the absolute figure was just $36.6 billion – $1,190 in per capita terms. On an annual basis, in other words, the federal government was sending about $20 billion less per year to the provinces, a cut in transfers that would either have to be made up with tax and user fee increases, or cuts in services, or a massive increase in provincial government debt, or a combination of all three.

These federal Liberal policies were directly complementary to the policies that were to unfold provincially under the Tories. They were policies deeply embedded in the bureaucratic institutions that comprise the modern state apparatus. Just days after winning the 1995 provincial election, Harris emerged from a meeting with Chrétien and announced that his government would "accept a reduction of transfers from the federal government, providing those dollars are going toward the deficit. I'm satisfied to date that they are."[11] (Three years into his mandate, there is some indication that Harris had buyer's remorse. "Ottawa must show it 'respects health care as a priority' by returning, over the next three years, the $6 billion it cut in transfer payments to the provinces, Premier Mike Harris says … 'This is money for health care that the people of Ontario have already paid with their federal taxes,' he said. 'This is money that has become part of the surplus in the federal budget.'"[12]) These Liberal policies were also reflective of class priorities shared across countries. In the summer of 2009, two figures from that era's Liberal administration – former top bureaucrat Jocelyne Bourgon and former Cabinet Minister Marcel Massé – flew across the Atlantic and met with leading British Conservatives including Philip Hammond, the shadow chief secretary to the Treasury.[13] We are not privy to the discussions which took place at these meetings. But it might not be a coincidence that the Conservatives in Britain in the twenty-first century embarked upon a serious austerity offensive that had many similarities with the Liberal austerity offensive Canada suffered through in the 1990s.

The Liberal policies leading to a reduction in transfer payments were at the core of the rationale for the CFS call for a day of strike and action, and the response to this call was extraordinary. The biggest rally was in Toronto, but there were also actions in Guelph, Moncton, Montreal, Ottawa, Regina, Saskatoon, St. John's, Vancouver, and Victoria. More than 60,000 in total participated in these events. If you include those who stayed away from classes, the figure of those involved rises to well above 100,000. And significantly, the mobilization had been done in conjunction with non-students – with social movement organizations, anti-poverty organizations, and trade unions.

> More than 140 local, provincial, and national organizations endorsed the Day of Action … Steelworkers Local 9196, miners in Stephensville,

Newfoundland, called in their support and congratulated students for "kicking butt." ... In some cities, Canadian Union of Public Employees (CUPE) members took the initiative to approach student unions and offer concrete organizational support. In other cities, postal workers participated in events leading up to January 25th. And throughout Canada, Public Service Alliance offices, CUPE offices and labour councils opened up their offices to provide students with access to photocopying. In Regina, 100 people defied temperatures of 22 degrees below zero and arrived on campus at 7:30 am to completely shut down the campus. The picket line was comprised of students, faculty and CUPE support staff who were not working that day. Cafeteria workers used their breaks to bring coffee to those staffing the picket lines. In Windsor, 250 Autoworker union members participated in the 2,000 strong rally.[14]

The different sectors of society do not exist in isolation. One of the key speakers at the rally in Toronto was Sunera Thobani, president of the National Action Committee on the Status of Women (NAC). Six months later, we will see the critical role of NAC and the feminist movement in helping to initiate struggle against the provincial Tories. Several union leaders also addressed the assembled crowd in Toronto, including Linda Torney from the Labour Council of Metro and York Region, Carolyn Egan from the United Steelworkers of America (USWA), Sid Ryan from CUPE and Buzz Hargrove, president of the Canadian Autoworkers, who closed the rally, saying: "The last time we had a crowd this big was when General Motors was handing out job applications."[15] Hargrove's reference would have been clearly understood by most in the crowd. On January 9, 1995, General Motors in Oshawa staged a recruitment drive to fill an expected four hundred to five hundred vacancies that would open that year. Some 25,000 stood in line in sub-zero winter weather for up to twenty-four hours "during a massive 'cattle call' at the Metro East Trade Centre." One year later, none had been hired.[16]

The January 25 student strike was an anticipation, a dress rehearsal if you will. Students had responded in numbers far bigger than any had predicted. The militancy of these young people – many demonstrating for the first time in their lives – caught labour activists unaware. It awoke memories in veterans of mass struggles in the past and began the process of spreading the idea that mass action was possible against the government cutback offensive, as related by Egan.

A Steelworker who marched with the students on January 25, said that when he saw 5,000 demonstrators from the University of Toronto round

Image 3.1. The January 25 student strikes.

> the corner to join the rally, a charge went through his body. "It was like a shot of adrenalin! I haven't felt that way for years, not since the Radio Shack strike, when busloads of miners came down from Sudbury and scattered the cops and the scabs. You can feel the power that we have."[17]

For the moment, it remained an anticipation. The story in Ontario shifted to the election. To no one's surprise, the NDP lost. To everyone's surprise, it was the Conservatives and not the Liberals who took office. Led by former golf club manager Mike Harris, these Conservatives were committed to an agenda of cutbacks on a scale never before seen in the province.

Tories Go on the Offensive

The scale of the Tories' offensive against the poor, against social services, and against workers' rights was unprecedented. On June 27, one day after being inaugurated, the Harris government announced a thirty-day review of all public housing projects.[18] Al Leach, the minister chosen by Harris to be responsible for housing, made no secret of his agenda. "As we've stated all along, it's our desire to get out of the housing business," he would tell reporters, later in July.[19] Three weeks into power, the axe really fell. It wasn't in a budget – the Tories would not present a budget until 1996 – but rather in something called a "fiscal overview." William Walker documented what we knew at the time.

- Social assistance for Ontario's poorest residents was slashed by 21.6 per cent, a cut of $938 million per year.
- New non-profit childcare spaces were cancelled, a $13 million per year cut.
- The JobsOntario training program was shuttered, an $86 million cut.
- The planned Jumpstart youth employment program was killed before it started, a cut of $60 million.
- $8 million was cut from the Employment Equity Commission, $10 million from the Advocacy Commission, and $16 million from the Workplace Innovation and Demonstration project.
- The Royal Commission on the Workers Compensation Board was scrapped.
- Pay equity funding was capped at $500 million annually.
- Payments to all social service agencies were cut 2.5 per cent effective October 1 to be followed by a 5 per cent cut in 1996–7.

The cuts totalled $1.9 billion in all, more than half of this coming at the expense of social assistance recipients.[20] Some of the cuts had effects that were both expensive and bizarre. Among the transit projects shelved was Toronto's Eglinton subway, even though $54 million had already been spent digging the tunnel. An additional $42 million had to be spent filling in the hole.[21] By December, it was clear that the extent of the cuts would go much further. Another "non-budget" with a huge impact, the November 1995 economic statement was, according to John Ibbitson, "the most important financial document tabled by the Harris government, eclipsing any of its budgets to come."[22] According to an analysis published by the CAW in their invaluable weekly newsletter *Contact*, over three years, the cuts would total $6.2 billion, and by 1999 would amount to $8 billion.

- Transfer payments to municipalities would be cut by 43 per cent.
- There would be a one-year 9 per cent reduction in transfers to school boards and an 18 per cent cut in hospital funding over three years.
- Spending on government administration would be cut by 33 per cent.
- There would be new user fees for prescription drugs for seniors and social assistance recipients.
- All of this was to be accompanied by extensive legislative changes to make it easier to close hospitals and keep wages low.[23]

There might have been an element of hyperbole when Robert MacDermid and Greg Albo called this a complete reordering of life in Ontario,[24] but it was certainly shocking and severe.

Some of the changes were ideological and not fiscal. In June of 1996, for instance, for the first time since the 1930s, the Conservatives would introduce workfare into the province. Up to 300,000 social assistance recipients would be forced to work up to seventeen hours a week. If they refused, they would be cut from social assistance. The implication, of course, was that the unemployed were out of work by choice, not because of poor economic conditions. Jamie Kristensen of the Ontario Coalition Against Poverty (OCAP) expressed a different view on June 12, at the raucous news conference where Social Services Minister David Tsubouchi announced the new program. "I've been through upgradings," Kristensen told reporters. "I've gone through college. There is no work for me out there."[25] The Ontario unemployment rate in June 1996 was 9.5 per cent. For young people, aged 15–24, it was 15.6 per cent.[26]

From the Beginning, Small Battles

The election of the Harris government, the open war on the poor, and the open war on workers were felt like body blows by working people everywhere. Despite the shock and disorientation that was widespread throughout the province, there was from the beginning a minority willing to take to the streets and protest. Harris rolled to his majority government on June 8, 1995. The next night, between 350 and 700 gathered in Toronto to mark the first anniversary of the defeat of Bill 167, the Equality Rights Statute Amendment Act, examined earlier, which would have "recognized same-sex relationships in law."[27] The bill – opposed by every member of the Tory caucus – was defeated when then NDP premier Bob Rae decided to allow a "free vote" by the NDP caucus. The demo was transformed into a denunciation of the "Tory bigots," a phrase used on what was probably the most popular of the signs carried by the protesters.[28]

Central to the developing movement against Harris was the June 26 demonstration against the Conservatives' swearing-in that was called by the Embarrass Harris coalition. This coalition had emerged not from the union movement, but rather from the feminist movement. The weekend after Harris was elected, there was an annual general meeting of what was at the time Canada's main feminist organization, the National Action Committee (NAC). Inspired by a speaker from Alberta who spoke about organizing against the Tories in that province, several Ontario women decided to form an ad hoc coalition to call a demonstration that would directly confront the legislature during the swearing-in. NAC's concerns about Harris were in part because of his stance on "women's issues." When the new cabinet was announced with just four women out of nineteen in total, then NAC president Sunera Thobani said, "there's no new ground broken here for women." But NAC's concerns went beyond this. The appointment of David Tsubouchi as community and social services minister was seen by Thobani as "bringing in a racial minority to do the dirty work in the province."[29]

Kam Rao, one of the key June 26 organizers, explained: "Some of us were really hell bent that it had to be there while they were on their stage. People know the difference between standing in front of an empty legislature building and standing in front of a legislature building where a government's about to dig its heels in on an agenda that's going to seriously hurt all of us. … We hoped that we wouldn't humiliate ourselves and that we'd have more than 500 people and in the end we had 2,500."[30] In large part this success came from the coalition-building approach taken by the NAC activists. They joined forces with OCAP and the Toronto Injured Workers' Advisory Group, among others. "More than 20 organizations representing labor, anti-poverty, women, seniors, students, the disabled, Indians [*sic*], co-op housing, gays and lesbians, visible minorities and child care, took part in the event."[31] Those 2,500 created an extraordinary scene. At times their angry chants could be heard inside the legislature. One Tory mocked the demonstration as consisting of "shaved heads" and "a lot of special-interest groups."[32] Out on the lawn, trade union leader Judy Darcy told the crowd: "The only special interest not represented here today is big business and the wealthy."[33]

For anyone with historical memory, it was a remarkable event. From David Peterson's lawn ceremony of 1985, and Bob Rae's love-in of 1990, Mike Harris's swearing-in of 1995 had devolved into an angry protest of 2,500. These were markers of significant shifts underway in Ontario politics.

Backlash Against Activism

For a while, many could not see these shifts. An atmosphere of demoralization permeated the union and social movements, reeling from the defeat of the NDP and unable to see the possibility of mass action against the Tories. Some pushed against this demoralization. President of the CAW Buzz Hargrove, responding to the Tories' promise to gut Ontario labour laws, said: "We're not going backward for the first time in the province's history. It could very well lead to some production being taken out of the system." President of the Canadian Union of Public Employees in Ontario Sid Ryan, responding to the Tories' threat to lay off 13,000 public-sector workers, said there would be "serious labour unrest."[34] But, their voices were a minority within the Ontario union leadership. Leah Casselman, president of the Ontario Public Service Employees Union, "said before issuing ultimatums she would try to work with the government to improve services."[35] Rather than build protests, Casselman, OFL president Gord Wilson, and Ontario director of the USWA Harry Hynd, according to Tony Van Alphen, wanted "to meet with him [Harris] and give the Conservatives' 'Common Sense Revolution' some different common sense."[36] Casselman refused to back the June 26 anti-Tory demonstration.[37]

Some outside the labour movement were similarly sceptical. Former Toronto mayor, John Sewell, in a full-page article in Toronto's *NOW Magazine*, said that while demonstrations against the cuts were welcome, they were simultaneously "marginal and impotent [*sic*]," unrealistically designed to "bring together masses of poor people – without realizing that they rarely have the energy or the wherewithal to fight back." According to Sewell: "At the end of the day, it's up to the urban middle class to do something."[38]

Sewell penned his piece in August, oblivious to the fact that in the previous month some very low-paid workers – very much not part of the urban middle class – had stepped onto centre stage in the struggle against Harris. One of the first attacks from the Harris Tories was directed at childcare. A key component of the attack involved cuts to funding that would "eliminate 3,580 child-care spaces, close some centres and throw 480 employees out of work."[39] On July 20, 1995, the day before Harris was to announce these cuts to subsidies, 1,000 childcare workers (who, given their low wages, would certainly qualify as poor) from eighty-plus day care centres in Toronto went on an illegal walkout and demonstrated at Queen's Park.[40] Andrea Calver from Embarrass Harris addressed the 1,000 in attendance at the demonstration, saying: "The Harris government plans to enact an agenda of pain that eliminates jobs, dismantles government programs and will leave the citizens of this province more vulnerable to poverty, homelessness and unemployment."[41] Their actions won a reprieve. Metro Toronto Council – by an extremely narrow 14–13 vote – used its corporate contingency fund to "save the spaces until the end of December at a cost of $1.8-million, and to spend a further $1.6-million in the first six months of next year to keep centres operating while the spaces affected by the provincial cut are phased out and other means of funding are found."[42] Sewell made no mention of this partial victory and the struggle which led to it.

But this scepticism notwithstanding, within months there would be tens of thousands on the streets against the Conservatives. What would have happened if Harris had taken office and the small marches, the small rallies, the small protests had *not* taken place? You don't create a mass movement out of nothing. Mass movements emerge when there is a growing feeling of confidence that action can make a difference. That confidence is not built all at once but is a culmination of battles, which of necessity begin on a much smaller scale. The lesbian and gay rights activists, day care workers, anti-poverty activists, social assistance recipients, and feminist "Embarrass Harris" organizers who took to the streets in the days and weeks following the Conservative victory helped nurture the flame of resistance during what were very difficult times.

The movement to come was anticipated in the many other anti-Tory actions that took place throughout the summer of 1995.

- July 2, at what was then called the Lesbian and Gay Pride parade in Toronto, 600,000 spectators watched 60,000 marchers, many of whom "waved rainbow flags while others carried Embarrass Harris signs."[43]
- July 21, the Embarrass Harris coalition rallied several hundred people outside government offices in downtown Toronto to denounce the attacks on the poor and on social programs. Embarrass Harris "paraded Harris' telephone number on a large banner" and "urged the public to 'flood' the Premier's office with calls of protest. At the same demo, "John Clarke of the Ontario Coalition Against Poverty," an organization present at virtually all of the early anti-Harris demonstrations, "called on the demonstrators to mobilize in 'unprecedented numbers' to 'defeat this man (Harris) and drive him out of office.'"[44]
- July 29, between 2,000 and 3,000 demonstrated at Queen's Park against the 21.6 per cent cuts to welfare slated to be implemented on October 1.[45] "They were joined by 150 people who marched 15 miles

from Scarborough, North York and Etobicoke."[46] The *Toronto Star*, while reporting a smaller figure of 500, featured the demonstration prominently on the second page of their Sunday edition, stating: "Injured workers, union representatives and welfare recipients were among the hundreds protesting." Significantly, it is at this demo that the term "Day of Action" first made its appearance. "Participants walked through the crowd ... handing out leaflets that announced a 'Provincial Day of Action' scheduled for what will likely be the first day of the sitting of the Legislature, Sept. 25."[47]

- August 2, some 300 demonstrated outside the provincial government building in Ottawa, also protesting the social assistance cuts. "The demonstration shut down the intersection at Rideau Street and Sussex Drive."[48]
- August 3, 150 demonstrators gathered outside the local Conservative MP's office in Peterborough.[49]
- August 5, 75 members and supporters of "Harmony Hollow Home Co-operative" in Hamilton pitched tents and slept outside overnight to protest cuts to 385 non-profit housing projects in Ontario.[50]
- August 22, 600 people in a march organized by OCAP made their way from Regent Park in Toronto, "one of Toronto's poorest neighbourhoods, to Rosedale, home of some of Toronto's wealthiest business tycoons."[51] The message, from the left-wing OCAP, couldn't have been clearer: Harris was ruling for the rich, and ignoring the poor.

These were just some of the actions across the province that summer. In places, the actions involved just dozens. Often, they involved hundreds. On at least three occasions they surpassed 1,000. But they proved to have an importance far greater than their numbers as events unfolded in the fall and winter of that first year of the Harris government. The small battles during the summer of 1995 slowly began to build confidence that the Conservatives could be challenged. Those "small battles" continued into the fall, documented meticulously by Jason Ziedenberg.[52]

- October 1, "Several hundred people attended a 'Rap and Rage against the Cuts' concert" in Allen Gardens in Toronto.
- October 4, in response to David Tsubouchi, minister of social services, suggesting that "welfare recipients could buy dented tins of tuna to cope with the 20 percent welfare cut, the Women's Centre of Grey-Bruce launched 'Project Tuna.' By the end of the

month, thousands of empty tins of tuna, sent by activists across the province, arrived on the minister's desk."

- The week of October 9, "Harris was met by protesters in Toronto, Kingston and Ottawa, and, in each city, had to be protected by lines of police in riot gear, armed with pepper spray."
- October 17, "three dozen women took over the social service minister's office to protest cuts to spousal abuse centres and counselling services."
- In the third week of October, a personage called "Mrs. Oktoberfest" had to "clean egg yolks off the premier's shoes after protesters showered him with produce at the annual German festival in Kitchener."
- In the fourth week of October, "an anti-Harris protester, dressed in a tuxedo, crept up to an open microphone at a charity dinner for Toronto's Catholic clergy, and berated Harris and other business leaders for five minutes before he was dragged away, kicking and screaming."

Reports from the CAW's *Contact* newsletter give a powerful sense of the breadth of the movement.

- From the October 22 issue – 60 anti-Harris activists embarked on a two-day "Journey for Justice" from Windsor to Chatham, organized by the CAW, the Windsor Coalition Against Poverty, Windsor and Area Coalition for Social Justice and the Windsor and District Labour Council. They were sent on their way by a 1,000-strong march through the streets of Windsor. On arriving at Chatham, the 60 were joined by folks from Chatham, St. Thomas, London, and Sarnia and established a "make-shift tent city dubbed HarrisVille. They said the tent city represented the Harris government's vision of affordable housing."[53]
- From the October 29 issue – After provincial ministry staff had prepared a "welfare diet" that included bologna, 125 protesters greeted a $300-a-plate Tory fundraising dinner in Concord, Ontario, presenting attendees with bologna sandwiches.[54]
- The same issue of the newsletter reported a rally of 55 in Owen Sound protesting the closure of a Women's Centre housing project – a rally to show solidarity with Women's Centre activists who were holding daily vigils outside the local Conservative MPP's office.[55]

It is significant that a key source documenting the "small battles" of the summer and fall is the newsletter of the CAW. That union was at the forefront of the labour movement, identifying the importance of the anti-Harris mobilizations, and finding ways to build links with community organizations. But for the challenge to Harris to become mass and effective, the ranks of organized labour beyond the CAW would have to be brought on board. In Ontario, that meant the forty-two unions grouped in the OFL, with 650,000 members, by far and away the biggest mass organization in the province. In Ontario, close to 40 per cent of working people were members of unions in the 1990s. If the anti-Tory movement could move from the streets to organized workers in the workplaces, then Harris would face a much bigger fight.

Return for a moment to the attacks on childcare. The July 20, 1,000-strong rally against attacks on childcare had temporarily stopped the worst of the cuts. However, Laurie Monsebraaten wrote that her newspaper (the *Toronto Star*) had been told by "sources" that, while cuts to an $8,000 wage subsidy had been deferred, other attacks were coming – including to pay equity settlements for the childcare workers, and subsidies provided to about 14,000 low-income families to help defer the costs to childcare.[56]

In November 1995 it was, again, Monsebraaten who broke the story, writing: "According to a confidential social services ministry report obtained by *The Star*, provincial Tories are considering killing more than 68,000 day-care subsidies and instead giving eligible parents day-care vouchers worth between $346 and $390 a month per child." This would be a real blow to low-income women, given the fact that childcare at the time was averaging $700 a month (and much more for infants under 2 years old), and also a blow to childcare workers, likely to experience layoffs as children were withdrawn from their care because of the expense.[57]

The response was explosive. The Metro Child Care Advisory Committee called a meeting to discuss the cuts for November 7, expecting 250 people. Something like 1,000 turned up and hundreds had to be turned away.[58] Monday, November 13, "about 5,000 staff, children and parents from about 100 day-care centres across Metro marched in area neighbourhoods to protest the province's rumoured plans to eliminate the subsidy system."[59] And on November 24, the struggle expanded to the entire province, another illegal strike closing not just 80 in Toronto as had happened in July, but 400 – across the province 1,100 out of all 2,800 childcare facilities. Another 600, while staying open, staged a "day of mourning." "Hundreds of Ontario day care centres were closed," according to the report in *Contact*, "as thousands of daycare workers staged a one-day strike. At the same time thousands of parents and their children rallied on the lawn of Ontario's legislature to support the workers."[60] Ibbitson put the size of the Toronto demo at 2,700, and reported on demos in other cities including:

- Ottawa – 1,000 on Parliament Hill
- Windsor – 200 outside a provincial government building
- Hamilton – 100 outside the offices of Conservative MPP Lillian Ross
- Waterloo – 80 at the downtown Market Square[61]

Leading childcare advocate Kerry McCuaig estimated that about 11,000 workers took part in total.[62]

The childcare strikes of July 20 and November 24 were notable for several reasons. First, as I wrote at the time, the July 20 strike was "the first illegal walkout by Ontario members of the Canadian Union of Public Employees (CUPE) since the 13,000-strong hospital strike of 1981."[63] Second, these two childcare worker strikes were *political* strikes – challenging government policy, anticipating the tactic of the political strike that would be the defining approach of the whole Days of Action movement. Further, these illegal political strikes were (a) carried out by a workforce comprised overwhelmingly of women workers; (b) emerging from workforces organized in CUPE, the union that would become (along with the CAW) one of two main centres in labour's fight against the Tories; and (c) driven by an issue deeply embedded in the history of the feminist movement – defending access to childcare. The galvanizing role of childcare – a core issue of the feminist movement – leading to the core tactic of the illegal political strike shone a light on how the "small battles" of the social movements might link up with the "big battalions" of the workers' movement.

Chapter Four

London Calling[1]

The breakthrough – organized labour joining the social movements in a mass way – came on September 27, 1995. It was earlier noted that at the July 29 demo at Queen's Park a call had gone out for a "Day of Action" when the legislature reconvened on September 25. As it turned out, the actual reconvening date was two days later, September 27. The Embarrass Harris Campaign was joined by two major Toronto-based union organizations – the Labour Council of Metropolitan Toronto and York Region and the Building Trades Council – in the call for a mass protest outside Queen's Park on September 27. For the first time, the ragtag army of anti-Tory activists had been joined by organizations with links to the mass organizations of the working class.

On Labour Day in Toronto, more than 10,000 flyers announcing the demonstration were distributed to union contingents. "Hundreds of workers carried signs calling for unionists to join the protest" on September 27. OCAP organized an overnight march from Markham to downtown Toronto, culminating in a rally and march from Allan Gardens to Queen's Park. Some reports put their contingent alone at 1,000.[2] The CFS built the action on campuses across the city. Busses from around the province were organized, including three from Guelph organized by the Guelph anti-cuts coalition and the Guelph and District Labour Council. "Solidarity actions are being planned for the same day in many communities throughout Ontario."[3] The anti-Tory street activists were now working in sync with student organizations, and key labour organizations had come onside. The "big battalions" of the labour movement were not yet involved, but for the first time, at least some of the labour movement's official organizations were backing the protests.

Labour Council and September 27

When September 27 came, it was clear that the anti-Tory movement would now be a *union-backed* anti-Tory movement. Laurie Monsebraaten wrote that the September 27 demonstration, "organized by the Labour Council of Metro and York Region and the Embarrass Harris Campaign, drew at least 17 busloads of demonstrators from communities across Ontario including Ottawa, Peterborough, Sudbury and St. Catharines."[4] In attendance were members of the Canadian Autoworkers, United Food and Commercial Workers, United Steelworkers of America, Canadian Union of Postal Workers, Canadian Union of Public Employees and the Ontario Public Service Employees Union – as well as hundreds marching with the Ontario Coalition Against Poverty.[5] Many put the size of the demonstration at around 5,000.[6] Some organizers put the figure at 7,000.[7] It was probably not the "tens of thousands" as described by Jim Turk.[8] But it was large and, importantly, beyond anyone's expectations. It was the largest protest yet against the Harris cuts, the first where the majority were organized workers, and the first that gave a sign of the mass movement building in the province.

The protesters were greeted by what Jim Turk describes as "heavily armed police who started lashing out, clubbing a number of women at the front of the doors" to Queen's Park.[9] In the ensuing confusion, the doors to the legislature were shut, keeping out not just protesters, but also some MPPs.[10] All of this was unprecedented. Never before in Canadian history had the opening day of the legislature for a newly elected government been greeted by a demonstration as angry and as large as the one that gathered on September 27. Traditionally, the Queen's representative – the lieutenant governor – arrives "by open carriage to be greeted by the firing of cannons." There was no such event this time, ostensibly for cost-cutting reasons, but probably, as Martin Mittelstaedt suggested, because staging such an "outdoor ceremony" would be difficult given the planned protests.[11] This turned out to be a good call. When September 27 arrived, there was no room on the lawn for this aristocratic dog and pony show, jammed as it was with angry anti-Tory workers and students.

The protest was also the first one to penetrate the workplaces. More than a demonstration, it involved workers collectively leaving their workplace and marching to the legislature.

> Workers streamed out of the hospitals on University Avenue, they came by the thousands out of government offices at Queen's Park. Clerical and administrative workers crossed the road from the University of Toronto.

> The Labour Council of Metro Toronto [and York Region] bucked the trend so common today in other labour bodies. Because of the urging of rank and file delegates, at its last meeting it unanimously decided that it would organize with other sectors to make Harris and his Tories understand that they were in for a fight. The Labour Council called on trade unionists in the Toronto area to come out and stand up for their rights, and the rights of every oppressed and exploited person in this province. The result of this call put a lie to earlier pronouncements by union leaders who declared that demonstrations were premature and wouldn't work.[12]

The OFL had not backed the September 27 demonstration. But its success created enough pressure to finally push the top union leaders in the province to call an anti-Tory action. The OFL would be having its convention in November, and the call went out from the OFL Executive Board that during the convention there would be a mass anti-Tory demonstration on November 22. From Embarrass Harris and OCAP to the Labour Council of Metro Toronto and York Region, the pressure had now built up sufficiently to put the ball in the court of the mass organizations of the Ontario working class. However, it was not yet clear which way the OFL leadership would go. Often in the past, there had been token action programs and token protests, sufficient to let off steam but insufficient to build a real movement. Would this time around be any different?

Two things ensured that it *would* be different: first, the deepening of confidence among rank and file workers that the Conservatives could be fought, as outlined above; second, the intensification of the Conservative assault.

Up to this point, the brunt of the Conservative assault had been on the poor and social programs. But in the summer and fall of 1995, the Conservatives turned their attention to labour. On August 8, 1995, the Workplace Health and Safety Agency was disbanded, leading to the layoff of many employment standards inspectors.[13] Most visible was the attack on Bill 40, introduced by the previous NDP government, at the core of which was anti-scab legislation, making strike-breaking illegal in the province. Bill 40 was an affront to the Conservatives and their big business backers. On October 31, the Conservatives rushed through Bill 7 in order to repeal the provincial anti-scab law, a day before a planned protest by public-sector workers. According to Steve Watson, the bill "included sixty-three last-minute amendments most members in the legislature had not read."[14] The new legislation would make it harder to unionize, easier to decertify unions, and would pave the way to large-scale privatization of services.

Elizabeth Witmer, minister of labour, tried to portray the Conservative approach as "restoring the balance, a very delicate balance in labor relations, and adding a few measures that will democratize the workplace."[15] But much more was at stake. David Rapaport, from 1991 to 1997 vice-president of OPSEU Region 5, an enormous region which included Toronto, says that while "Bill 7 was a major assault on the rights of all unions in Ontario, it had greater implications for civil servants, because it removed our successor rights from the Crown Employees Collective Bargaining Act (CECBA)." Without successor rights, when a section of the public sector was privatized, the old collective agreement was null and void, and unions had to go back to square one, conduct an organizing drive, and negotiate a "first contract."[16] This analysis was confirmed by none other than Dave Johnson, chair of the Management Board of Cabinet, who was quoted as saying that "civil servants must be stripped of their union rights for the economic good of Ontario."[17]

If the first round of cuts had been a war on the poor, this new Bill 7 was a war on organized workers. Suddenly, the union movement moved to the front of the line in the battle against the Harris Conservatives. The summer of street activism had given people confidence that the Conservatives could be fought. The September 27 breakthrough had shown that if major union organizations put out a serious call, thousands of workers would respond. The vicious attack on workers' rights intersected with this rising confidence, leading to an explosion of anger in the ranks of organized labour.

After the Labour Council of Metro Toronto and York Region, the next major mass workers' organization to respond was the CAW. On October 31, the day Bill 7 passed into law, "almost 600 leaders of the Canadian Auto Workers ... voted unanimously to lead a general strike before the end of the year."[18] It was a very aggressive, very bold resolution: "that the CAW continue the fightback against the Harris and corporate agenda, and that we organize with the rest of the labour movement and working people of Ontario to stage, as one part of the fightback, a shutdown of the Province of Ontario."[19] Suddenly, the top leaders of the Ontario union movement were caught between two opposing forces. From above, they were being hammered by the most vicious anti-union legislation in Ontario since the 1930s. From below, they were being pressed – first by the Labour Council of Metro Toronto and York Region's 10,000-strong September 27 protest, and now by 600 local leaders of the province's strongest private-sector union – to call strike action against the attack.

The weekend before the bill was passed, "Both Gary Parent, president of Windsor and District Labor Council, and Gord Wilson, Ontario

Federation of Labor president, said … a joint labor action to protest the repeal of Bill 40 and its replacement by Bill 7 is being planned and the auto industry has been targeted,"[20] with Wednesday, November 1 – the date the bill was to be passed – floated as a possible date. The threat of a political strike targeting automobile production was taken very seriously by auto executives. Steve Lowe, director of public relations for GM in Oshawa, said: "A work stoppage would be illegal and we will react strongly to that."[21] It was taken seriously, for quite different reasons, by anti-Tory activists. "Faxes went out on Friday [October 27] to labour leaders across the province. As we write this (Saturday morning) we are aware of at least two emergency meetings taking place: one at the OFL building in Toronto; another of OPSEU members specifically regarding action against Bill 7."[22] But November 1 came and went, and no strike call was issued. "There was talk in a lot of our Cambridge plants that people were upset they didn't have it [the strike] today," said Tom Rooke, president of CAW Local 1986 in Cambridge. Friday, November 3 was floated as a new strike day, but when the day arrived instead of a strike there was a meeting of top OFL union leaders.[23] The truth is, there was considerable opposition at the top of the movement to taking *any* strike action against the Conservatives. Many union leaders simply did not believe that workers would heed the call. Further, the auto industry made it very clear that any work stoppage would be illegal and "might result in reprisals."[24]

Then in the second week of November, word spread like wildfire through union and activist circles in Ontario: on November 14 the CAW was going to strike the Autoplex complex in Oshawa, at the time the biggest centre of vehicle production in Canada. The walkout would have been illegal. There were then, and are to this day, severe restrictions on what strike activity is allowed between collective agreements. But there was such anger against the Conservatives that there was every reason to believe the walkout could have worked, and a successful walkout would have inspired the fightback across the province. This was particularly true for a job action involving the CAW, whose "social unionism" (or "movement unionism" in Sam Gindin's words) meant it had a much greater affinity with the social movements – particularly the anti-poverty organizers – which had been at the forefront of the anti-Harris movement to date.[25]

The leadership of the Oshawa local, CAW 222, backed the call and threw themselves into organizing it. The Social Action Committee of the CAW was enthusiastically working to bring in activists from other trade unions and social movements. The strategy was to call on the day shift to stay away from work and to reinforce this call with picket lines starting at 6 a.m. and staffed by other trade unionists, anti-poverty activists, and others opposed to the Conservatives. In our office, we received telephone reports about plans for busses of activists to go to Oshawa from Toronto and Kingston to support the stay-away. For students, anti-poverty activists, and trade unionists from the public sector to stand side by side on picket lines with one of the country's strongest private-sector unions would have seriously built the solidarity necessary in the fight against the Conservatives. But after setting the wheels in motion for the stay-away, on November 9 the plug was pulled. The phones rang across the province to tell people the strike was off. This account of events in November 1995 was first drafted in real time, while phone calls and reports flooded into our newspaper office. Very little of this intense activity has been captured in any subsequent press accounts. The closest I could find was a cryptic reference in a *Toronto Star* article a few days later. Theresa Boyle reported that "plans to protest" the anti-labour Bill 7 "before it was passed were scuttled because of the Tories' haste in pushing it through." Boyle quoted Dean Lindsay, then recording secretary for CAW Local 222 in Oshawa, saying, "Labor was starting to organize but the government had to make sure to cut the legs out from under us."[26]

CAW officials were not forthcoming with the reasons for calling off the November 14 stay-away. There was, apparently, fear at the highest levels that the rank and file of Local 222, many of whom, as we documented in the previous chapter, voted for the Conservatives in the provincial election and for the Reform Party (predecessor to the Canadian Alliance, now folded back into today's federal Conservative Party) in the previous federal election, would not respond to the call for a stay-away.

But was this fear justified? Reform Party arguments did have a hearing in a section of Local 222. We saw earlier that right-wing Reform Party supporters had led a call for the local to disaffiliate from the NDP. The Reform Party based much of its politics on, among other things, welfare-bashing. But in October, the month before the announced strike date, anti-poverty activists from OCAP met with 200 stewards from Local 222. At the meeting was a single mother on welfare who explained her plight to the stewards. There was an enthusiastic response from the stewards at the meeting. John Clarke, provincial organizer of OCAP put it clearly.

> In the course of our work, we've had dealings with local leadership and with rank and file members of 222, and have always found that if the issues were presented from the standpoint of working class unity, we have got nothing but a warm reaction.[27]

Regardless, the strike was off. The elation of November 9 gave way to dejection. There would be no Oshawa strike on November 14.

"Let's Do a Community" – CUPE, CAW, and the OFL

Harris was exerting intense pressure from above. There was pressure from outside of organized labour in the ragtag volunteer army of the social movements. Left there, it is not clear that a general strike movement would have been called. Importantly there also developed intense pressure from two key unions in the province – the Ontario division of CUPE and the CAW, whose presidents were Sid Ryan and Buzz Hargrove.

CUPE at the time had about 200,000 members in Ontario organized into eight hundred locals. Within the union, an intensive education and mobilization campaign was underway, to both increase understanding about the nature and danger of the Harris cuts, but also about the possibility of organizing against it. Thousands of CUPE members were involved in this internal campaign. CUPE's René Fortin, who would in March 1996 be the co-chair of the Sudbury Day of Action, outlined this very clearly.

> We held a series of consultations with the local leadership, which culminated in massive conferences throughout Ontario in which direction was given by the local leadership. In every community or concentration of membership, we called leadership meetings and then membership meetings.[28]

There was a specific goal at these meetings, to have members vote on a general strike, "for the withdrawal of all public services in the province." CUPE – the biggest union in the province – could impact public services through strike action. But having a real general strike would require the support of unions in the private sector. Fortin says that "the Steelworkers and other industrial unions were reticent." The one private-sector union where the call for a general strike resonated was the CAW.

Herman Rosenfeld, at the time working in the education department of the CAW, describes a process of education and mobilization inside the CAW, both in the run-up to the first Day of Action and in all subsequent ones. This internal campaign differed in its specifics from that in CUPE – a union with a very different structure than the CAW – but pushed in the same direction and with the same kind of impact.

> We set up meetings in union halls, or informally in bars and donut shops. We produced leaflets and materials specifically targeted to the workers

> in the workplaces in the community, zeroing in on issues that we knew would touch a chord with them. They were handed out in union meetings, informal meetings, and inside workplaces. We encouraged activists and local union officials inside workplaces to talk to co-workers, and suggested tactics for them to do this. This was a planned component of building the Days of Action in each of the target cities. While most of the meetings were with small numbers of people, they eventually involved thousands of workers.[29]

The complete picture of the CAW's role is more complex. Then CAW president Buzz Hargrove was a complicated figure – capable of fiery oratory and calls for mass movements and social action – and simultaneously willing to explore avenues of improbable compromise. After the election of Harris, he chastised corporate Ontario, saying, "the corporations can't have it both ways; they can't expect stability in shop floor relations while they cheer-lead the Harris government's gutting of labour laws."[30] The same article which reported this anti-corporate rhetoric also reported on a joint letter signed by the CAW and Chrysler Corporation "urging caution with respect to the government's announced wholesale dismantling of labour laws." Hargrove in the article said that "Chrysler is not the only corporation expressing doubt about massive regressive changes to labour law" and indicated that other corporations intended "to sign a similar letter."[31] Nothing came of a corporate-centred strategy to stop the labour law amendments. The CAW's principal role would be as a core part of the building social movement – focussing on the call for a general strike.

To have the largest public-sector union and the largest private-sector union in the province campaigning for a general strike was unprecedented. But to really mount such a strike would require at least the cooperation, and at best leadership, from the umbrella organization of Ontario labour, the OFL and its executive board. That executive board and its president, Gord Wilson, were at best lukewarm to the notion of mass collective action against the Tories. Reshef and Rastin quote an unnamed CAW executive member saying that "the labour movement," specifically the executive board of the OFL, "was dragged into this protest kicking and screaming."

> The vast majority wanted to do nothing except just to educate our members to vote NDP the next election. That was, more or less, the consensus. But we had a strong sense that that wasn't going to work. We started out thinking that we could organize a Day of Action and build it up to three or four or five events. But it was absolutely clear that we couldn't get the

> majority of the unions, both public and private, on side, and that it would be a challenge for us.
>
> It [i.e., a community-based protest] was actually [then-OFL president] Gordie Wilson's idea. As we were trying to get the people to agree on a Provincial action, Gordie said, "Let's do a community; let's just start it at some community and see what kind of response we get." I grabbed on to it like a drowning man who grabs the branch of a tree, 'cause there wasn't much else we were able to get through our consensus politics in the labour movement.[32]

Significantly, the unnamed CAW executive member put the weight of the organizing responsibility on the CAW. "Gordie was smart enough to know that if you're going to make it successful the CAW had to lead it. So he told me that he would support whatever community we selected. We looked at London because it had to be a place where we could mobilize; it had to be one that we could come out of it with credibility."[33]

On November 12, the OFL Executive Board recommended a motion for the upcoming biennial OFL convention that a one-day general strike take place in London on December 11. This was the second-best choice. Striking Oshawa at the heart of the Canadian economy would have sent a quick message to the Conservatives that the movement was serious. It would have galvanized hundreds of thousands – in Ontario and the other provinces – that a fightback was on the cards, a serious fightback. No one could question the power of the workers of Oshawa. That city, along with Winnipeg, Windsor, Sept-Îles, and a few other places, is iconic in Canada as a location of historic working-class militancy. London was more of an unknown quantity. Some in our office felt that the OFL Executive Board was putting forward London in the hope that it would be rejected out of fear that London workers would not respond. Nonetheless, a date had been proposed, a place had been chosen, and all eyes turned to the upcoming OFL convention and its decision on December 11 and London.

When the time came for the OFL convention to vote, there was no stopping the general strike call. The top leaders were preoccupied with the issue of labour's relation to the NDP and what some of us called, at the time, "an extraordinarily uninspiring executive election." There was little push from the top to build support for general strike action. But when the vote came on November 20, the 2,000 delegates, "much closer to the shop floor anger than the officials at the top of the movement, pushed these petty disputes aside to massively endorse the action plan" and its call for a one-day strike in London, December 11.[34]

It was, in fact, a very ambitious action plan, summarized by Marcella Munro as calling for "a series of escalating actions, including workplace disruptions, that would build towards a general walkout of organized labour in the province."[35] Suddenly, there was a road map for activists, showing the way to building a mass movement against the Conservatives. Shut down London on December 11. Target another major city in early 1996. Build towards a province-wide general strike to stop the Conservative attacks. Throughout the province, organizing meetings took place – both inside and outside the union movement – to prepare for the London Day of Action. One of the most important was a CAW Council with 650 delegates, culminating in a 1,000-strong rally against the Harris Tories, a council which voted unanimously to endorse the OFL's Fightback program, "including the call for a Day of Protest in London on December 11."[36]

In 1972, 300,000 Quebec workers staged a massive general strike, which included seizing control of radio stations and other workplaces.[37] On October 14, 1976, one million stayed off the job protesting then Prime Minister Pierre Trudeau's policy of wage controls.[38] Since those events, the phrase "general strike" was rarely on anybody's lips. But now, many were reaching back in time to the 1970s and imagining a general strike to stop Harris. A general strike had brought the Conservative government in Britain to its knees in the early 1970s. A general strike in Ontario would reveal the extent of the isolation of the Conservatives and build the confidence of people who wanted a way out of the devastation the Conservatives were leaving in their wake. As the busses were booked to travel to London, as the leaflets and picket signs were being prepared, there was a sense throughout the province that we had everything to play for.

If you looked closely enough, though, there were also warning signs of troubles to come. Return for a moment to the OFL convention's "extraordinarily uninspiring executive election." The run-up to that election revealed clear signs of tension between the OFL executive, particularly its president Gord Wilson, and the CAW. A cryptic report in the CAW newsletter of September 18, 1995, complained about a letter from Wilson to the CAW, which the article's author said could "best be described as intent on dividing the labour movement, indeed dividing the CAW delegation, at the upcoming federation of labour convention when leadership elections will be held." The article's author went on to say: "To unite the OFL affiliates around a fight-back means pulling together a leadership team. Solidarity cannot be built on manipulation but on taking strong principled stands on issues, on taking action against the corporations that will profit from the Harris rollbacks."[39]

Cryptic or not, harsh phrases such as "solidarity cannot be built on manipulation" speak to a sharp, factional division. When that "uninspiring election" took place, the CAW caucus supported Julie Davis for secretary-treasurer and Sid Ryan for vice-president. Both lost – the pro-social movement Ryan being defeated by John Murphy, president of the Power Workers' Union.[40] Murphy would emerge less than a year later as one of the most prominent "pink paper" union leaders, opposed to continuing the Days of Action. Perhaps it was true that Gord Wilson "was smart enough to know that if you're going to make it successful the CAW had to lead it." We will see that the CAW would play a central role throughout the Days of Action. But the CAW was not to be rewarded with having people they endorsed win leadership positions in the OFL – reflecting the ambivalence in the OFL towards a mass movement response to the Harris cuts, an ambivalence that existed throughout the OFL hierarchy.

General Strike Movement Begins – "It's Not as Cold as Harris"

When the day arrived, December 11 showed that we had the power to build a province-wide mass movement. In weather that was minus thirty with the wind chill, a crowd which protest organizers said was 15,000 strong[41] marched through the streets, chanting "it's not as cold as Harris."[42] Gord Wilson estimates that 40,000 stayed away from work that day.[43] General Motors's London diesel plant (2,200 workers), Cami in Ingersoll (2,300 workers), and Ford Talbotville (2,500) – all were shut for the day,[44] as were the Labatt brewery, Kellogg's, the McCormick cookie factory, 3M, the Accuride auto parts plant, the Canada Post sorting plant,[45] the municipal transit system,[46] and "all workplaces in three CAW locals – 88, 1520 and 27," including (besides some already mentioned above), AWL Steego, Burgess Wholesale, Connor's Eastown Chev Olds, Dale Downie, Globe Envelopes, Form Rite, Gentek, Hayes-Dana, Kimpex, London Machinery, Phillips Electronics, Siemens Electric, Spareton, Trailmobile, Unifin, Universal Engine, and Vytec Corp.[47]

All the work stoppages were illegal. Ford management received a court injunction banning pickets at the gates of the Talbotville plant, but workers from Cami showed up anyway and picketed the plant shut.[48] "Police watched the scene, but did not enforce the court injunction."[49] The 15,000-strong march felt like the beginning of a movement, the coming-out party of an opposition to Tory austerity plans. "Some demonstrators beat drums and blew whistles, while others carried signs like, 'Stop the Harris-ment' and 'Save the Social Programs.'"[50]

The most eloquent report of the day's events comes, again, from the pages of *Contact*. It is worth quoting the newsletter at length.

> At Burgess Wholesale the first CAW picket line went up Sunday afternoon, December 10. By 10:00 pm Sunday thousands of workers, CAW members, braved the bitterly cold winds that plunged temperatures to the minus 30 degree mark, to set up picket lines at the General Motors Diesel plant, the CAMI auto assembly plant, Ford, 3M, Accuride, Siemens and the list goes on.
>
> Warmed by the spirit of success and the coffee and food provided by USWA Local 1005 from Hamilton, the picket lines were solid – estimates place 1,000 to 1,500 workers at the gates of the three largest facilities, CAMI, Ford, and GM Diesel.
>
> By 5 am the next morning cell phones were ringing as picket line organizers called central headquarters to report all lines were up. On Highway 401 in the black of night, buses with 'charter' signs blazing began turning off at the London exit. By 8 am all plants were down and 11,000 CAW members of Locals 27, 1520, and 88 were part of a mass day of protest. ...
>
> At the airport, more than 300 CAW retirees set up an information picket and Santa Claus gave out lollipops. Air Canada cancelled several flights.
>
> More than 175 busloads of supporters from union locals, anti-poverty groups, and university student groups across the province rolled into London in the early hours. ...
>
> Later in the morning, nearly twelve thousand people rallied in the streets and marched to the London Western Fairgrounds jamming two cavernous buildings.
>
> The CAW Rank and File Band warmed up the crowd along with truckloads of hot chilli prepared by London area church groups.[51]

The mood of the day was captured perfectly by the title Slim Evans gave to his documentary of the day. "London Calling" evoked the great 1979 Clash album of the same name – a day of resistance against Ontario's Tories paying homage to a movement of resistance against Britain's Tories.[52] The Days of Action campaign had begun. The debate about moving to a province-wide general strike was now by far the most important political issue in the province.

Some Preliminary Conclusions

This chapter has returned to a theme that will recur throughout the book: the ongoing tension between the base of the movement – both in the unions and outside – and the institutional representatives of that movement itself. It is too simple to paint a picture of a rebellious rank and file, chomping at the bit, being held back by "misleaders of the class." However, what can be said is that the routinism, conservatism, and resulting lack of imagination and vision displayed by the principal representatives of the trade union movement again and again led to squandered opportunities and confusion in the movement. This was clear right from the movement's beginning. The anti-Harris movement began in the context of mass anger over the attack on social assistance and the poorest of the poor. The 21.6 per cent cut in social assistance rates was horrific to many. However, this did not galvanize the union leaders into action. It was Bill 7, which was seen as an affront to their authority and influence viz. both government and the employer, that moved the anger from the streets to the union offices. This is interestingly symbolic of a leadership more attuned to its own institutional concerns than to the plight of the poorest in the province.

This tension between the institutional representatives of the workers' movement and the movement itself (the "rank and file") needs to be approached very concretely through an appreciation of the ups and downs of the class struggle at the workplace. Unions present themselves in two different ways in modern society – as agents of collective bargaining and as agents of mass struggle, typically represented through actions on the picket line in strikes and lockouts. The background to the Days of Action in Ontario in the 1990s – not dissimilar from the experience in the United States, Britain, and other advanced industrial countries – was a background of many years where the level of class struggle, as measured in the statistics of strikes and lockouts, was exceedingly low. Figure 4.1 documents this, measuring workers involved in strikes and lockouts in Ontario and Canada from 1946 to 2018. To capture the "social weight" of these strikes, the numbers involved have been expressed per 1,000 population. It shows a steady decline from the peak levels of strike activity in Ontario in the late 1960s, to the very low levels in 1992, 1993, and 1994, the years just preceding the Days of Action when the NDP was in office in the province. In such an environment, it will not be surprising that the often-conservative traits of the institutionalized collective bargaining routine would come to dominate the union leaderships while the characteristics appropriate to the "war of manoeuvre" on the picket line would recede.

The "Days of Action" moment presents itself at one level as a classic confrontation between a party sympathetic to big business (the Conservatives) and the "serried ranks" of organized labour. That dimension is of course present. But what this and the previous chapter have

Figure 4.1. Workers Involved in Strikes and Lockouts – Ontario and Canada, 1946–2018 (per 1,000 population).

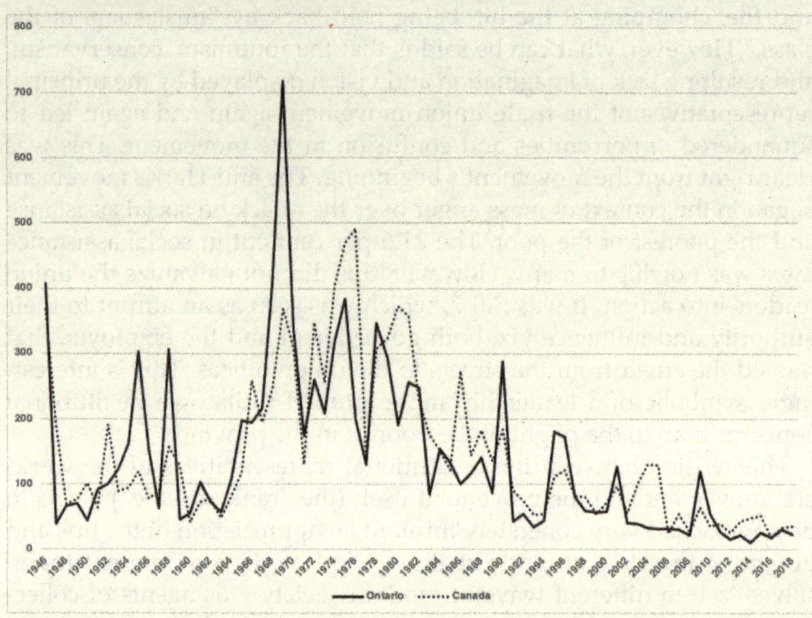

Source: Authors compilation from data in Statistics Canada and Government of Canada.[53]

tried to show, is that without the activity and presence of thousands outside the ranks of organized labour, the Days of Action movement would not have even begun. The "serried ranks" of labour were in fact quite passive in the first months of the Mike Harris government. It was the actions of students, social assistance recipients, feminists, community-based social movements, and heretofore relatively isolated left activists who provided the initial spark for the movement. It is no longer tenable, if it ever was, to conceptualize class struggle as solely a workplace-based affair including as agents only those organized into unions. This is clearly of pressing importance in the newly industrializing world where millions exist in a kind of "class limbo" – halfway between the countryside and the city, halfway between a life of hustling on the streets and collective labour in a sweatshop. But even in a fully advanced industrial society such as Canada, where the question of urbanization was settled a long time ago, this "broadening" of our sense of class and class struggle remains critical.

It is no longer tenable, in other words, to see class and class struggle with anything except an intersectional lens. The powerful term, "intersectional," while introduced to left discourse by Kimberlé Crenshaw three decades ago,[54] was not yet part of the everyday lexicon of left and union militants in Ontario in 1995. However, it precisely captures the dynamics without which the Days of Action would have been impossible. The attacks by Mike Harris occurred at an intersection of the poor, people of colour, women, and organized workers. When a parallel intersectional response of the poor, people of colour, women, and organized labour began to resist and, importantly, began to resist by at least in part "recognizing" each other in the struggle, then a mass movement became possible.

Think only of the Embarrass Harris moment. It was a key component of the initial response to the Harris attacks, and it emerged not from organized labour, but from the feminist movement. The class struggle of workers against Tories in Ontario in 1995 has as a key component: the deliberations and discussions taking place in the annual general meeting of NAC, the central feminist social movement in English Canada in the 1990s. The idea of class struggle in the context of the Days of Action, then, cannot just be an idea of the workplace and unions. It must also be an idea of women's oppression and resistance, whether in the workplace or not. To restrict our notion of class struggle in this instance to unions and the workplace is to make it an idea which cannot grasp the totality of the forces that were to create a vast, class-based movement.

All these themes will recur in the following chapters. But with the passage of time, the "feel" of the movement can become lost as memories fade and history moves on. Sam Gindin, at the time director of research for the CAW, captured the hope and prospects that many could feel opening up on that very cold day in London. It is appropriate to give Gindin the last word.

> The London protest was the first time during any of our lives that workers in mass walked off the job over social issues. What happened in London didn't just surprise others; in many ways it also surprised us. London reminded us of our potential. London showed workers at their best: discussing the issues, generating a wider debate, organizing for action, and stubbornly carrying out that action in spite of employer intimidation and a steady barrage of "there-is-no-alternative-so-why-fight-back." London was about turning our back on cynicism, and finding some hope in solidarity. London was about putting the movement back in labour, and putting labour at the head of the movement. ... Something beyond militancy and numbers was happening. Something that had to do with politics and political consciousness.
>
> Workers were saying that they were no longer content to leave politics to the politicians. Workers gave up a day's pay and risked employer

retaliation because they understood the dangers of the Harris direction to themselves, their families, and their communities. London was the beginning of a new politics in which workers, as individuals and through their organizations, would take dramatic action to focus attention on the kind of society we were becoming. …

By itself, the London protest won't change the direction of the Harris government. But it changed the labour movement – and that makes broader future changes possible.[55]

Chapter Five

Outrage Against the "Bully Bill"

The December 11, 1995, London Day of Action and strike had been a magnificent beginning to the Days of Action social movement. The austerity agenda announced by the new Conservative government had shocked the province. As we saw, the cuts that had motivated the protests had come, not in a budget, but in a mere "economic statement." Despite the emergence of mass opposition, the Harris Tories were determined to push ahead with austerity.

The cuts announced in the November 1995 economic statement were not going to be enough. The first two quarters of 1995 saw the Ontario economy slip back into recession, leading to revenues falling $1.4 billion below expectation.[1] The government, set on balancing the budget at all costs, was determined to find an additional $2 billion in expenditure reductions. To accomplish this, the Tories turned their attention to municipalities, universities, schools, and hospitals, the so-called MUSH sector. An orientation developed to, in general, reduce or eliminate provincial transfers to this sector and then give the MUSH sector the authority, through regulation, to levy new user fees (tuition in the case of universities and colleges). There were to be changes to dozens of pieces of legislation, and this created a problem. If each change was presented on its own, each change might become a focus for the growing anti-Tory opposition that had announced itself on the streets of London. To avoid this, a three-fold strategy was adopted. First, to combine everything into an omnibus bill – "the hospital-restructuring commission, the curbs on doctors' privileges, the tuition hikes, the municipal user fees, and all the rest."[2] Second, to package it as if it was simply a series of relatively technical, unimportant measures and third, to announce it at the same time as the November economic statement, a statement that would garner considerable attention. Perhaps the omnibus bill, titled "Bill 26, Savings and Restructuring Act, 1995," would fly under the radar.

Alvin Curling's Direct Action

For a few days, the strategy worked, the press concentrating on the "seismic cuts contained in the economic statement."[3] But in the end, Bill 26 was a little too big to go unnoticed. John Ibbitson described it as "perhaps the largest bill ever put before the legislature of any province." It was over 200 pages long. It amended forty-seven different acts on the books in Ontario. A compendium attached to the bill photocopied the pages of the acts being amended. This compendium ran to 2,225 pages. The government's senior media adviser, Paul Rhodes, "chose to downplay the bill, shrugging it off as a compendium of housekeeping measures."[4] But as people started to read the bill, it began to seem more like house demolition. Rick Witherspoon of the London and District Labour Council said: "The bill has been more aptly described as the bully bill, despicable, dictatorial, astonishing, controversial, octopus-like, and a bill that was prepared with military-style secrecy."[5]

Here's what the Conservatives wanted to accomplish with their housecleaning.

- Schedules F, G, H, and I were the "health package" of the bill. They gave the health minister the power to close hospitals if s/he deemed it to be in the "public interest."
- Amendments to the "Private Hospitals Act" allowed the government to revoke a hospital licence or reduce the level of government financial assistance to hospitals without notice.
- The bill went on to redefine the term "facility fee" to allow for an expanded use of user fees. It redefined the term "independent health facilities" for all such user-fee charging facilities so that they could play a greater and greater role in the health care system.
- Seniors and people on social assistance would have to pay increased deductibles for drug plans. Drug prices would be deregulated, something that had happened in no other province.
- In amendments to the Health Insurance Act, all references to services being insured when they are "medically necessary" were removed and replaced with "under such conditions and limitations as may be prescribed." This gave the ministry greater leeway in removing services from health insurance coverage. This opened up the possibility of a potential attack on abortion clinics in the province, which had only recently won the right to have their services covered by health insurance.
- Schedule "J" effectively killed pay equity. It did this by ending the "proxy" method of pay equity as of January 1, 1997. The

proxy method was vital to real pay equity. Some sectors of the job market – in day cares, nursing homes, etc. – are comprised primarily of women and are very low paid. Their pay can't be compared to groups of men doing the same work because by and large this work is done by women. To get around this, pay equity legislation allowed for "proxy" comparisons – choosing a primarily male-dominated employment field requiring equivalent training, experience, and skill, and comparing wages in those sectors to their "proxy" in the women-dominated, low-paid job ghettoes. Without the right to make such proxy comparisons, pay equity became a meaningless law for approximately 100,000 women in Ontario.

- Schedule M amended the Municipal Act and twelve other related statues. Most were designed to facilitate the privatization of utilities and to allow municipalities to charge user fees.
- Privatizations of local utilities used to require referenda. This would be done away with through Bill 26.
- The end of the bill, in particular, "Schedule Q," was a broadside assault on trade union rights and wages. In the event of an impasse in collective bargaining, arbitrators would be required to consider "the employer's ability to pay" when they arrive at a settlement.

With one hand, the Conservatives were ripping billions out of the system – $1 billion from support to public school boards for instance – considerably reducing "the employers' ability to pay." Then, with the other hand, they were giving extraordinary new powers to arbitrators to say, "sorry, but we have to slash jobs and wages because the employer doesn't have the ability to pay."[6]

By Tuesday, December 5, Bill 26 started to get considerable attention and sparked a series of actions not normally seen as part of social movement organizing, actions in the Legislative Assembly and in committee hearing rooms across the province. As social movement and labour activists were gearing up for direct action in London, members of the opposition parties were taking direct action in the Legislative Assembly. The government was insistent that the bill be passed before the holiday break. Opposition politicians, focusing on the bill's contents, became furious that these massive changes were going to be passed on such a compressed timetable. "There were walkouts, angry insults, desk pounding – everything short of actual fist fights at the Ontario legislature," said a report filed by *The Canadian Press*.[7] On December 6, thirty-three opposition members refused to participate in a routine vote concerning the bill and were therefore asked to leave. Liberal Alvin Curling – former housing minister and the province's only black member of the legislature – refused. "In a hand-written note passed to a reporter, Curling said he was inspired by the example of Rosa Parks, the black woman who ignited the U.S. civil rights movement by refusing to give up her seat on a bus to a white man."[8] The speaker ordered the sergeant-at-arms to eject him by force, but Curling was surrounded by other opposition MPs, and short of an extreme escalation, there was nothing that could be done. The speaker ordered a recess and left the legislature, "but Curling stayed, all night as it turned out. Surrounded by a praetorian guard of opposition MPPs, sustained by pizza, propped up with pillows, and warmed by a blanket that covered a bottle discreetly brought in for calls of nature, Curling sat out the night."[9]

The direct action worked. A government suddenly on the defensive agreed to delay passage of the bill till the end of January and to hold an unprecedented number of public hearings across the province, overseen by the Standing Committee on General Government. "From Monday to Friday during the weeks of December 18, 1995, January 8 and January 15, 1996, from 9 am to 9 pm," the committee will meet "to receive public submissions on the bill."[10] Starting in Toronto, the Standing Committee held hearings throughout the day, with hundreds of different groups and individuals speaking for up to half an hour to the all-party committee. Then after the holiday break, from January 8 to 19, the committee travelled the province, visiting Windsor, Timmins, London, Sudbury, Kitchener, Thunder Bay, Niagara Falls, Ottawa, Hamilton, Kingston, and Peterborough. So great was the demand for an opportunity to make a submission, that (a) the committee had to split into two so it could hold simultaneous sessions, doubling the number of delegations that could be heard, and then (b) had to visit each of the cities a second time. John Ibbitson counted 367 deputations.[11] In reviewing the transcripts for every day of the hearings, the actual count was even higher. An astounding 476 groups and individuals testified before the committee, and more would have been heard had the hearings lasted longer. Never before had this usually obscure government committee been the centre of such attention.

A Province Polarized

How to assess the views that came forward in this remarkable moment of public debate? One way is to get a "feel" for the emotional divide that permeated the hearings. Martin Mittelstaedt, reporting on the January hearings in Windsor, said: "Travelling public hearings on Ontario's controversial omnibus bill got off to a stormy start yesterday as proceedings were punctuated by catcalls, jeers and hyperbolic rhetoric by many witnesses."[12] Once we get past the heckling, the voices that can be heard through the transcripts from these hearings were passionate, informed, and informative – and they give a powerful sense of the different political currents at work in the province in the early months of the Harris government.

A content analysis of these submissions suggests that these 476 submissions can be divided into sixteen sectors (ranging from the provincial government and business associations to advocacy groups and labour organizations), and four categories ("strong support" of the legislation, "some concerns," "serious concerns," and "strong opposition").

Strong Support – These were submissions that expressed their support for the omnibus bill without reservations. Representative of this category was Hazel McCallion, mayor of Mississauga, December 18, Toronto. "As mayor of the fourth-largest city in this province, I'm very delighted with this bill as it applies to municipalities. We've had a noose around our neck for years under the Municipal Act. In fact, the province has treated us as children."

Some Concerns – These were submissions which clearly indicated support for the bill but asked for amendments or indicated some reservations. Representative of this category was Doug Smith, Thunder Bay Chamber of Commerce, January 17, 1996, Thunder Bay. "The Thunder Bay Chamber of Commerce supports the government's initiatives in Bill 26 while respectfully requesting amendments to Bill 26 to restore citizens' participation and rights to appeal bureaucratic and undemocratic decisions and bylaws by the Ontario Municipal Board."

Serious Concerns – These were submissions that did not always explicitly say they were opposed to the omnibus bill but indicated very strong opposition to or reservations about key aspects of the legislation. Representative of this category was Chief Gordon Peters, Chiefs of Ontario, December 1, 1995, Toronto. "We've never accepted the provincial view in regard to lands and resources within this region that we're restricted to the small reserves that we're placed on. In fact, our people are very adamant in understanding their interpretation of the treaties and their access to the traditional land use areas that they've had, and most of those are protected by the treaties. It's very clear to say that in dealing with any kind of legislation, our people are very concerned that on anything that alters the situation there must be adequate dialogue with ourselves to understand what's going to happen in those particular areas."

Strong Opposition – These were submissions that, without reservation, came out against the omnibus bill. Representative of this category was Cheryl Lucier, Public Service Alliance of Canada, January 8, 1996, Windsor. "In Ontario, there is a huge outcry against Mike Harris and the provincial Conservatives because of the massive cuts, and rightly so. But at the same time, Jean Chrétien and the federal Liberals are gaining in popularity, even though it is their budget that is ultimately responsible for the cuts we face in Ontario today. Jean Chrétien and the federal government have successfully transferred the blame to Mike Harris for betraying us, and now Mike Harris is playing the same game with Bill 26 by letting the municipalities take the blame. We do not support Bill 26 and we will continue to put the blame where it belongs: on Mike Harris and Jean Chrétien and on any politician who puts profits over people."

The transcripts of submissions made during the unprecedented Bill 26 hearings are an extraordinary resource. The four excerpts used as exemplars here provide a very small window into what is a fascinating record of the emotions on display. An appendix to this book provides further examples, as well as a complete list of all 476 submissions, by category and sector.

Table 5.1 reveals the results of the content analysis of all 476 submissions, organized by sector and category: 5.1a – those expressing "strong support" for the legislation; 5.1b – those expressing "some concerns"; 5.1c – those expressing "serious concerns"; and 5.1d – those expressing "strong opposition."

Both a "top-level" and a more granular analysis of the data are fascinating. A "top-level" analysis shows that of the 476 submissions made, just 52 (11 per cent) expressed strong support for the legislation compared to 195 (40 per cent) that were strongly opposed. Only two (effectively 0 per cent!) had no opinion. The largest number of submissions fell between these two extremes, 135 (18 per cent) expressing some concerns, and 98 (21 per cent) expressing serious concerns. This "top-level" analysis reveals serious opposition to and concern about the legislation outweighing those with some concerns and the quite small number of submissions expressing support.

A more granular analysis brings things much more clearly into focus. Three sectors fit clearly into category 5.1a, those largely expressing "strong support" for the legislation: business associations, the provincial government, and taxpayer associations. None of the submissions from members in these three sectors came out against the legislation.

Table 5.1. Submissions to Bill 26 Hearings, by Sector and Response

	Number of Submissions	Strong Support	Some Concerns	Serious Concerns	Strong Opposition	No Opinion
Total, All Sectors	**476**	**52 (11%)**	**135 (28%)**	**98 (20%)**	**195 (40%)**	**2 (0%)**
5.1a. Sectors Largely Expressing "Strong Support"	**46**	**27**	**19**			
Business Associations	30	16	14			
Taxpayer Associations	9	6	3			
Provincial Government	7	5	2			
5.1b. Sectors Largely Expressing "Some Concerns"	**60**	**8**	**39**	**7**	**5**	**1**
Municipal Government	28	3	22	2	1	
Professional Associations	11	1	8	2		
Individual Businesses	11	3	5		2	1
Police Services	6		3	2	1	
Education	4	1	1	1	1	
5.1c. Sectors Largely Expressing "Serious Concerns"	**211**	**17**	**70**	**67**	**56**	**1**
Health Care	95	5	46	28	16	
Individual	71	12	11	22	25	1
Service Provider	18		8	6	4	
Environment	16		5	5	6	
Fire Services	11			6	5	
5.1d. Sectors Largely Expressing "Strong Opposition"	**159**		**7**	**24**	**134**	
Labour	78			4	74	
Advocacy Groups	74		6	19	50	
Faith	7		1	1	5	

Source: Author's calculations derived from content analysis of Government of Ontario.[13]

None expressed serious concerns. Almost two-thirds registered strong support, while 40 per cent expressed some concerns, but leaned towards support. Here we see the coalition that the Harris Tories were gathering to implement the Common Sense Revolution – a coalition expressing unambiguous support for a deregulated economy, a reduction in taxes, a reduction in social service spending, a balanced the budget, and all the other trappings of the Common Sense Revolution.

Category 5.1b lists sectors whose submissions largely expressed "some concerns" – 60 submissions from four sectors – municipal government, professional associations, police services and education. Of the 28 submissions from municipal government, only 3 expressed unreserved support for the legislation. There were 3 strongly opposed it and 2 expressed serious concerns. The large majority – 22 out of 28 – were supportive but with ambivalence, expressing some concerns. Ambivalence is not surprising given the implications that deregulation and a reduction in transfer payments from the province to the municipalities might entail for the pressures of governing at the local level. In this category, we also find submissions from individual businesses. Only 11 made submissions, so it is hard to draw definitive conclusions – but these individual businesses were much more prepared to express reservations and concern about the legislation than were the business associations whose mandate was to represent the interests of business. Two sectors – education and police services – had very few individual submissions, making the drawing of conclusions a little difficult. Of note, however, is the fact that police services – usually seen as allies of Conservatives when in office – in their majority expressed some or serious concerns about Bill 26.

In these first two categories, six sectors are represented – four strongly supportive of the legislation and two expressing some concerns. The other ten sectors of the population expressed either serious concerns or strong opposition.

Category 5.1c lists those sectors largely expressing "serious concerns." Heading the list is the health care sector – not surprising given the huge emphasis in Bill 26 on restructuring in that sector. Reading the submissions, you can feel the tension of the moment – very few coming out strongly opposed or in favour of the legislation, but almost all expressing serious reservations and concerns. The large category of individual submissions captures the polarized nature of the moment. Of the 71 individuals who made submissions, 12 were strongly in favour, and twice as many (25) were strongly opposed. The largest category came from individuals with some (11) or serious (22) concerns about the legislation.

Image 5.1. Ester Reiter was ejected from Ontario's legislature in 1996 …

Finally, when you examine the 159 submissions in category 5.1d, from sectors largely expressing strong opposition to the legislation, you can see the contours of the Days of Action coalition that was to challenge the Tory rule for three contentious years. The largest number of submissions came from labour (78), and an astonishing 74 of these were easily put into the category of "strong opposition." Four expressed serious concern, and precisely none could be placed in the category of strong support or "some" concerns. The second largest number of submissions (74) came from advocacy groups – 49 of whom opposed the legislation outright, 19 expressed strong concerns, 6 expressed some concerns, and none came out in favour of the legislation. Faith groups rounded out this category, with 5 out of 7 of their submissions expressing strong opposition to the legislation.

Here in one table is the physiognomy of the Days of Action. On one side, a pro-Tory coalition dominated by the provincial government and business associations that was advocating deregulation, reduction in services, and cuts in taxes. On the other side, an anti-Tory coalition dominated by organized labour and advocacy groups representing the poor, women, and racialized minorities that was advocating a defence of social services, opposing the backlash against employment equity, and opposing the tax cuts that would jeopardize social services. In the middle, you can see the complete spectrum of Ontario society – some leaning towards support for the legislation but hesitantly (e.g., municipal governments, professional associations), and some with very serious concerns (e.g., the health care sector and many individual citizens), leaning towards opposition. The stage was set for the next three years of contestation between the Common Sense Revolutionaries and their opponents.

"The End of Democracy"

The vast weight of the submissions opposed Bill 26. Nonetheless, on January 29, 1996, the bill received final reading in the legislature, where the galleries, as David Rapaport writes, "were packed with

Image 5.2. … and again in 2018, protesting Tory policies.

opponents, and the speaker had to clear them a few times. Ester Reiter, a York University sociologist who was removed by Queen's Park security, remembers screaming at the Tory MPPs, 'This is the end of democracy in Ontario!' There was a front-page picture in the *Toronto Sun* of Reiter being thrown out of the gallery."[14] Interestingly, twenty-two years later, the same Reiter again had her picture in the paper, thrown out of the legislature in opposition to new Tory premier Doug Ford invoking the "notwithstanding clause" to slash the size of Toronto City Council. Before being thrown out, she "yelled from the balcony ... 'I am 77-and-a-half years old and I hate the destruction of democracy.'"[15]

Reiter's voice bridges the opposition in the Harris years to the opposition in the Doug Ford years. The appendix provides a small sampling of the voices from the Harris years, excerpted from the hundreds of pages of testimony in response to the omnibus (bully) bill. These are the voices from all sides of the Days of Action moment – a "Common Sense Revolution" committed to austerity, cuts, restructuring, and backlash; a deep concern from many sectors of society about the speed of the changes and their effects; and finally, a massive, deeply rooted social movement in formation articulating clear and intelligent opposition to the Conservative's agenda. Unable to stop this agenda through the available channels of consultation and legislation, that movement returned to the streets.

Chapter Six

Watershed 1: Steeltown Shutdown[1]

Given the draconian intensification of the Conservative attacks, symbolized by Bill 26, and the Tory insistence on pushing the legislation through even after a province-wide outcry against the bill, it is not surprising that anger in the province increased, and with it the mass movement. As the dust cleared following the London Day of Action, the province was abuzz with anticipation. The very success of London had inspired activists everywhere. We could mobilize thousands. Workers would strike, and strike illegally, against both their boss and against the Conservatives. And support for the Conservatives – which had looked so solid in June – was withering quickly. Elected with 45 per cent of the vote in June, their support had climbed to 50 per cent in September. But by January of 1996, after the magnificent London general strike and after intense and negative publicity around the "bully bill," it had dropped precipitously to 36 per cent.[2] The Harris majority was unravelling.

A sign of the growing opposition to the Tories came from an unlikely quarter. An organization not known for its militancy, the Ontario English Catholic Teachers Association (OECTA), called for a January 13 demonstration against the Harris cuts to education. OECTA President Marilies Rettig said, "there's no way an additional $400 million can be cut without extremely serious impact on children in the classroom."[3] Organizers were hoping for a turnout of 12,000 to 13,000.

The run-up to the demonstration was marked by a chill in relations between OECTA and other teacher unions, including the Ontario Secondary School Teachers Federation (OSSTF) – conspicuously absent at the January 10 press conference announcing the demonstration. OSSTF had its own action plan and was divided from OECTA on the question of public and Catholic school boards: OSSTF was calling for them to be combined.

But on the day, these differences seemed irrelevant. As many as 37,000 turned out, including teachers from other unions – the biggest anti-Tory demonstration to date.[4] Many of the thousands on the demo were from outside Toronto, with 380 busses bringing people in from as far away as Sudbury and Ottawa. Most came from towns that had voted overwhelmingly Tory the year before. But those towns in voting Tory had not voted for the massive cuts announced by Harris.[5]

On January 17, four days after the massive OECTA protest, the OFL Executive Board announced that the next target of the Days of Action protest would be Hamilton. If there had been some questions about the possibility of shutting down London in a political one-day strike, there were no such doubts about Hamilton. This, one of the historic hearts of the industrial union movement in Ontario, would without question respond when the call came. A one-day illegal walkout was scheduled for Friday, February 23, followed by a community demonstration on Saturday, February 24, to coincide with the Conservative Party's annual general meeting, which was scheduled for that day in the city.[6] In and around this second Day of Action, two big processes were underway: an internal one clarifying how the Days of Action were to be organized, and an external one activating the province's public-sector workers in the OPSEU.

Organizing the General Strikes

Among the ways in which the Days of Action were unique as a social movement was how it was organized. Table 6.1 documents the local leadership structure for each of the Days of Action from 1995 to 1998. Even this two-dimensional institutional analysis reveals some unique characteristics.

There were co-chairs for each, a labour co-chair, and for all except the London Day of Action, a community co-chair. In every Day of Action except for one (Sudbury), the labour co-chair was the president of the local labour council. The community co-chair was a leading representative from social justice or other advocacy groups in the community.

Dan La Botz claims that "union leaders were clear from the beginning that a general strike could not be organized by the union movement alone. It would also need allies among the social movements and community organizations."[7] The reality is a little more complex. At London, the co-chairs had both been from organized labour, Rick Witherspoon coming from the private sector (CAW) and Elaine Ellis coming from the public sector (OPSEU). As David Rapaport has pointed out, this created both "gender balance and also a balance between public-sector and private-sector unions." However, he goes on to say, "another

Table 6.1. Local Leaderships, Days of Action, Ontario, 1995–8

	Date	City	Co-Chair	Affiliation	Co-Chair	Affiliation
1	Dec. 11, 1995	London	Rick Witherspoon	CAW; London and District Labour Council, president	Elaine Ellis	OPSEU Local 102, London and District Labour Council
			Labour Co-Chair		**Community Co-Chair**	
2	Feb. 23–4, 1996	Hamilton	Wayne Marston	CEP background (Bell Canada); Hamilton and District Labour Council, president	Andrea Horwath	Hamilton-Wentworth Coalition for Social Justice Chair
3	Apr. 19, 1996	Kitchener-Waterloo	Bob Cruickshank	CAW (Budd Canada); Waterloo Regional Labour Council, president	Lucy Harrison	Waterloo Regional Coalition for Social Justice
4	Jun. 24, 1996	Peterborough	Tom Veitch	CAW Local 1987 executive member; Peterborough and District Labour Council president	Jill Ritchie	Peterborough Coalition for Social Justice Co-Chair
5	Oct. 25–6, 1996	Toronto	Linda Torney	OPSEU background; Labour Council of Metro Toronto and York Region, president	Margaret Hancock	Metro Network for Social Justice Chair
6	Mar. 21–2, 1997	Sudbury	René Fortin	CUPE, assistant regional director	Bobbie Cascanette	Laurentian social work student

7	Apr. 28, 1997	Thunder Bay	Evelina Pan	COPE (Canadian Office and Professional Employees Union); Thunder Bay District Labour Council, president	Chris Mather	Thunder Bay Coalition Against Poverty
8	Sept. 26–7, 1997	North Bay	Dawson Pratt	OPSEU Local 657; North Bay and District Labour Council, president	Lana Mitchell	Low Income People Involvement of Nipissing
9	Oct. 17, 1997	Windsor	Gary Parent	CAW Local 444; Windsor and District Labour Council president	Helen O'Keefe	Chair, Regional Women's Committee, Public Service Alliance of Canada
10	May 1, 1998	St. Catharines	Ed Gould	CAW Local 199; St. Catharines and District Labour Council, president	Linda Rogers	Golden Horseshoe Social Action Committee
11	Jun. 8, 1998	Kingston	Charlie Stock	CAW Local 1837, president; Kingston and District Labour Council, president	Natalie Mehra	Kingston Action Network

Sources: London;[8] Hamilton;[9] Kitchener-Waterloo;[10] Peterborough;[11] Toronto;[12] Sudbury;[13] Thunder Bay;[14] North Bay;[15] Windsor;[16] St. Catharines;[17] Kingston.[18]

political balance was overlooked, since both co-chairs were from the labour movement."[19] This issue was central to a meeting of the Ontario Coalition for Social Justice (OCSJ) held four days after the London Day of Action. According to Jim Turk, "most representatives felt that the days had to continue and that there had to be a more significant role for the broader community."

> In this regard, it was essential that the community (non-labour) groups have at least as large a role as the unions in planning the days. Out of this OCSJ meeting came a series of recommendations: that the days continue in other centres, that in every case there be a community co-chair and a labour co-chair; that there be as many community speakers as labour speakers; that representatives of the OCSJ join labour leaders in choosing sites and dates; and that the days of protest be on weekdays to put pressure on employers.[20]

From that point on, as table 6.1 makes clear, these principles were adhered to – a remarkable structure of leadership representing an attempt at coalition building between organized labour and social justice advocacy groups. But it is a structure that was not automatically given. It evolved with experience – under the pressure of a movement that very much consisted of both organized labour and social justice advocacy organizations.

Table 6.1 also reveals other important dimensions of the Days of Action. There was gender parity in the leadership, reflecting what has already been pointed out in this book, that from the beginning women played an indispensable, leading role in the anti-Tory movement. However, this parity was only achieved because of the leadership involvement of social justice advocacy groups from outside the labour movement. Only three of the labour co-chairs were women (Elaine Ellis in London, Linda Torney in Toronto, and Evelina Pan in Thunder Bay) – the rest were men. By contrast, every single one of the community co-chairs was a woman.

Another important aspect of labour's participation in the Days of Action is revealed in this table. Of the labour co-chairs, more than half (6) came from the CAW. This underlines the extraordinary role that the CAW played in the Days of Action themselves. Only one of the labour co-chairs (Wayne Marston from CEP [Communications, Energy and Paperworkers]) had a background in the pink paper unions that would play such a decisive role in derailing the Days of Action. One final point is worth mentioning. Among the community co-chairs was Andrea Horwath, who would later rise to prominence as leader of the Ontario NDP and is today the mayor of Hamilton.

Underneath this unique structure, a movement unfolded that was new to almost all involved. While strikes have always been part of the tool kit of the contemporary labour movement, when we think of strikes, we think of *economic* strikes – walking the picket line over issues to do with wages, working conditions, benefits, etc. What had commenced with the London Day of Action was a movement of *political* strikes, which as Marcella Munro emphasized, was something that hadn't been seen in the province in a generation.[21] The two one-day strikes of childcare workers, examined earlier, were harbingers of the tactics to come. Both were illegal (as earlier pointed out, the first CUPE illegal strikes since 1981) and both, while they had a clear economic content to do with attacks on wages and subsidies, were clearly in the category of *political* strikes – withdrawing labour to pressure a government to change or modify a policy.

The political strike posed some unique challenges. For something like a political strike – for which there is no provision in any collective agreement, and which in that sense is an *illegal* action – there had to be some level of understanding of the Tory policies against which the strikes were being conducted, a level of understanding at a whole different level than that of a strike over economic conditions at the workplace. We earlier documented the intense educational campaigns carried out inside both CUPE and the CAW to prepare for the first Days of Action. That intense educational effort was a necessary, bedrock component for any political strike movement to succeed.

To deal with the "illegal" nature of the strikes, unique tactics were developed, including most significantly, "cross-picketing," whereby workers didn't picket their own workplaces (which could bring sanctions from their employer) but rather picketed workplaces of other unions, whose members could then stay away from work based on an old union tradition – respecting and not crossing a picket line. Reshef and Rastin point out that it also meant "that people who had chosen not to participate in a given DOA would not have to cross a picket line set up by their co-workers."[22] The tactic proved quite successful. Little came of the various threats of legal sanctions by employers against workers for taking part in these strikes.

Cross-picketing was an active strategy by definition, involving the mobilization of hundreds of people to show up at workplaces with picket signs (and often disguises), trying to persuade the workers there to participate in the action. Other tactics were completely passive and bureaucratic. For the Kitchener-Waterloo Day of Action, the CAW made a deal with Lear Seating Canada Ltd. – a company that produced car seats – that production lost from a shutdown during the Day of Action would be compensated for by having that production finished *before* the strike. The steelworkers used a similarly bureaucratic and passive tactic for the Hamilton Days of Action, where "two of the city's main employers, Stelco Inc. and Westinghouse Canada Inc., allowed employees to work a holiday earlier in the week in exchange for a day off on Friday, the first of a two-day DOA."[23]

Finally, there was the question of financing the strikes. Some were completely or in their majority underwritten by the OFL, such as the initial Day of Action in London, for which it "funded all the costs [about $110,000]," according to Jim Turk. For the second Day of Action in Hamilton, OFL money was still significant, but the OFL "president indicated that the OFL would cap its contribution to Hamilton at $45,000 (later raised to a total of $54,000)."[24] Others were funded locally, including the Kitchener-Waterloo action, which was "entirely financed by supportive unions and community groups,"[25] and Peterborough, where "all financial support was to be raised by the supporting organizations, with no contribution from the OFL other than the release of two staff who would serve as coordinators."[26]

However, regardless of whether OFL or local union resources were used, it created an absolutely unique organizing situation for activists in the communities. Resources normally reserved for economic strikes were now being mobilized for political purposes, intersecting with the actions and personnel of community activists, giving them suddenly unheard-of access to funds and staffing. Marcella Munro captures this perfectly:

> Cashed-starved community groups suddenly had the kind of infrastructure necessary to successfully organize. When organizers got to Hamilton, for example, the local coalition didn't even have their own phone number. Suddenly, they had office space in a downtown building, and a host of other bare necessities most community coalitions (and, for that matter, community organizations in general) can't afford – a phone number, an answering service, and a fax machine. Through the organizers assigned to help them, they had instant connections to the provincial, and in many cases, national offices of unions and other social movement groups. They had signs, placards, t-shirts, leaflets, and other popular materials designed and printed, which gave them a local profile and visibility they had never had.[27]

There was another organizing characteristic of most of the Days of Action – the absenting of a formal presence of the NDP. "At protest after protest, local organizers turned down demands to allow NDP leaders to address the crowd. On several DOA they were not even allowed on stage. This made the NDP-backing pink unions furious."[28]

OPSEU Joins the Fray

If those were some of the internal elements structuring the unfolding movement, an enormous external factor burst on the scene in early 1996 – a confrontation between the Harris Tories and the 67,400 members of the OPSEU.

It is slightly inaccurate to categorize this as an "external" factor. In fact, the Days of Action movement had been central to building the morale and self-organization of the civil servants – a section of the workforce in Ontario which had no strike traditions because, until granted the right to strike by the Rae government, they had been prohibited from walking a picket line.

Just how distant OPSEU members were from the strike traditions of the labour movement is drawn out clearly by David Rapaport in his indispensable book on the OPSEU strike. A July 1995 internal union poll, conducted after the election of the Harris Tories, indicated that almost 40 per cent of OPSEU members had voted for Harris, and more than one-third agreed with the Common Sense Revolution.[29] Three years earlier, in November 1992, while the NDP was in office discussing whether to grant the right to strike to civil servants, Rapaport recounts how he and then-OPSEU President Fred Upshaw had travelled to London to debate with other OPSEU leaders who opposed civil servants getting the right to strike. "The opposition had filled the room with busloads of members, and it was most discouraging to see hundreds of union members wearing buttons opposing the right to strike."[30] According to Rapaport, this opposition to the right to strike was strongest in Kingston, Brockville, Eastern Ontario – and the Southwestern region in which London is situated.

Flash forward to December 1995 and London was playing a very different role. One OPSEU staff organizer, Pam Doig, is quoted by Rapaport saying: "The London Day of Action was significant. It gave us the ability to say to the membership that OPSEU can hit the streets."[31] The London strike did not simply inspire OPSEU members from the city itself. Rapaport quotes Marilou Martin, an OPSEU Executive Board member who organized the busses from Toronto, saying: "I was shocked by the numbers of people signing up to go to London on buses leaving at three in the morning."[32]

> The London Day of Action was a preview of the strike – the biggest show of militant support we had ever seen from OPSEU. There were picket lines in front of every Government of Ontario building in the city. It was a turning point for the two thousand OPSEU picketers who showed up that

day. And it was a turning point for OPSEU. At our regular December meeting, the OPSEU Executive Board placed the union on strike alert.[33]

The relationship between the Days of Action movement and the OPSEU strike did not end with London. At the second site for the Days of Action movement, the private-sector steel town of Hamilton, thousands of OPSEU members took part. For thousands of civil servants to be marching side by side with thousands of private-sector workers "made a big difference to us," writes Rapaport. "It seemed as if a strike by civil servants was receiving, if not an endorsement, then certainly a wink from a wide range of people right across Ontario. This made the idea of a strike by civil servants more plausible and less marginal, and it helped buoy our spirits when, two days later, the strike began and we had our first day of picketing."[34]

> In retrospect it all makes sense – the anger of an Ontario reacting to a reactionary reordering of society, done in a bully fashion, with no real mandate. The Common Sense Revolution had created the opposition – it had created the anger and militancy – and the OPSEU strike had grown in the belly of the opposition. Too much was being changed too fast.[35]

In other words, the political strikes of London and Hamilton, and the dynamic changes in mass consciousness represented by these actions, were an intrinsic part of the gelling of an OPSEU membership willing to take to the picket lines. There were, of course, very serious economic reasons to take strike action. OPSEU members had been working without a contract for months, they "hadn't seen a pay raise since 1991, and had actually seen their average pay of $40,000 temporarily cut during the Social Contract." However, "the union was not pressing for increased wages. Instead, it was fighting to preserve job security."[36] This was understandable. On October 4, 1995, the Conservative government moved to repeal the NDP's Bill 40. The most visible change would be ending Bill 40's ban on the use of replacement workers (strike-breakers) during labour disputes. But probably more significant in the short term for the Harris government was the elimination of successor rights for public-sector workers. "Successor rights protect the pay and privileges of employees whose companies are sold to another concern."[37] But the government's more than $8 billion-plus deficit reduction target could not be met without a drastic downsizing of the public sector. Central to this downsizing would be contracting out – having the same work done but by a private-sector corporation that offered reduced pay and

Image 6.1. Hamilton – February 1996: "Woodstock of the Labour Movement."

fewer benefits. With successor rights protecting wages and benefits, few private-sector employers would be interested in taking over work formerly done by the government – so successor rights had to go. A key negotiating demand of OPSEU was to reinstate successor rights in a new contract. However, the Harris government "had no intention of giving back to the public servants through collective bargaining the successor rights it had just legislated away." The first-ever provincial government workers' strike looked increasingly like an inevitability.[38] When the votes were counted on a poll that had begun February 15, OPSEU members had voted 66.7 per cent to take strike action.[39] They would be in a legal strike position on Monday, February 26.

Woodstock of the Labour Movement

The possibility of coordinating the Hamilton Days of Action with an OPSEU strike was clear to many. A ready-made plan was waiting to be implemented: build the one-day Hamilton strike on the Friday, link both it and the mass demonstration on Saturday to the struggle of the OPSEU workers, and then use these two events to build a series of escalating solidarity strike actions beginning Monday, the first legal strike day for OPSEU. In this sense – making the Days of Action a springboard for active solidarity with a major striking group of unionists – a province-wide general strike against the Conservatives and in solidarity with OPSEU was both possible and necessary.

For anyone who participated in the Hamilton events, this was abundantly clear. The city was shut on Friday. The federal agency responsible for tracking labour disputes said that 100,000 struck[40] (examined in more detail in the sidebar at the end of this chapter). An eyewitness report written on the day by John Bell captured the mood.

> Workers came from all over the province. I spoke with a hospital worker from London, transit workers from Chatham and a group of teachers who were still lively in spite of having driven all night from Sault Ste. Marie. It is a measure of how passionate workers are in their hatred of Harris and his right-wing government, that they are willing to go to great lengths, literally, to make their anger heard. While it was significant that supporters came from across the province, the success of the strike depended on the workers of Hamilton and district. And they stayed away from work in their thousands.[41]

The next day saw the largest labour mobilization ever in Ontario's history. The mood of the day was captured perfectly by Sid Ryan. "At the time I called it the Woodstock of the labour movement and I still think that fits."[42] Organizers anticipated an anti-Tory demonstration of between 50,000 and 70,000.[43] Either figure would have made it the largest-ever anti-Harris demonstration in Ontario. Wayne Marston, president of the Hamilton and District Labour Council, wouldn't predict a number, except to say that it would be "broader" than the events in London.[44] By the end of the day, somewhere between 100,000 and 120,000 had tramped through the mud and streets of an eerily quiet downtown Hamilton to vent their rage against the Tories.[45] The latter figure, 120,000, was suggested by then-president of the Canadian Labour Congress, Bob White. He pointed out that such a turnout would mean that 1 out of every 73 residents of Ontario were assembled outside the Tory convention that day.[46] "By 11 am, the park where the march was mobilizing had long since filled up and had overflowed into the grass and mud. And still they came, banners flying, signs blowing in the wind."[47]

The CAW's newsletter – covering the event in reverse chronological order – captures the mood brilliantly.

> The busses snaked along the highway edging the harbour for as far as the eye could see – hundreds of yellow school busses one after another … Tens of thousands carrying flags, banners and picket signs streamed into the music-filled harbourfront park following the path down the bluff to the damp windblown assembly area. Close to 120,000 people gathered for the second day of the historic two-day protest against the Ontario Conservative government led by Mike Harris.
>
> The day before, Friday, February 23, plants shut down, busses didn't run, postal services ceased, and the city core was emptied as thousands of unionized workers led off the two-day protest …
>
> Union members boarded busses and travelled into Hamilton to stand on picket lines in solidarity with their co-workers. Twenty-five thousand rallied on a workday in the city centre. All told, close to 150,000 participated in the two-day event, the largest in Canadian history …
>
> There were nurses, teachers, workers – from firefighters to auto workers, public service employees, church and anti-poverty activists, the unemployed, and seniors. They came from all over the province to give voice to their democratic right to say no to the government's cut and slash actions.[48]

In his account of the strike, John Ibbitson emphasizes the divisions within the union movement. "The day before, union protesters had shut down Hamilton's public transit, garbage collection, and libraries – but not the steel mills. The Steelworkers were having none of it. And many of the bigger unions were becoming increasingly resentful of resistance by the public-sector unions to the idea of donating to the NDP a portion of the funds raised for the Days of Action."[49] Without question, the divisions outlined by Ibbitson were real. But the situation was more complex than the one he painted. Above we pointed out the arrangement made between the steel union and employers to take holiday days in lieu of strikes. James Rusk puts a quite different spin on this than Reshef and Rastin. "A steel mill cannot be closed down and restarted in a day, so the company and the United Steelworkers of America arranged for the plant to run on a holiday schedule by switching a designated holiday from Monday to yesterday."[50] Of course, getting a day's paid holiday is not the same as participating in an illegal picket. Later in the Days of Action, there would be an active abstention by the USWA from events in Sudbury. But in Hamilton, there were Steelworkers present in numbers.

Image 6.2. OPSEU – March 1996: "No Justice. No Peace."

"No Justice No Peace"

On the Monday after the two Days of Action in Hamilton, OPSEU did walk out, in an enthusiastic and surprisingly popular strike against the Harris Tories. Ultimately involving more than 50,000 strikers, it was claimed by union leaders – probably accurately – that it was the largest (economic) strike in Ontario's history.[51] Earlier we documented the resistance David Rapaport and Fred Upshaw had encountered when campaigning for the right to strike in 1992 and that among OPSEU members there was considerable sympathy for the Common Sense Revolution and the Harris Tories. But on February 18 when votes on proposed strike action were tabulated, a significant shift was revealed. Almost 48,000 valid votes had been cast – representing just over 70 per cent of the union's membership – and two-thirds, 31,664, had voted to reject the employer's offer.[52] The movement against the Tories was having a radicalizing effect inside the union.

It was also having a similar effect elsewhere. John Ibbitson articulated a widespread sentiment when he suggested that "many ordinary citizens" would be unsympathetic to the strike because of OPSEU members' $40,000 average annual salary, benefits, and job security – out of reach for many outside the public sector. Ibbitson argues that because of this, "the union knew it couldn't count on public sympathy."[53] The major daily newspapers, in the run-up to the OPSEU strike, had been replete with similar coverage about how a strike by civil servants would prove manifestly unpopular. "'There is not a lot of sympathy for civil servants,' said Jane Armstrong of Environics Research Group."[54] These reports proved to be completely wrong. They did not factor in the sense of shared grievance between many Ontario workers, public and private sector, trying to deal with the Harris cuts – a shared grievance that had coalesced into shared actions in the two Days of Action at London and Hamilton. The OPSEU strike found a huge resonance throughout the province. The truth is, the slogan of the strikers – "No Justice, No Peace" – spoke to thousands outside of OPSEU, outside of the union movement.[55]

The radicalization of the movement was reflected in the actions at the base of the union. On February 26, locals all over the province walked off the job simultaneously, not in the "staggered" fashion preferred by the union leadership. "Head office in Toronto can't direct the regions," said Ron Elliot, vice president for the Southwestern Ontario region. "We wanted it to be a disruption to the employer first, before we fully wanted to do it to the public," said Rapaport in his capacity as union vice-president for the Toronto region, "but when you start getting people who want to join the action as soon as possible, who are we to say no?"[56]

It was a bitter strike, most clearly revealed in what became misleadingly known as the "Riot at Queen's Park" on March 18. It was not the first time that there had been a violent confrontation during the anti-Harris movement. Most notably, on February 7, during a demonstration by several hundred students against pending tuition fee hikes, a group broke from the main demonstration, dismantled the metal barricades separating them from the front entrance to the legislature, managed to then get through the barred doors, and entered the lobby of the building. The resulting standoff with the police lasted about twenty minutes. In the aftermath, several charges were laid, including a little-used one called "intimidating the legislature" – a charge that would ultimately be dropped[57] – but would for several months provide grist for ridicule of the Tories in the Days of Action movement.

The March 18 incident was, however, on a much bigger scale and left a much greater mark. The spring session of the Ontario legislature was scheduled to open that day, and OPSEU chose the occasion to organize a rally on the lawn outside Queen's Park. Somewhere around five thousand answered the call, from Toronto of course, but also from all over the province – including "Oshawa, North Bay, Sudbury, London, Windsor, Hamilton, Kingston, Ottawa and Cornwall," according to Rapaport.

> Queen's Park was a celebration of opposition that morning. There were thousands of us – autoworkers, teachers, community activists, steelworkers, students, and OPSEU strikers. At the west door of the Legislative Building was a chorus singing labour songs. Steelworkers had occupied the tunnel connecting the government buildings to the Queen's Park subway station, and pickets had taken up their positions at the doors of all the government buildings.[58]

The celebration soon turned into a battle. Queen's Park security had closed both the centre and west gates, leaving the east gate as the only way into the Legislative Assembly. "By dawn Monday, that entrance was surrounded by hundreds of demonstrators, most of them teachers and steelworkers. Steelworkers also guarded the subway entrance to Queen's Park – called 'scab alley,' it had been a convenient way for strike-breakers to get to work until the steelworkers shut it down – as well as the entrances to the adjacent office complex, where much of the provincial bureaucracy worked."[59]

What happened next was unprecedented in contemporary Ontario history. Without warning, fifty members of the Ontario Provincial Police riot squad, "dressed to intimidate," burst into the crowd, waving batons and using pepper spray. Their ostensible purpose was to "create a corridor" for Tory MLAs to get into the Legislative Assembly.[60] What they succeeded in doing was igniting anger throughout the province at an extreme use of force, covered that night by every news outlet in the province. John Ibbitson was not the only commentator to use "Darth Vader" as a metaphor for the outfitting of the riot squad. The metaphor fits not only a description of the riot squad's uniform but also their mood. "Witnesses said they heard the police beating their shields and vowing to 'whack 'em and stack 'em' as they got ready to engage the strikers."[61]

The OPSEU workers waged a magnificent fight. For five weeks, they challenged the Conservatives, confronted the pepper spray and batons of the police, and battled to keep the scabs out of the workplace. The latter was successful, with just 10 per cent of OPSEU's membership crossing the lines according to Steve Watson,[62] national representative in the CAW education department.[63] There was a tremendous sentiment for solidarity with the strike. Steelworkers and Autoworkers joined the lines, as did postal workers and teachers. Rapaport characterizes the support from the labour movement as "huge," represented by "$16 million in interest-free loan guarantees, picket line training and support, donations, financial advice, soup trucks, the twinning of other union locals with striking OPSEU locals, the organizing of rallies, and even music."[64] The strike was the dominant theme at Toronto's International Women's Day event in March. OPSEU's "No Justice, No Peace" picket signs became a standard of the labour movement across the province.

The Union the Tories Could Not Break

On Friday, March 30, after five weeks on the picket line, a tentative deal was reached. It was ratified by 95 per cent of OPSEU members who voted.[65] In light of what was to come, it is important to realize that this settlement, in the moment, "felt" like a victory. OPSEU president Leah Casselman said that "public sector workers have made major gains."[66] Gord Wilson said: "We could declare a victory. We had been able to hold the government off, and we had made people feel better about the labour movement."[67] Steve Watson called the new contract "a major improvement over the government's 'final offer'" and emphasized that "the Harris government had to negotiate seriously with an organization they thought would collapse once forced to strike. There was no collapse."[68] This feeling was reflected in an article with the same title as this section, "The Union the Tories Could Not Break," that I wrote the Monday after the announcement. What was to have been an article covering a "Toronto fund-raising party for the five-week-old OPSEU strike" turned into an article on a party that had "turned into a celebration."

> The 500 strikers and supporters who turned out at the Music Hall were there to celebrate the solidarity which had forced the Tories to back down. The tentative agreement, reached hours before, had been ratified by an overwhelming 95 per cent of the OPSEU members who voted. On the Monday, contingents of strikers formed up outside their workplaces, marching into work as a block with their heads held high.[69]

However, besides the (extremely important) victory in preventing union busting, the specific gains, while important, were in truth quite modest.

> The Tories had wanted to discipline workers, particularly in the prisons, for violating the "essential services agreement." They were forced to

> accept an agreement that promised no reprisals. They had wanted to be able to "temporarily" lay off workers for two months pending resolution of final plans for privatization and job losses. They had to back down. They had to improve the seniority protection for OPSEU workers facing job losses through improved "bumping" provisions.[70]

The latter point is the key. Improved "bumping" provisions – while ameliorating the situation for those with seniority – would do nothing to prevent mass layoffs, and the Tories were committed to just that. There was some new language – but that was all.

> Bill 26 stripped unions of successor rights. In the event of privatization, employers are no longer obligated to respect the collective agreement of the employees. But in the deal worked out with OPSEU, the Tories were forced to make half a nod in the direction of successor rights. Their first offer gave no protection to OPSEU workers whose jobs were privatized. There was no guarantee they would be rehired. And if they were offered a job and refused (because of a massive pay cut, or worse conditions), they would forfeit their right to any severance pay from the government. Now, the new employer of a privatized government service will have to make a "reasonable effort" to hire the OPSEU members, on the basis of seniority. And all OPSEU members, even those who refuse new employment, are entitled to severance pay.[71]

I optimistically described this tortured language as "a foot in the door that a militant local can use as a lever to organize a defence of their members' jobs." In the end, it was not much of a lever at all. Public-sector workers were about to experience horrendous layoffs.

On April 11, the grim new reality came into focus with the government announcing a series of cuts whose changes were "almost too numerous to list." Among these changes, 10,600 of the province's 81,000 public servants would lose their jobs over two years including:

- Ministry of Natural Resources – 2,170 out of 5,000 employees
- Ministry of Agriculture – 954, or half the staff
- Ministry of Transportation – 1,239
- Ministry of Community and Social Services – 919
- Environment and Energy – 752
- Management Board – 682[72]

This was less than the 13,000 to 27,000 job cuts that had been floated before the strike, but nonetheless represented devastating job losses.

Some of the leading militants who held the lines through the bitter dispute would find themselves out of work within a matter of months.

Lost Opportunity

There is another plane on which the OPSEU strike needs to be evaluated – what *might* have been the result if the strike had been approached differently, not just by OPSEU leaders, but by the union leadership as a whole. The very context of the Days of Action clearly put on the agenda the possibility of different paths forward other than the one taken.

Everywhere during the strike, strikers speculated on the OFL putting its resources into building a general strike in solidarity with OPSEU. "People are ready to move the struggle up to a new level because they know that's what it will take to win. According to Leslyn Jones, President of OPSEU Local 515: 'If we have a general strike I believe it's going to show [Harris] that it's not a few people, but thousands and thousands of people, and that is really going to do it.'"[73]

Petitions began circulating, demanding that the OFL leadership recognize that "the Harris government intends to use the OPSEU strike to try to smash the union." Further, that "the enormous success of the Hamilton general strike and days of action shows the solidarity and anger which exists amongst working people in Ontario." Therefore we "call on the Ontario Federation of Labour (OFL) to call a province-wide general strike in support of the workers of OPSEU."[74] But the OFL did nothing. The busses rolled into Hamilton and rolled out again, and the OPSEU strikers were left to fight alone. Even Leah Casselman, president of OPSEU, refused to advance the call for wider solidarity action. She "received a petition of 1,400 names calling for a general strike in support of the OPSEU strike. Yet she did not raise it at the March 12 meeting of heads of unions."[75]

Marcella Munro, an organizer for the Action Canada Network who worked closely with the community organizations in the province building the Days of Action,[76] put the issues very clearly, saying that the OPSEU strike "could have been a real opportunity to build on the Days of Action strategy."

> Yet to the best of my knowledge, no discussions were held about how, for example, to use the OPSEU walkout to move from the Days of Action strategy into a multi-city strategy of more general strikes and protests. This is not to say that community coalitions didn't respond to the OPSEU strike, or show solidarity through contributing time and resources. But, imagine

> the impact if instead the union leadership had stated that they were going to assign two organizers to set up a strike support office in each of the communities where Days of Action had already occurred and perhaps in other communities identified as priorities by the OPSEU leadership. These offices could have built on the work already done in the community and involved the coalition in working out local strategies to support the OPSEU strike in that area: to strengthen picket lines; to organize community information nights; to organize OPSEU workers to talk to other union locals and other local groups about their struggle; and to organize community-based strategies to make the links between OPSEU demands and the larger issues, such as cuts to public services, that their struggle entailed.[77]

CAW president Buzz Hargrove did instruct all CAW Ontario locals to "immediately establish OPSEU Strike Support Committees. Hargrove said the strike by Ontario government employees is an important fight for all workers in this province."[78] However, Hargrove envisaged these as committees to bring solidarity to the OPSEU strikers, not as bases from which to escalate and broaden the action.

The OPSEU strike was certainly a lost opportunity, for both the political fight against Harris and the economic fight of OPSEU workers for job security and wages. The OPSEU workers had fought hard and long and preserved their union against an employer that had wanted them broken. But without a solidarity general strike from the rest of labour – a strike that was eminently possible – these gains felt hollow as employee after employee was given the pink slip.

The "business plan" announcing the layoffs also included further attacks on the poor. Welfare benefits were eliminated for 17,000 single parents and couples attending university and college.[79] On top of this, the Conservatives continued a push to introduce workfare.[80] By now, the Conservatives had announced "$8 billion in cuts over three years to social programs, school boards, hospitals, municipalities."[81] The need for wider action to stop these cuts was growing by the month. Anger against the Conservatives and enthusiasm for action against the cuts remained high. Days of Action were called in city after city.

The Economic and the Political

The OPSEU strike / Hamilton Days of Action dichotomy revealed one of the biggest issues facing the Days of Action movement. The Days of Action themselves were political strikes – a mass movement focussed on changing government policy. The organizing centre of that protest had been inherited by the largest of the mass institutions in Ontario civil society, the trade union movement. To be more specific, the leadership of the Days of Action could be found among the heads of unions of the Ontario Federation of Labour. But the bread-and-butter activity of trade unions is not, in the first instance, political action, but economic action to protect the wages and benefits of their members. The OPSEU strike was a clear example of such an economic struggle.

For Harris and the Conservatives, the political and the economy were not separate spheres. Their political changes were being done with an eye to economics – facilitating the class position of the employers in the province of Ontario. Sometimes it is difficult to perceive the class basis of governments in office. In the case of Mike Harris, his pro-corporate bias was almost undisguised. Ending employment equity, capping pay equity, ending the ban on strike-breakers, opening the door to contracting out in the public sector – all of these *political* decisions were clearly of *economic* interest to the private-sector employers in the province. Given this close relationship between the political and the economic from the standpoint of the attacks coming from the Conservatives, for any anti-Conservative strategy to be effective, the political struggle would have to be tied closely to the economic struggle. Rosa Luxemburg saw this same issue extremely clearly nearly a century before the Days of Action. In her analysis of the mass strikes in Russia in 1905, she emphasized "the reciprocal action of economic and political struggle," criticizing the German trade union and socialist leaders for not seeing this clearly and for constantly approaching politics and economics as if they operated in two separate spheres.[82]

However, this is precisely what the heads of unions in the OFL did throughout the entire period of the Days of Action. The political strikes of Hamilton in February and the economic battles of OPSEU that began a few hours later were always kept apart and never connected. This separation of the economic and the political was not only visible during the walkout carried out by OPSEU but was characteristic throughout the entire Days of Action. On March 31 more than 300 CUPE contracts expired. The Power Workers' Union voted almost 100 per cent for strike action in its dispute with (what was then) Ontario Hydro. On April 19, the third Day of Action was scheduled for Kitchener-Waterloo. But the two – the economic fight against the boss and the political fight against Harris and the Conservatives – proceeded on different tracks.

Throughout the entire period, there was little if any thought by the union leadership that was now at the front of the anti-Tory movement of combining the political protests with the ongoing economic struggles of workers in their unions. OPSEU was the first big lost opportunity of 1996 – but it would by no means be the last.

The Politics of Numbers 1: Who Counts and Who Doesn't

The Politics of Numbers first reared their head in a big way at Hamilton. At issue was how many stayed away from work on Friday, February 23.

At the time, a publication from Ottawa called *Collective Bargaining Review* collected strike statistics from the provinces and compiled national statistics every month. (It ceased publication in January 1998). The process was simple. Once a week, every provincial ministry of labour was phoned, a list was made of major disputes going on, and a preliminary estimation was made of the size of those disputes. Once a month, a written report from the provinces was sent to Ottawa.

That process meant that there had to be some adjustments between the preliminary figures and the final figures. During the first eleven months of 1995, those adjustments were made nine times. The biggest adjustment was in May when the number of strikers was revised downward by 2,450.

But the Days of Action caused problems. The first one, in London, was initially completely ignored. But one month later, the Conservatives concluded that 23,000 people had struck that day, revising the figure upward.[83] While less than the 40,000 claimed by Gord Wilson,[84] this was a not unreasonable estimate, in line with the kinds of figures cited in this book.

Then came Hamilton. The provisional figure, first reported in April, was 100,000 participating in the Hamilton strike on February 23. Remember – this is not a figure for those who demonstrated that day (in the neighbourhood of 25,000) – but a figure for those who stayed away from work, which would be considerably higher than the number of those demonstrating. That figure of 100,000 stayed on the books until the summer. But in the July-August edition, the February 23 Hamilton strike was downgraded – to 25,000![85] The publication describes it as a strike against "various employers, Hamilton Ont. And other areas," involving "various unions" striking for "union solidarity against Ontario government Labour and Social Policies."

I asked an official with *Collective Bargaining Review* about the discrepancy. "Our hands are tied," he said. "We have to go with what the provinces decide. In some cases, what matters is not the number itself, but what is politically correct."[86] The implication of this revised figure was that the Hamilton strike was only marginally bigger than the London strike of December 11, 1995, muting the story of the strike and minimizing the sense of its impact.

Without trying to further test the arithmetic, here's what we do know of the workplaces and industries which were struck on February 23. According to Jim Turk, "most major unionized workplaces were shut, as were most non-emergency public services and workplaces."[87] As Jack Lackey reported:

- Public transit workers struck – there was no bus service.
- All libraries were closed.
- There was no garbage collection.
- All public schools were closed for a professional activity day.
- Federal and provincial government offices had only skeleton staffs.
- There was no mail delivery, and the large postal sorting plant in Stoney Creek was struck, as was the city's main postal station.[88]

Lackey goes on to say: "Friday is pay day for many in this blue-collar city, one of the biggest shopping days of the week. But the streets were barren of shoppers yesterday morning and it didn't get any better as the day wore on." Turk's and Lackey's descriptions are borne out by the CAW newsletter.

> Thursday, February 22 the CAW members at El-Met Parts put up the first picket line that signalled the Hamilton Days of Protest were underway. By midnight, lines were up at Westinghouse, Wabco, and Camco. Early the next morning every CAW-represented plant was shut down tight.
>
> CAW members closed operations at the following facilities: A.H. Tallman Bartek Industries; Burlington Technologies; Boston Insulated Wire; Brown Boggs Foundry; CAMCO; El-Met Parts; Fisher Ludlow; Hickeson-Langs Supply; John Bear Pontiac Dealership; Laidlaw, Hendrie Trucking; Langs Cold Storage; Loomis Courier; Navistar; Wabco; Westinghouse.[89]

No amount of tinkering with the numbers can obscure the fact that the February 23 Hamilton strike was massive and effective.

Chapter Seven

The Extraordinary Becomes Ordinary

On March 12, a remarkable meeting of the Ontario heads of unions took place to make plans for the next steps in the campaign against Harris. It was remarkable in that it was attended by representatives from the Ontario English Catholic Teachers' Association and the Ontario Secondary School Teachers' Federation. Not only were the two only recently affiliated with the Canadian Labour Congress, but their members were on the front lines of the cuts being implemented by Harris. OECTA's impressive January 13 demonstration had shown a capacity for mobilization on an unprecedented scale. Their joint presence showed the impetus towards a unified fight against the Harris agenda. The meeting was also remarkable because it took place: (a) not three weeks after the Hamilton Days of Action; and (b) while the OPSEU strike was in full swing. This was the opportunity to sketch out a road map for the next Days of Action, to *strategically* plan them to reinforce the bitter and important strike by government workers against the provincial state. While the heads of unions did vote to increase financial support for the OPSEU strikers,[1] they made no attempt to link their Days of Action planning with the strategic needs of the strike.

Tri-Cities in the Spring

However, the heads of unions did set a date for the next mobilization – April 18 in the Tri-Cities of Kitchener-Waterloo and Cambridge. When the day arrived, the movement on the streets was, again, magnificent. Picket lines were set up at seventy workplaces in the three cities, leading to the closure of Canada Post operations, government offices, transit, liquor stores, high schools, and garbage dumps, as well as the cancellation of operations at some hospitals. Students were able to take part in the protest because elementary and high schools were closed for the day as teachers took an "in-school professional activities day." As usual, the CAW took the lead in picketing its workplaces shut. The CAW plants and offices shut for the day included: Advance Metal Industries Ltd., A.G. Simpson, Apex Metals, B&W Heat Treating, Browning-Ferris Industries, Budd Automotive, Butler Metal Products, Crowe Foundry Ltd., Conestoga Meat Packers, Derlan Technologies, Fasco Motors, Go Plastics, Heron Cable Industries, Keene-Widelite, Kitchener Transit, Lear Seating Canada, Ledco Ltd., McRobert Spring, MTD Products, Ornamental Moulding, PJ Wallbank Mfg., Pebra Inc., and Zettel Mfg.[2]

The day had the feeling of a community mobilization.

- The faith community held a mid-morning worship service, opened by Lutheran pastor Rev. Robert Kelly who warned that "the creator of all the universe is not fooled by propaganda … or a 69-cent can of tuna,"[3] referencing the shocking argument from Tory minister of social services, David Tsubouchi, that the poor could weather the welfare cuts by buying cheap tuna. Joining the Lutheran minister were faith leaders from other denominations (Roman Catholic and Mennonite) and religions (Jewish, Muslim), as well as the Spirit Nation Singers and Drummers.[4]
- Anti-poverty activists marched through Upper Beachwood, a well-to-do neighbourhood in Kitchener, chanting, "cut the rich." The Cooperative Housing Federation of Canada devoted two staff members to helping the OCAP create a tent city called "Harrisville" on a downtown lot in Kitchener.[5] Michael Shapcott told reporters, "This was going to be a public housing project for needy people, but Harris cancelled it."[6]
- Students rallied at the University of Waterloo and marched about 1,000 strong to join the main rally downtown, "teachers, students and university faculty walking and carrying signs and banners with slogans such as 'underfunding education is child neglect.'"[7]
- Before the rally, several hundred people gathered outside an old building at King and Victoria Streets, once the site of the Epton factory. Jim Webber, former president of the Steelworkers local at the now-closed plant, told the crowd that "this was where the first strike took place for union recognition … The rubber workers local was started in 1937, and the strike took place in 1946."[8]
- In Cambridge – the smallest of the three components of the Tri-Cities – around 2,500 marched from Pinebush Road to the offices of Tory MPP Gerry Martiniuk, and then boarded busses to join the main rally in Kitchener. In addition, approximately 5,500 were

> bussed into the city from other communities to take part in the demonstration, including busloads of OPSEU trade unionists from Toronto.[9]

All of this culminated in a mass rally outside City Hall Square in Kitchener.

> As phalanxes of banner-waving demonstrators marched down King Street on Friday towards Kitchener's Civic Square, their chants of "No Justice, No Peace" were echoed by the crowd waiting for them outside City Hall … Roaring its approval through most of the speeches, the crowd gave a special ovation to Leah Casselman, president of the Ontario Public Service Employees Union. The union is now dealing with the first wave of public sector layoffs after a five-week strike that has put OPSEU deeply in debt.[10]

The enthusiastic reception for Casselman and the presence of a mass OPSEU contingent was a sign of the militancy with which OPSEU members had waged a desperate battle against Harris. It was also a reminder of the cost incurred by the heads of unions stubbornly separating the political strike movements of the Days of Action from economic battles such as that waged by OPSEU.

There were the usual controversies over the size of the crowd, with one Southam reporter estimating that it was just 12,500 strong. The director of Kitchener's traffic and parking put the size at a "maximum of 15,000." Given the presence of 2,500 from Cambridge, 1,000 from the University of Waterloo, and more than 5,000 from outside the Tri-Cities, these figures, if true, would have meant that attendance from those who lived in and around the Tri-Cities was risible. However, all of us present on the day knew very well that the crowd was composed, in its majority, of folks who lived and worked in the area. A police spokesperson guessed that the rally was anywhere from 15,000 to 20,000 strong. Sid Ryan of CUPE was among many who said it had to be closer to 40,000 in size. Jim Turk pegged it at 30,000.[11] But whether it was 20,000 (the smallest plausible size) or 40,000 (the highest estimate), it was as CAW Area Director Wayne McKay said, "the largest protest ever held in the area."[12] The size of the demonstration was reflected in the enthusiasm of some of the participants and the reach of the demonstration into segments of the population not known for militancy – including students from Waterloo Lutheran Seminary who joined the protest singing the South African freedom hymn, "We are marching in the light of God."[13]

Image 7.1. Discussing 1990s politics on the Toronto Road, Welcome Ontario.

"It's Our Hospital – You Can't Close It"

With the shutdown of the Tri-Cities, the Days of Action story had already become a very big story. Just months into its mandate, the Harris Tories had been confronted by the London general strike, that city's largest-ever mass protest action; the Hamilton general strike and mass demonstration, the latter not only that city's largest-ever mass protest, but Canada's largest since one million workers struck on October 14, 1976 against Pierre Trudeau's wage controls; the OPSEU strike, the largest-ever work stoppage against an employer in Ontario's history; and the largest-ever mass-mobilization in Kitchener-Waterloo and Cambridge. Further – beginning with the childcare strikes of July and November 1995, continuing with the London shutdown of December 1995, the Hamilton shutdown of February 1996, and the Tri-Cities shutdown in April 1996 – Ontario workers were engaging in *political* strikes, far outside the norms of everyday labour relations. In addition, the five strikes listed had all been, in the sense that there was no provision for them in their collective agreements, illegal – and yet still tens of thousands had walked off the job. Finally, this whole massive confrontation between labour and capital and labour and the state was simultaneously a moment of developing unity between organized labour and social justice community movements and coalitions, some of which had previously operated in an orbit that only rarely intersected, at least in a consistent way.

Sometimes when caught up in big events, we start to take them for granted. For those of us immersed in this big movement, mass actions against Tory cuts had become an expected part of daily life. With a quarter-century perspective on the events, it is clear that we were treating as "ordinary" events that in any other circumstance would have been seen as "*extra*ordinary." This was true from the very beginning. London and the Tri-Cities were places that did have union traditions but also long traditions of electing Conservatives. To cross-picket and close dozens of workplaces and pull tens of thousands onto the streets in these communities just months after a Tory landslide? That was extraordinary. The Hamilton general strike was less surprising as the city was long known as a union stronghold, no stranger to mass labour protests. However, that labour movement was dominated by the Steelworkers union, the leaders of which were deeply suspicious of the entire Days of Action movement, and yet tens of thousands struck and marched. Below we will tell the story of the Toronto general strike, surprising simply because of the challenge involved in building a movement capable of closing down, even for a day, a city of some millions.

Like London, Hamilton, and the Tri-Cities, Toronto was (and is) a *city*. Mass movements were not an everyday occurrence. But they did *occur*. However, examine the list provided last chapter of some of the other sites of the Days of Action, a list which includes Peterborough, North Bay, and Kingston. Despite certain pretensions (drive along the 401 and you will be proudly welcomed to the "Greater Kingston Area" while still surrounded by forests and fields), if still formally "cities," these are in a very different category from Hamilton and London – let alone the megacity we call Toronto. This author has a certain familiarity with some of these communities – I grew up in Cookstown (south of Barrie), Kingston, Cornwall, and Belleville, and my parents grew up on farms in what is today Northumberland County – near the hamlets of Welcome and Wicklow – with aunts, uncles, and cousins in the orbit of Peterborough, Lindsay, and Bowmanville.

There are of course traditions of mass struggle in these communities. Cornwall, for instance, was shaped by the monstrous industries of extraction – monstrous both because of the noxious by-products which emanate from cotton, rayon, and paper mills, but also monstrous because of the manner in which the owners of these industries discard worn-out workers like blue jeans gone out of fashion. Organizing against these conditions has a long history in Cornwall. In an old nineteenth-century British imperial document, we read that, in 1888, "a strike amongst cotton mill operatives in Cornwall, Ontario, was settled by arbitration."[14] During World War II there were at least two strikes at the (now-closed) rayon mill owned by Courtaulds.[15]

But building a province-wide movement that pulled together social movements whose deepest roots were in the urban areas, side by side with workers and farmers from much smaller communities, was going to be a challenge. In many parts of rural and small town (or small city) Ontario, the word "Toronto" was (and is) a swear word. These are parts of Ontario that watched the societal changes of the 1960s and 1970s with a mixture of fear and suspicion, holding onto a way of life they felt to be under threat, confronted by images and ideas – and immigrants from places other than the British Isles – that were to them both new and disturbing. The depth of these emotions is hard to exaggerate. For my dad's father – a farmer from the hamlet of Welcome – even a town like Cornwall was a disturbing and foreign place. I remember like it was yesterday, my dad driving through Cornwall, my wonderful grandpa in the passenger seat, expressing his outrage at the "long hair" he saw on the young men on the street – an outrage that was really directed towards myself and my similarly long-haired brother sitting behind him.

These small towns and rural areas were a large part of the reason that Mike Harris had swept into office. Not, of course, the sole reason. In the awful backlash moment that was the 1995 Ontario provincial election, the Tories emerged as the dominant party, not just in small city, small town, and rural Ontario, but also in the megacity of Toronto. But without question, the backlash that propelled him into office was more furious and powerful in the small cities, towns, and countryside outside of the big urban areas. Table 7.1 provides some information to quantify the extent of this backlash, comparing the 1990 election where Bob Rae's NDP won a majority to the 1995 election where Mike Harris's Conservatives swept into office, focussing on the fifty-six ridings in the eleven communities where Days of Action were staged between 1995 and 1998.

Table 7.1a shows Members of Provincial Parliament (MPPs) elected by each major party in the eleven Days of Action communities. The scale of the NDP victory in 1990 is evident – electing thirty-eight MPPs as against thirteen for the Liberals and just six for the Conservatives. The change in 1995 is dramatic. The number of NDP MPPs falls to just nine, the Liberals increase their numbers modestly to seventeen, and the Tories capture fully thirty-one of the fifty-six ridings in question.

Table 7.1b provides vote totals highlighting this dramatic shift. In the eleven Days of Action communities, the Liberal vote is virtually

Table 7.1. Political Characteristics, Days of Action Communities, 1995–8

7.1a. Members of Provincial Parliament Elected by Major Party, 1995 and 1990

	MPPs elected 1995				MPPs elected 1990		
	Liberal	NDP	Cons.		Liberal	NDP	Cons.
All 11 Communities	17	9	31	**All 11 Communities**	13	38	6
London		1	2	**London**		2	1
Hamilton	1	1	2	**Hamilton**		4	
KWC			4	**KWC**		3	1
Peterborough			2	**Peterborough**		2	
Toronto	9	5	18	**Toronto**	11	18	3
Sudbury	1	1		**Sudbury**		2	
Thunder Bay	2			**Thunder Bay**	1	1	
North Bay			1	**North Bay**			1
Windsor	2	1		**Windsor**		3	
St. Catharines	1		2	**St. Catharines**	1	2	
Kingston	1			**Kingston**		1	

7.1b. Total Vote by Major Party, 1995 and 1990 (Highest Vote Total Shaded)

	Total Vote 1995				Total Vote 1990		
	Liberal	NDP	Cons.		Liberal	NDP	Cons.
All 11 Communities	563,630	427,087	710,933	**All 11 Communities**	551,863	733,303	361,333
London	29,364	29,992	50,720	**London**	31,448	49,280	33,255
Hamilton	40,145	34,158	39,139	**Hamilton**	28,007	75,356	15,862
KWC	34,433	33,810	73,792	**KWC**	37,598	64,910	32,500
Peterborough	14,382	15,909	38,922	**Peterborough**	17,913	25,096	19,271
Toronto	311,559	224,919	394,699	**Toronto**	316,856	362,844	201,056
Sudbury	21,943	19,934	16,773	**Sudbury**	17,494	30,943	4,776
Thunder Bay	29,962	12,051	13,670	**Thunder Bay**	22,683	22,372	8,154
North Bay	7,885	4,350	18,722	**North Bay**	10,745	7,039	15,469
Windsor	31,633	28,662	13,754	**Windsor**	30,028	52,995	3,609
St. Catharines	32,010	15,250	42,171	**St. Catharines**	30,999	32,284	20,302
Kingston	10,314	8,052	8,571	**Kingston**	8,092	10,184	7,079

Author's compilation from data in Elections Ontario.[16]

Figure 7.1. Per Cent Change in Vote by Major Party, Days of Action Communities, Ontario, 1990–5.

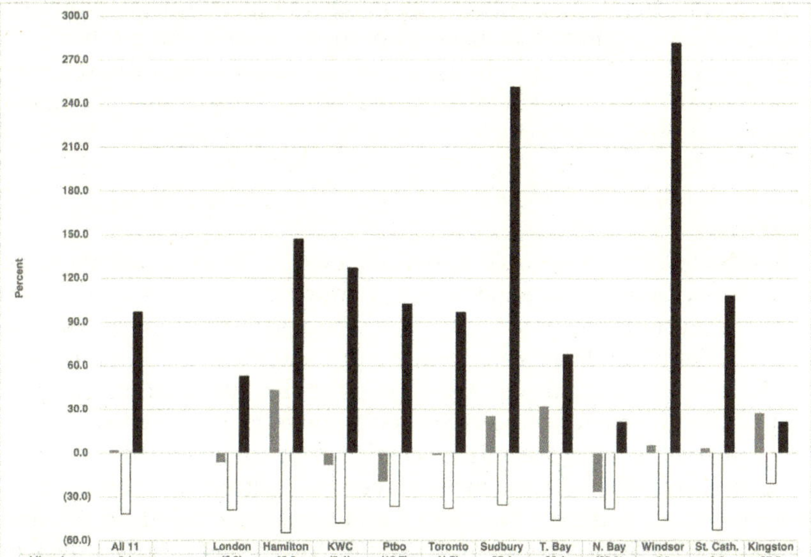

	All 11		London	Hamilton	KWC	Ptbo	Toronto	Sudbury	T. Bay	N. Bay	Windsor	St. Cath.	Kingston
Liberal	2.1		(6.6)	43.3	(8.4)	(19.7)	(1.7)	25.4	32.1	(26.6)	5.3	3.3	27.5
NDP	(41.8)		(39.1)	(54.7)	(47.9)	(36.6)	(38.0)	(35.6)	(46.1)	(38.2)	(45.9)	(52.8)	(20.9)
Conservative	96.8		52.5	146.7	127.1	102.0	96.3	251.2	67.6	21.0	281.1	107.7	21.1

Author's compilation from data in Elections Ontario.[17]

identical in the two elections. But for the NDP it is a different story. The party's vote went from just under three-quarters of a million to less than half a million. By contrast, the Conservative vote almost doubled – from 360,000 to just over 700,000. The table highlights (through shading) the highest vote total in each community for each election. In 1990, the NDP outpolled the other two parties in nine of the eleven communities. In 1995 that figure fell to zero, the Conservatives topping the polls in six of the eleven communities, the Liberals in five.

Figure 7.1 provides a visual reference to capture the extent of this political swing, showing the per cent change in the vote by major party between the two elections for the communities involved in the Days of Action campaign.

The key dynamics at work in the election are clearly visible. There was a substantial drift away from the NDP, their vote dropping on average by 40 per cent. But there was an even more pronounced surge in the vote for the Conservatives, their vote almost doubling – and in some communities (Sudbury and Windsor) increasing by more than

200 per cent! Given the relatively unchanged nature of the Liberal vote, we can provide a plausible explanation for these swings. Disillusion with the NDP in office saw a substantial drift away from the NDP, including parts of its base who voted in 1990 staying home in 1995 – and others who switched their votes to the Conservatives. Other factors – earlier I suggested an emotional backlash against employment equity and other NDP policies – propelled an even bigger movement of voters out of apathy and into open support for the Tories. The left was demoralized and disoriented while the right was energized and mobilized.

In this context, what would be expected would be a prolonged period of passivity from labour and social movements. And, as we saw earlier, this was precisely the trajectory of key sections of the union movement in the wake of the Harris electoral victory and the smashing defeat of the NDP – a "wait and see" stance arguing that mass action was premature. But when activist-centred social movements nonetheless took to the streets – against the cuts to social assistance, against the attack on childcare, etc. – it sparked a mass movement centred on labour, a mass movement much bigger than any could have anticipated. In the first shock of the Harris revolution, it did not feel like a movement was in the works. Within months, we were immersed in the biggest and most protracted mass movement seen in the province since the 1970s.

There existed other, more "gut-level" reasons for the surprising emergence of a united anti-Tory movement – uniting social justice and organized labour, rural farmers with town dwellers, workers from both large and small cities. Among these were the scale and callousness of the Tory cuts. Towards the end of Mike Harris's first term, my uncle – my father's brother – had a near-fatal heart attack, and one summer day I stopped by the farmhouse on "Toronto Road" near Welcome, Ontario, to see how he was doing. As I parked the car, I was surprised to see on the lawn a protest sign with big letters saying something to the effect of "It's Our Hospital, You Can't Close It." I sat down with my uncle, surrounded by big men of his generation, with their calloused hands and sunburnt faces, sitting in lawn chairs, drinking sugary Kool-Aid, chatting about the weather, the crops … the usual. When it was appropriate, I asked my uncle, "tell me the story of that sign on your lawn – what does it mean, 'It's our hospital'"? One of the big men angrily interrupted. "It *is* our hospital. We paid for it." He explained that as a young man, he had been working in a factory – I think Goodyear near Napanee, but I could be wrong – and that "every pay cheque, we authorized a few bucks to come out, so that we could have a hospital built in Port Hope, a hospital with an emergency room."

I did a bit of research and found out that – yes – the hospital had been built through donations from local farmers and workers, "paid for out of their own pockets and pay cheques, scraping up dimes and quarters and slowly but surely filling any number of tin cans sitting on store counters – and down at the library, and the Legion, and the newspaper office, and anyplace else where somebody might just lift up their kid or their grand-kid and, hoisting them way up to that counter like never before, let them hear the metal-on-metal noise of a hospital being built one nickel at a time."[18] But, as part of a province-wide health care restructuring, the boards of Port Hope and nearby Cobourg hospital had been amalgamated, and the new board, "faced with too little money from the province" voted, narrowly, to consolidate hospital services in Cobourg – effectively meaning the closure of the Port Hope facility.

The fight against that closure was bitter. Eight hundred people crammed into the Port Hope Legion,[19] April 30, 1997, to voice their displeasure.[20] Lawn signs went up, and farm families had stories to tell and anger to express when their urban nephews drove down the highway to sit and chat. The anti-Harris movement was united by the deep work and long hours of social movement activists and rank and file worker militants, doing the work that activists and militants do. It was also united by the righteous anger of ordinary small-town and rural folk, who could not believe that "their government" had the nerve to try and close "their hospital" – a hospital built with the sweat and sacrifice of generations. The anger I encountered on the Toronto Road near Port Hope was being felt across the province – the Tories' Health Services Restructuring Commission recommending closing hospitals, laying off staff, and saving money in not just Port Hope, but also Hamilton, Ottawa, Kitchener, Thunder Bay, Sudbury, and elsewhere.[21] So yes, Mike Harris won a landslide in a backlash election accompanied by an ugly discourse that we have become sadly familiar with in today's backlash era. But no, he did not have a mandate to do this type of damage. More people – far more – voted for the other two major parties, both of which came out in opposition to these cuts. And so, despite a seemingly overwhelming majority, and despite a crushing defeat for the left, the province's biggest-ever social movement took root and took to the streets.

Peterborough – "They're Here for Us, George"

Thursday, May 2, just days after the Day of Action in the Tri-Cities, OFL heads of union met and announced that there would be a fourth Day of

Action, June 24 in Peterborough. Gary Parent, an OFL vice-president, said, "we want to keep the momentum going,"[22] but not all were reassured. London was a city with an established NDP presence, including MPP Marion Boyd, who withstood the Harris avalanche of 1995. Hamilton of course was a traditional NDP stronghold, all four of its seats going NDP in 1990. It lost three of them in 1995, but David Christopherson won re-election. The Tri-Cities were a different story, the NDP being shut out in 1995, losing all three seats it had formerly held to the Conservatives. And Peterborough? The city's two seats had gone NDP in 1990 – but by the narrowest of margins, Jenny Carter winning her seat by just 185 votes, Elmer Buchanan by just 896. In 1995 they were both defeated decisively by a resurgent Tory party, Buchanan losing by 7,859 votes and Carter dropping to third place, trailing the Tory victor by more than 15,000 votes.[23] This seemed to be returning Peterborough to its more conservative "norm" – a town not known as a friendly refuge for proponents of mass movements.

With this as a background, there was some trepidation heading into the June 24 Peterborough Day of Action. With just 67,000 residents, Peterborough would be the smallest of the communities struck to date – and even without its Conservative political background, any action there would inevitably involve fewer people than in London, Hamilton, or the Tri-Cities. Many trade union activists feared that the union leaders were hoping to wind down the momentum by calling smaller and smaller actions and using that as an excuse to stop calling any more Days of Action.

But events were quickly to brush aside any such trepidations. On May 27, for the first time since being elected to office, Harris agreed to meet face-to-face with the heads of Ontario's unions. In what William Walker described as a "lavish dinner in the Royal Suite of the Royal York" in Toronto, Harris and his chief political lieutenants, including Finance Minister Ernie Eves and Labour Minister Elizabeth Witmer, met for three hours with Gord Wilson from the OFL, Sid Ryan from CUPE, Buzz Hargrove from the CAW, Leah Casselman from OPSEU, "and leaders from the Communications, Energy and Paperworkers Union, the Service Employees International Union and the United Steelworkers of America."[24] There was much to discuss. Bill 7 had made the use of scabs legal. Bill 26 had set the stage for the privatization of many government services and made it easier for employers to rid themselves of their unions. And on May 13, Ontario Labour Minister Elizabeth Witmer announced that there would be significant changes to the Employment Standards Act. The act was to be changed so that unions would have "to negotiate their own standards for hours of work, public holidays, overtime pay and severance pay."[25] In other words, after three mass mobilizations – part of arguably the biggest mass movement in Ontario's history – not only was Harris not budging, but he was escalating his attack on workers' rights. The lavish dinner settled nothing – following the meeting Wilson announced that the Days of Action campaign would in turn escalate and escalate quickly, Peterborough to be followed by Metropolitan Toronto on October 25 and 26.[26] The issue of Peterborough was now settled. It would not be a safety valve to quietly let the movement lose steam but rather a stepping-stone towards shutting down Canada's largest city.

In the run-up to Peterborough, small direct actions continued to target the Harris Tories. To name just one, in June, members of the CAW and injured workers' organizations "staged a peaceful sit-in at the Ontario Ministry of Labour at 400 University Avenue ... protesting cuts to worker health and safety, plans to rollback Ontario's Workers' Compensation system, and government plans to end the right to refuse unsafe work."[27]

And when June 24 rolled around in Peterborough, the actions that day were without question, "the largest demonstration this community has ever witnessed."[28] Estimates of the size of the main rally ranged from an improbably low figure of 5,000 up to a more realistic 12,000.[29] Sam Gindin said that the protest significantly included "a higher percentage of young people than at any of these previous protests."[30] Some press reports of the event were dismissive. Barbara Shecter, writing in the *Financial Post*, said: "Turnout for the rally, on a rainy day, was far below the crowd of 25,000 that hit the industrial heart of Hamilton on a sunny Friday in February."[31] Shecter was using Hamilton's Friday citywide general strike as the point of reference. Wendy McCann said that some estimates "put the crowd at no more than 5,000, considerably smaller and more subdued than the boisterous 100,000 who marched the streets of Hamilton last February."[32] McCann was using Hamilton's even larger Saturday mass protest as her point of reference. But these dismissive accounts – besides being absurd, making a comparison between a protest in the large city of Hamilton and the much smaller city of Peterborough without pointing out this population difference – really missed the mark. As James Turk pointed out: "Virtually every industrial workplace was closed, as were municipal services, libraries, the transit system, provincial government offices and federal services including the Trent-Severn Waterway." Turk estimated that 10,000 participated in the main rally. "Given the size of the community, this was proportionately a much larger turnout than in London, the Friday in Hamilton and Waterloo Region."[33]

In that small city:

- Assembly Lines at General Electric and Quaker Oats were silent for the day.[34]
- Most public services came to a halt, including transit and garbage pickup.
- Libraries, liquor stores, and the post office were shut.[35]

CAW members organized on the evening of June 23 to cross-picket plants in the area, closing, in addition to General Electric and Quaker Oats:

- Johnson & Johnson; Camco; Messier-Dowty Electronics; Pan-Osten Ltd.; Pebra Inc.; Pebra Inc. (office); NHB Industries; and Meyers Transport.[36]

Sam Gindin, in his report on the day, captured the "feel" perfectly.

> At the rally in the park, a couple in their fifties stood on the margins, watching the crowd but with different responses. "What are they all doing here? Who needs them!" growled the man impatiently. The woman, her head bobbing around to read the different signs, calmly and almost absent-mindedly replied: "They're here for us, George."[37]

An ordinary conversation of a middle-aged couple had become a moment of political education and, perhaps, radicalization. At this point, I should perhaps reverse the title of the chapter. The ordinary had become extraordinary.

The Spirit of the Days of Action

In the wake of the Days of Action in the Tri-Cities and Peterborough, economic disputes continued to bubble to the surface. What was becoming clear was that the Days of Action were feeding the confidence of Ontario workers. Telemarketers, workers at the Ontario Jockey Club,[38] and others ignited a series of small disputes, encouraged by the sight of tens of thousands striking back against Harris.

Most importantly, Westin hotel workers in Toronto, members of Local 351 of the Textile Processors, Service Trades, Health Care, Professional and Technical Employees International Union, went on strike on June 9. They were up against management demands for the imposition of piece work, shifts as short as two hours, and the dismantling of the seniority system. Management used the Conservatives' Bill 7 to hire between 300 and 450 scabs to continue operations.[39]

However, the workers used mass pickets to disrupt operations. The spirit of the Days of Action permeated the strike.

> From the beginning, lively pickets, complete with percussion and loudhailers, challenged scabs at Westin's entrances. Designated "scab days" were organized to demoralize the scabs, who were chased from door to door by groups of strikers. Solidarity pickets – some seemingly emerging spontaneously – kept up morale and rattled the nerves of Westin's management and goons. In a burst of creativity, several workers built a coffin – complete with an effigy of a Westin manager – which stood upright and open for all passers-by to behold.[40]

On June 24, activists from Toronto who had travelled to the Peterborough general strike showed how the Days of Action could be used as a springboard for building solidarity with these economic disputes. They arranged for their busses to drop them off at the Westin picket line, leading to a fantastic and spirited mass picket.[41] This kind of initiative, however, remained the property of a very small minority. Finally, at the beginning of August, management caved. Workers won a wage increase and forced management to back down on all of its key demands. The political strike action against the Conservatives was starting to invigorate industrial militancy for workers in their economic fight against management. And as summer turned to fall, all eyes turned to Toronto.

Chapter Eight

Watershed 2: The Streets of Toronto

Taking the Days of Action to Toronto – the largest city in the province and the country – was an enormous commitment for the Days of Action movement. Toronto was not just any city, and everyone knew that. This would have implications for the entire province. Toronto labour leader Linda Torney articulated a widespread sentiment when she said that a province-wide strike would enter the realm of the possible "if we can do it in Metro."[1] In that spirit, in the run-up to these Metro Days of Action (MDA), the CAW spread the word across the province, putting up billboards – in Hamilton, Kingston, Kitchener, London, North Bay, Ottawa, Peterborough, Pickering, Sudbury, St. Catharines, Toronto, and Windsor – "saying 'Demonstrate for Democracy' with a picture of the 120,000 people who rallied in Hamilton" in February 1996.[2]

Making Toronto's event a success would require careful, effective organization. The co-chairs were Torney, long-time president of the Metro Toronto and York Region Labour Council, and Margaret Hancock from the Metro Network for Social Justice. Joining them were Bill Howse, long-time executive assistant at Metro Toronto and York Region Labour Council, and Paul Forder from the OFL. Forder has a unique place in the Days of Action story. Recall that when Gord Wilson finally agreed to "do a community" and launch the Days of Action campaign, we quoted an unnamed CAW executive saying: "Gordie [Wilson] was smart enough to know that if you're going to make it successful the CAW had to lead it."[3] That led directly to Forder, with a long CAW background, being tasked by the OFL to work full-time on the Days of Action. Jason Ziedenberg calls these four – Torney, Hancock, Howse, and Forder – "a real dream team, and along with 70 other staff seconded from unions, and those hired by unions to help organize community groups, they wear the accolades of MDA's success."[4]

As important (or more so) were unpaid (and often unsung) volunteer organizers. Helen Kennedy, at the time on the executive of Metro Toronto and York Region Labour Council as well as secretary of CUPE's Toronto District Council, gives an insight into one corner of that network of activists.

> Just after Mike Harris was elected, we created a grassroots organization that brought together both community and labor organizations, the North York Fight Back coalition. We didn't have funding from anybody. We went to community organization meetings where we explained what was happening to the budget and funding for social programs. And we organized our own information meetings where we explained the 22 percent cut to welfare. We grew to become a much larger organization reaching across the whole community.[5]

The intensity of feeling in the run-up to the October Days of Action could be felt at the annual Labour Day parades in Toronto and across the province. In Windsor, 7,000 marched including 2,000 from CAW.[6] In Hamilton, 3,000 marched. Saul Antanaitis, a member of Local 105, International Brotherhood of Electrical Workers, said, referring to the Harris government: "We're pretty upset with the cuts, the reforms, and the bills that are destroying our labour movement."[7] Toronto had the biggest Labour Day event, the CAW describing "a massive turnout of 30,000" with many talking up "the importance of taking part in the Toronto Days of Protest."[8] You had to be on the ground with the movement to know about these events, ignored, for instance, by *The Globe and Mail.* The Council of Canadians' Maude Barlow chastised the newspaper's editors for having "failed to report one word about this extraordinary national demonstration of labour's political strength or the growing solidarity between labour and social activist groups that it represented."[9]

One opportunity to escalate the anti-Tory movement had been missed during the OPSEU strike. But now, another one was in our laps. As I wrote at the time, "the argument against a province-wide strike has always been, 'well, you can strike a union town like Hamilton, but Toronto will never go out.' Well, Toronto was going out. And if we can shut down Toronto, we can shut down the province."[10] All eyes, both anti-Tory and pro-Tory, turned towards October. This was the big challenge. Would Toronto workers respond to the call to strike illegally in protest at the Conservative cuts?

"We're Occupying the Plant to Try and Save Our Jobs"

In the run-up to the October strike date, the challenge of uniting the economic and political dimensions of the struggle was posed once again, but this time on a much bigger scale than with previous economic strikes in 1995 and 1996. The most powerful and left-wing union in the country – the Canadian Autoworkers – was up against the "Big Three": Ford, Chrysler, and General Motors. Just as Harris was attacking jobs through outsourcing in the public sector, the Big Three were attacking jobs through outsourcing in the private sector.

The confrontation focussed on General Motors. At issue were outsourcing of jobs and plans by GM to sell two Delphi auto parts plants. The strike began October 3, when 15,000 GM workers in Oshawa and Ste. Thérèse walked off the job – actually October 2 for 3,000 workers in Oshawa, who jumped the gun and walked out in advance of the midnight strike deadline.[11] Four days later, they were joined by 5,300 workers in St. Catharines, and three days after that by another 4,660 in Windsor, London, and Woodstock.[12]

A strike is not just about walking picket lines, but about building mass meetings both to gauge the scale of support among the strikers and to share information about the issues at stake. Those issues had been well-articulated by people like Jim Stanford and Sam Gindin, who had carried out the research that rebutted GM's arguments on competitiveness and effectively "juxtaposed GM's record profits to company demands for more cost-cutting."[13] By Wednesday, October 9, nearly 10,000 union members had shown up at membership meetings in Windsor, Ste. Thérèse, Oshawa, St. Catharines, London, and Woodstock, expressing their determination to "stay out as long as it takes" – including 900 from the Windsor transmission plant, 1,000 from the Windsor trim plant, 3,000 gathering in Oshawa's Civil Arena, 3,500 in St. Catharines, and 1,000 in Ste. Thérèse. CAW/GM Master Bargaining Committee Chairperson Dave Vyse said: "Workers are angry at GM's lack of respect for the work they do and how they've contributed to the enormous profits. I've never seen the membership so united in every location."[14] By midnight October 9, all 28,510 of GM's unionized workers in Canada were on the picket line.[15]

The strike was a lightning rod for discontent everywhere. On (Canadian) Thanksgiving Monday, October 14, more than 100 workers from Detroit, including members of the United Auto Workers and striking *Detroit Free Press* workers, joined the picket lines in Windsor and brought food for the strikers' Thanksgiving dinners. "We came to bring a message today that U.S. workers should be down with the CAW to bring GM around and to solve it," said Pat Meyers of UAW Concerned. "We thought it was a significant message to send to Canadian workers today. The message is total support."[16]

In the midst of the strike, on Tuesday, October 15, GM reported new profit numbers which only fuelled the anger of the strikers. For the period July to September 2016, GM's worldwide profits had almost doubled from the same period the previous year, climbing to $1.27 billion (US). GM did not release quarterly figures for profits from its Canadian operations, but we do know that GM profits for Canadian operations in 1995 were $1.39 billion (Canadian) and Hargrove estimated GM's Canadian profits from July to September 1996 to be about $300 million.[17] "The workers on the picket line in Oshawa saw those [profit] numbers and they want us to stick to our guns more than ever," said Oshawa Local 222 president, Mike Shields. "We have made too much money for them and this is how they repay us – by trying to get rid of our jobs," said Ron Hulett from Local 1973 in Windsor.[18]

The confrontation escalated when, also on October 15, GM applied for an injunction to move seventy-five manufacturing dies out of one of the Oshawa plants. Hargrove wrote that GM "was sending a tough message … that if we didn't settle, GM would operate in spite of the strike. Moving the dies could have kept GM in business while our members walked the picket line. An injunction could seriously have undermined the effectiveness of our strike. 'We have to take over GM's Oshawa fabrication plant,' I told our bargaining committee."[19] Elsewhere, he is quoted as using less diplomatic language – "You will not get one goddam die out of the city of Oshawa."[20] One day later, on October 16, the occupation happened, when in numbers variously reported as 100, 150 or 300, CAW workers led by Shields stormed the GM parts plant,[21] evicting managers and guards, and welding the plant doors shut, "vowing to occupy the building indefinitely" to stop GM moving the dies.[22] "We're occupying the plant to try and save our jobs," said Shields.[23]

The workers did not have to stay indefinitely. After just five and a half hours, GM backed down. The return of an almost forgotten tactic to further the demands of labour, the factory occupation, was like an electric shock through both the striking GM workers and the entire movement. The next week, at a special CAW convention, this energized mood was evident: only 2 out of 700 delegates voted against doubling union dues so that CAW could, if necessary, sustain a long, drawn-out strike.[24]

As it turned out, the strike would be over quickly, a settlement being reached on October 23, with strikers voting 88.7 per cent in favour of the

Image 8.1. Toronto – Ontario 1996.

negotiated agreement. When 6,400 production and skilled trades workers attended a standing-room-only meeting in Oshawa, "the enthusiasm built during the strike and from the occupation of the Oshawa Fabrication plant was in evidence from start to finish."[25]

Here again, however, we see the political and the economic running on separate tracks. One part of the CAW was deeply immersed in the colossal task of shutting down Toronto on October 25 for a *political* strike. Another part of CAW was deeply immersed in the colossal task of organizing an *economic* strike against what had historically been the world's biggest corporation. The political and the economic missed each other … by forty-eight hours! Why not merge the two tracks? Perhaps an all-out province-wide strike wasn't yet on the cards. The difficulties in organizing such an undertaking would have been daunting. But at the very least, strategically link the two big events – bussing in Day of Action anti-Tory organizers, for instance, to support the picket lines and provide information on the political demands of the Metro Days of Action; bringing strikers from the line into Toronto for mass meetings organized by MDA to link the two movements. But each event – the political strike against the Tories and the economic strike against GM – were treated as discrete events, not strategically linked one to the other.

Toronto – 24 Hours, 300 Picket Lines

When October 25 finally arrived, it was a moment unlike any we had seen. Across the city, 300 picket lines were thrown up, closing hundreds of workplaces. According to René Fortin, responsible for the citywide strike on the twenty-fifth, CUPE alone, with about 145,000 members in the city, had "100 or 111 places we want to shut down" and "began to close things down at 5 o'clock in the morning."[26]

- "The Toronto Transit Commission, which moves some 1.3 million people daily, was shut down …
- Mail delivery in Canada's largest city ground to a halt as postal workers set up picket lines at giant mail sorting facilities.
- Basic municipal services, including garbage pickups, were cancelled across much of Metro because workers either didn't show up or couldn't get through picket lines.
- In some schools, teachers outnumbered students … At the Metro separate school board, only 12 percent of 15,575 high school students showed up for scheduled classes at the 15 Roman Catholic high schools and six elementary schools that were open. The other schools were closed for a professional activity day."[27]
- "The Toronto Board of Education estimated that up to 40 percent of its teachers booked off … Principals kept schools open, but in many cases, parents did not send their children."[28]

The strike suspended most social services, closed landfill sites, liquor stores, the Toronto Stock Exchange, city hall, the Hydroelectric Commission (power facilities), school boards, the Science Centre, museums, universities, high schools, and malls.[29] The CAW picketed and shut seventy workplaces where it had members.[30] When Toronto's largest industrial employer, Bombardier-de Havilland, was threatened with picketing, the employer simply told its employees not to show up, "docking them a vacation day instead."[31] "The Toronto Eaton Centre was a retail graveyard – while security guards wearing bulletproof vests protected the desolate mall, store clerks searched for things to do in their empty shops."[32] Those who wanted to go to work, but knew that the strike would disrupt transportation, did boost one section of the economy – hotels – as thousands of office workers booked rooms to stay "close to their desks. In many office towers, they found themselves bedding down in impromptu dormitories."[33]

Fortin knew that to make the city come to a halt, its transportation would have to be shut down – not just transit (whose unionized members, as we found out on the night of the 24th, had no intention of crossing picket lines), but also the enormous highway network that brought workers into and out of the city every day.

> Our plan was to stretch cars across the freeways and just drive at a slow rate, causing traffic congestion. So we had people get up at 5 o'clock in the morning to set up those barriers. But on that day, everybody decided to stay home, because the subway was going to close down, and people presumed there would be major havoc on the roads, so when we got there in the morning the highways were deserted. Our cars traveling at a slow speed got pulled over by the police. Toronto was a ghost town, nobody came that day.[34]

The day was not simply about picket lines and ghost-like highways.

- A group of Days of Action cyclists, between 50 and 100 strong, put down their bikes on Bay Street and sat beside them until moved along by the police. They went from intersection to intersection, again and again, moved along by the police. At 7 p.m. they blocked traffic on a downtown section of Yonge Street till almost 8 p.m.[35]
- At the shuttered Toronto Stock Exchange (TSE), 1,000 people gathered to demonstrate the links between Bay Street and Queen's Park. A section of the crowd briefly made it into the lobby of the exchange, before peacefully retreating.[36]
- A group of professors and graduate students held a teach-in at the Ontario Institute for Studies in Education. "'We hope to bring back the constructive activism of the '60s by bringing issues and discussion back to the streets' said organizer Don Young, a graduate student in adult education."[37]

"Hey Mike, Hey Harris ... We'll Shut You Down like Paris"

The next day saw what was, "by any measure of counting," the largest demonstration in Canadian history,[38] not to be matched until the great anti-war protests of the early twenty-first century. The march – certainly more than 200,000 strong – took hours to gather, and hours to march from our starting points to our destination at Queen's Park (for a discussion of the numbers, see the sidebar at the end of this chapter). There were several marshalling points, but the one at Coronation Park was the largest, and its route stretched five kilometres, east on Lakeshore Boulevard, north on Spadina Avenue, so we could swing east on Front Street, and then north again up the widest street in Toronto, University Avenue – where we took over every lane – to take us to the "pink palace" at Queen's Park.[39]

The route had to take us past the Convention Centre, because inside, meeting in convention, were the Tories responsible for the so-called Common Sense Revolution – better-labelled counter-revolution – that was making all our lives so miserable. When we got to the Convention Centre, the contempt felt by the crowd for the delegates huddled inside – architects of attacks on the poor, attacks on childcare, attacks on public housing, attacks on health care, attacks on employment equity, attacks on workers' rights – that contempt and anger became palpable. As the ranks of protesters marched past the centre, the thunderous cry of "Shame" was shouted again and again and again.[40] "Hey Mike, Hey Harris – We'll Shut You Down like Paris,"[41] a chant started by the contingent I was in, was taken up by thousands. It had been our calling card in the first of the big anti-Tory actions, the shutdown of the city of London on December 11, 1995 – linking it to the general strike in France on November 24 that same year, protesting cuts to social security in that country.[42] The slogan was newly relevant, as one week before the Toronto protests, another one-day strike against attacks on the public sector had again brought the economy of Paris to a grinding halt.[43] As Marcella Munro has noted, that chant "was possibly the best popular example of the sentiment that this is not the only battle ground."[44] We felt that we in Ontario were just one part of an international movement against austerity.

Aftermath

On the eve of the MDA, two labour history experts, Bryan Palmer and Laurel Sefton MacDowell, did not doubt the scale of what was coming to Toronto. Palmer, then at Queen's University said, "there's no question" that there would be "a huge mobilization." MacDowell, then at York University, called the scale of the protests "unprecedented."[45] Linda Torney, in the immediate aftermath of the protest, offered a careful analysis. "I think the important thing is that we demonstrated that we can shut down a big chunk of the city and that despite all the rhetoric about danger and violence, that we can do it peacefully." She also captured the enthusiasm of the day. "There was a lot of festivity on the picket lines ... It was quite a party."[46]

Some involved became *extremely* enthusiastic. The CAW's Hargrove put on the agenda the probability of a serious escalation of the movement against cuts. "This is a first in Toronto, but there will be more across the province. And the entire province and country is going to be shut down at some point, I would predict within the next year or year and a half."[47]

Thomas Walkom was less enthusiastic. The massive protest was without doubt a "spectacular success." The organizers had demonstrated the scale of opposition to the Tory cuts. They had shut down a major city "without violence, without trashing buildings and with a considerable amount of good humor." They had put together "at a very local level, a working coalition of groups opposed to these cutbacks." But he cautioned: "The question for the demonstrators now becomes: once the good feelings die down, what's next?"[48]

Gord Wilson posed the question of a province-wide shutdown abstractly – putting out the date of May 1, 1997. Buzz Hargrove posed the question enthusiastically, suggesting not just a province-wide but also a national shutdown. But in truth, no one posed the question *strategically*. There were no plans in place to operationalize these big projects.

The MDA had taken place under the banner of "Organize, Educate, Resist"[49] – fine as a headline for collective action, but only as a headline. The challenge would be to come up with a *strategic* plan to provide goals for the movement and benchmarks by which to achieve those goals. A real strategic plan would have expressed more than just these fine sentiments. Stop the war on the poor. Repeal the anti-labour laws. Stop workfare. Stop the cuts to social assistance – give back the 21 per cent stolen by the Tories. Restore funding to schools and hospitals. That kind of a program of action could have been the foundation for a strategic plan to build the movement towards the province-wide shut down that had been talked about for months. Such a program of action was never, however, on the table.

Increasingly, in spite of (or perhaps because of) the momentum created by the MDA, tensions within the movement became harder and harder to ignore. Two weeks before the great Toronto shutdown, an enterprising *Toronto Star* reporter noticed that while Linda Torney and Margaret Hancock were handing out leaflets at Kensington Market and St. Lawrence Market, making the case for the coming mass actions, Wilson – president of the Ontario Federation of Labour and nominally head of the Ontario union movement – "spent the day at home sweeping out his garage." Wilson acknowledged there was a "turf war" between the OFL and the MDA organizers but insisted the OFL would put its resources into the Toronto strike. An aide for Torney denied there was any dissension.[50]

On October 26, the dissension was there for all to see. At the very moment of what was, at the time, the largest-ever mass demonstration in Canadian history, Wilson was absent – deciding instead to travel to Sudbury for an NDP fundraiser.[51] After the event, Wilson rewarded Paul Forder for heading up the massive two Days of Action by *demoting* him, ostensibly for "insubordination." Using a strained but quite insulting metaphor, Wilson said about the demotion, "when you hire a dog, you don't bark for it."[52] So rather than organizing mass mobilizations against the Tory cuts, Forder's job would be to write a stewardship manual.[53]

If the proponents of mass action did not have a strategic plan, the Tories certainly did. Their wars on the poor, the public sector, and workers' rights were proceeding apace. And ominously, one section of the workers' movement – heretofore relatively silent and in the background – also had a strategic plan, but one that would derail the movement, not build it.

Pink Paper Pessimism

The seventh of November was slated as the date for union leaders to meet and decide how to build on the MDA. But rather than a road map for pushing the movement forward, we were confronted with the worst factional split Ontario labour had ever witnessed. Leaders of thirteen so-called pink paper unions emerged from a joint meeting to announce they would not be supporting any further Days of Action but would instead concentrate on working to elect the NDP to office.[54] The OFL at the time was an umbrella organization for unions, whose total membership was 650,000. As we saw earlier, the unions who were now backing out of the Days of Action had cohered as a bloc during the Bob Rae administration. Some referred to this grouping as the Steelworkers-CEP-UFCW bloc[55] – referencing the three big private-sector unions at their core – United Steelworkers of America (USWA, 64,000 members); Communications, Energy and Paperworkers (CEP, 38,000 members); and United Food and Commercial Workers (UFCW, 32,000 members). Together with several other private-sector unions, including International Association of Machinists and Aerospace Workers (IAMAW) and Amalgamated Clothing and Textile Workers Union (ACTWU), and two largely public-sector unions, the Power Workers Union (PWU) and Service Employees International Union (SEIU), the thirteen unions counted 210,000 members, almost one-third of the entire

OFL membership.[56] This mass backlash against activism was a devastating blow to the Days of Action, from which it never really recovered.

Part of what was at issue was economic resentment. Unions had provided the lion's share of the financing for the Days of Action budget – already exceeding half a million dollars – and some objected to paying all this money and then sharing decision-making with social justice community groups who had far fewer financial resources to contribute. Part of what was at issue was political resentment. Again and again, Days of Action organizers had refused to allow NDP politicians to speak from the platform, and the unions that were now turning their back on the movement were the most pro-NDP unions in the OFL.

John Murphy, president of the 15,000-member PWU, gave the clearest articulation of the pink paper group's thinking. He called it "counter-productive" to challenge the Harris Tories without putting forward an alternative. But the alternative about which he was musing had nothing in common with the missing program of action, sketched out here. "The alternative for us, as working-class people, is the New Democratic Party."[57] Leaders of twelve major pink paper unions had co-signed a document on August 30, 1995, titled "Toward the Renewal of Social Democracy in Canada." The document argued that "Liberals, Conservatives and Reformers" are "poised to engineer the most abrupt political transformation in the history of this country." It also clearly argued that to challenge this right-wing offensive, the left and the workers' movement had to embrace political action. To pretend that unions could restrict their activities to the economic front, as in the United States, would be a disaster.

The document took issue with those who saw disconnected, single-issue social movements as a sufficient vehicle for change. "The NDP has at least 100,000 signed-up members – that is, people who have explicitly chosen to join a left-of-centre, pro-labour organization. There is no coalition or single-issue formation that can point to the same level of sustained support."

The document acknowledged that the principal vehicle for political action in Canada, the NDP, had at best a chequered record. The Rae government in Ontario in particular was targeted for helping "to usher in the political equivalent of nuclear winter." But these observations were used, not to put forward a program of action that could challenge both the Harris cuts and the problematic policies of the Rae government, but to minimize the consequences of the actions taken by the NDP in office, saying, "we do not intend to dwell on the political events here in Ontario which provided the occasion for this review." To make such a statement was, to say the least, astonishing, given the enormous crisis which was unfolding under their feet.

The logic of the document was that workers had no choice but to step back from mass social movement activism and work for the re-election of the NDP. There was an implication – more than an implication – that the real problems were not the policies of the NDP in office, but the lack of political sophistication among union members. The document argued that labour "must re-examine its own linkages with its membership base, to rekindle, spread and strengthen the social democratic values that too few of our members recognize as their own today."[58] In other words, the problem was not the problematic lead from the top, but the backward politics at the base of the movement.

The pink paper unions did not *explicitly* counterpose electoralism to mass action in their 1995 document. One year later, at the moment they were announcing their withdrawal from the Days of Action campaign, they argued that "the strategy of partial general strikes must be replaced by militant targeted actions against employers who ignore workers by using scabs and lockout out workers."[59]

There was a clear need for the "militant targeted action" suggested by the pink paper unions. The ongoing strikes were often bitter and difficult – and sometimes went on for months. One of them, occurring right in the middle of the Days of Action campaign, involved 90 members of the USWA Local 6917, on strike against the Scarborough-based S.S. Armstrong, where the employer did exactly what was feared following the Harris rollback of the NDP reforms – employing scabs to try to break the strike. At a late September press conference, USWA District 6 Director Harry Hynd said that the strike "would have been over much sooner if the company had not been able to hire scab labour. He said it is the first time replacement workers have been used to replace USWA members in an industrial plant since the Tory government scrapped the ban on replacement workers last November."[60] However – in restricting union action to legally sanctioned strikes, distancing themselves from the tactics required to engage in *political* direct action against the Tories, and restricting their notion of politics to the electoral arena and the election of NDPers, the pink paper unions were turning their back on the heartbeat of the anti-Tory movement.

They were not alone in this approach. A case in point was Gord Wilson who, while coming from the pro-Days of Action CAW, was much more comfortable with the pink paper approach. In a telephone interview with John Ibbitson, he said that "we have to do something dramatic" to stop strike-breakers who had been deployed at four ongoing labour disputes in Ottawa, Brampton, and the Toronto area. "We have to stop the use of the plant. And there's only one way you do that. You seize the plant."[61] Wilson of course – the same man who had missed the largest demonstration in Canadian history to attend a fundraiser in another city – never authorized even a single "plant seizure" against the use of scab labour. Like the pink paper rhetoric, his was a case of verbal militancy masking passivity in practice.

From the very onset of the Days of Action campaign, there had been an undercurrent from the Steelworkers-CEP-UFCW bloc that opposed the whole approach of (a) reaching out to the social justice community organizations and (b) engaging in mass street protests and illegal strikes.

The former was quite serious. We earlier looked at the debate that emerged after the London Day of Action, in which community organizations felt out of the loop because both co-chairs of the event came from the labour movement. From that point on, that practice shifted – all future events were chaired by both a local labour leader, as well as a local social justice community leader. However, after the Tri-City Day of Action, the OCSJ wanted to go further. The key decisions about the direction and future of the Days of Action were being made at the heads of union meetings, referred to throughout this book. The OCSJ argued that these meetings should be expanded to include "all provincial and national organizations" in the OCSJ. James Turk says that "this recommendation was forwarded to the OFL and distributed to all unions." However: "Union leaders split along the same fault line that had run through all other discussions of the days of action. Because of this division, the nonlabour group leaders were again not allowed to participate in the post-Waterloo heads of unions meetings."[62]

The latter, the reluctance to participate in strikes being labelled as "illegal," was often articulated from within the Steelworkers-CEP-UFCW bloc. Typically, the largest union in the pink paper group, the USWA, would arrange its participation in the Days of Action through deals with employers. At Kaiser Aluminum in London, the union agreed that its members would work Sunday in exchange for getting the Friday off to participate in the London Day of Action, a strategy similar to the one mentioned earlier, where workers at Stelco and Westinghouse got a day off for the Day of Action in exchange for extra work earlier in the week. It would be wrong to argue that only the pink paper unions engaged in this kind of strategy. We earlier saw that during the Tri-City shutdown, the CAW had made a similar kind of deal with Lear Seating Canada Ltd., and during the London events, the CAW worked out with Accuride Canada that CAW members could book off the Friday as a holiday.[63] But during every single Day of Action, the CAW could also proudly list the dozens of plants around which it had organized cross-picketing, a tactic that the pink paper union leaders were much more reticent to employ.

This preference for a handshake with the employer rather than mobilized cross-picketing for an illegal political strike reflected scepticism about the whole Days of Action exercise. In the run-up to the very first Day of Action in London, Connie Maile of UFCW Local 1977, representing workers at thirteen Zehrs stores in the area, said: "We are not going to go on strike against a good employer," arguing that "thousands of dollars will be lost" and in any case, "people will go and do their shopping in non-unionized grocery stores." She was joined in her scepticism by Patrick Warlow, president of USWA Local 88, representing several hundred Kaufman Footwear employees. "I cannot back a strike. We'd get fired. I supported the NDP, now it's too darned late. I'm not going to make the company more mad at me." Jim Webber, president of the Steelworkers union at Epton Industries, said he had a "real problem" with members of the local labour council, "who chose to lead their people into the wilderness."[64] Jason Ziedenberg quotes from a memo by Ed Nelson, a CEP vice-president, opposing the London Day of Action. "We believe that a majority of our members have not yet been directly affected by this government and therefore there is little support for action of this kind."[65]

This echoed the view of Howard Hampton – then-leader of the ONDP. His name was frequently put forward as someone to be invited to speak to a Day of Action rally, a request that was just as frequently refused by the Day of Action organizers, still furious at the Social Contract experience. But even if willing to speak at rallies, Hampton was a Days of Action sceptic. "There's a whole bunch of people out there who believe that Harris is on their side. If we shut down transit and the hospitals, are we going to persuade all these people that we are on their side?"[66]

The Politics of Numbers 2: How Big Was That Demo?

Numbers, as we have seen, had become political footballs at previous Days of Action. At Toronto, the "number games" verged on the ridiculous. The strike on October 25 brought the economy of a megacity of three million to a standstill. But the preliminary estimate for those participating in the strike was 75,000,[67] a figure that was without question far too low. All measurements of a strike count not just those on the picket line, but also those who stay away from work. In a city the size of Toronto – to shut it down so completely that the highways are empty, the shopping malls are silent, and the schools are closed – that would take hundreds of thousands of strikers, not tens of thousands. My guess is that the total of those who stayed away from work amounted to one million people.

On the Saturday, organizers and participants were very comfortable with calling the demonstration a quarter of a million strong – some saying it pulled in as many as 300,000.[68] Veteran performers Bruce Cockburn and Billy Bragg had entertained the crowd at Queen's Park – Cockburn's rendition of "Lovers in a Dangerous Time" bringing many to tears.[69] Bragg estimated the crowd at a quarter of a million. "He's done lots of concerts," said Linda Torney. "I'm going with Bill Bragg."[70]

Many didn't. Toronto police came up with the extremely low figure of 40,000, a figure so unbelievable that they had to quickly increase it to 75,000.[71] The *Toronto Star* gave identical sets of aerial photos to a group of experts, photos "showing the crowd at the height of the Queen's Park rally." Their experts weighed in as follows:

- 25,000 according to Phil Coppack, geography professor at what is now Toronto Metropolitan University
- Between 33,000 and 49,500 according to "experts at the Institute for Space and Terrestrial Science at York University"
- Probably 54,000, no more than 75,000, according to Metro Toronto Police Staff Sergeant Stan Belza
- 75,000, according to the Ontario Provincial Police, "who counted 63,000 people passing a given point during the parade and allowed 12,000 for those who went directly to Queen's Park"

Based on these estimates, and similar ones made by *Toronto Star* staff, they arrived at a figure of 52,800 for the crowd size.[72]

Belza says that they had "measured the area from Queen's Park to College St. and included 'every blade of grass' to come up with 27,000 square metres able to be occupied by crowds." For the staff sergeant, this was definitive, because if there is a maximum of four people per square metre, then the absolute maximum who could be present at any one time would be 108,000. "That's it," said the sergeant. "They did not have four people per square metre crammed into everything down to College St. It never happened, and we have the aerial photography and the video to prove it."[73]

But we *did* have a continuous march five kilometres long, a march where, as the first group was arriving at Queen's Park, the last marchers had not even begun to march. And – many who arrived at Queen's Park left – in fact, thousands left – before the rest of the demonstration had arrived. There was never a moment when the entire crowd was present at Queen's Park and surrounding streets.

Further, it was a march with multiple staging points, Coronation Park but also Gore Park for some of the overflow. Non-labour protesters marshalled at Nathan Phillips Square, which "was packed to its 50,000 person capacity."[74] In addition – and this is important – Paul Forder knows that 1,120 chartered busses were used to bring people into Toronto, and reasonably estimates that these busses would account for about 50,000 of those demonstrating.[75]

That latter fact alone – 1,120 busses carrying 50,000 people to the demonstration – makes any of the figures from the "experts" simply ludicrous.

Walter Podilchak, who at the time was teaching collective behaviour at the University of Toronto, applied his skills to the crowd size. For the record, it is worth quoting him at length.

- There are four lanes on one side of University Ave.
- Five people can occupy a lane, making it 20 people across on one side.
- Let's say it takes a line of people two seconds to cross my vantage point, making it 40 people per two seconds or 1,200 per minute.
- There were two sections of protesters, the first from City Hall took a minimum of 30 minutes, and the Coronation Park group took a minimum of two hours. This is a total of 150 minutes for the parade.
- Simple counting of real people marching, not restricted pictures of the rally (Queen's Park lawn) would conclude: 1,200 people per minute times 150 minutes for a minimum total of 180,000 people. My numbers are the conservative lower limits. About one-third of the parade time included marchers on both sides of University Ave. This would put the estimate above 200,000. Admittedly there were pockets in the crowd occasionally. At times the density of people was more than the estimate of 20 people crossing my vantage point every two seconds.

  I was a scientist watching reality on the street, not some photographic images. You can't get any more simple than that – count real people and provide facts by which the estimates are made.[76]

Podilchak's math is, if anything, conservative. The crowd took at least three hours to empty from Coronation Park, as anyone who had to stand there and wait to get out will attest. The demonstration was easily 250,000 strong.

But you didn't have to be "an expert" to know that the crowd was in six figures. Vicky Hargreaves was waiting with friends for her section of the march to arrive. "We waited at a restaurant, half a block from the convention centre. We sat there for 90 minutes until our group passed. In that time, we figured 150 to 200 passed in front of the window every five seconds, which means that over the first hour we saw about 72,000." That makes 90,000 a conservative estimate for the number who passed in the 90 minutes Vicky and her friends were waiting, and they joined the march halfway through, again coming up with a minimum figure of 180,000.[77] Add in the 30,000 from Nathan Phillips Square, and the figure goes over 200,000. Call the Nathan Phillips Square crowd in the range of 50,000, as Ziedenberg does, and suddenly the figure for the number demonstrating that day is closing in on 250,000.

Chapter Nine

Life in Some Northern Towns[1]

The year 1996 ended in acrimony. On December 9, forty public and private-sector union representatives from the OFL gathered in Toronto to assess the Toronto events and look to the future. The divisions were palpable. John Ibbitson reported that at the meeting, Wilson, in a voice so loud it could be heard in the hallway outside the room, warned that "If we leave this room without having taken steps that are meaningful, then ... this federation will start to fall apart."[2] Tom Collins from the USWA said: "If the Federation of Labor isn't going to perform its function anymore, let's get rid of it." Wilson intimated he might soon leave his post as head of the OFL. Another said: "We're immolating ourselves."[3] The great hopes raised during two magnificent days in Toronto were now disappearing in the noise of a horrendous internal faction fight.

Tensions had been visible before the open break announced by the pink paper unions. Part of the reason Gord Wilson took a pass on the October 26 massive demonstration in Toronto was his personal anger towards Linda Torney over her insistence that the Metro Days of Action would be run locally, and not from the OFL.[4] Torney saw these and other tensions through a feminist lens.

> Sometimes it looks to me like a bunch of male egos, and all the women want to get on with the job. Gord thinks put Howard on a podium and then the world will unfold as it should, Sid thinks there should be another party because he's pissed off at the NDP. You've got the boys out there fighting, flexing their muscles and doing their, "My Dad's bigger than your Dad" routine or whatever they do. Margaret [Hancock, Days co-chair] and I were friends going in and we were bigger friends coming out. It was a wonderful experience for the two of us.[5]

Judy Rebick, who from 1990 to 1993 had been president of the National Action Committee on the Status of Women – an organization whose central role in launching the Days of Action was examined earlier – saw the issue as one of "new forces coming into the labour movement" that were "threatening the old boys' network, the old alliances between the private-sector unions and the NDP."[6] The contrast between the magnificent events of the Toronto general strike and the bitter factionalism inside the mass organizations of labour was warning enough that our movement had problems.

The Two Souls of the Days of Action

These bitter internal disputes had not broken the Days of Action movement – but there was damage. The three cities to host Days of Action after Toronto – Sudbury, Thunder Bay, and North Bay – were all in Northern Ontario, and each displayed, in different ways, "two souls" of the movement:[7] one, reluctant and demoralized; the other, energized and militant. It was the former that we witnessed first.

On November 26, three weeks after the pink paper unions' abandonment of the Days of Action, the heads of unions met with representatives from the OCSJ, and the meeting voted that the next target would be Sudbury in February 1997. This was a very questionable decision. In the room for the discussion was just one representative from Sudbury, who voted *against* staging a Day of Action in that city. They should have listened to this Sudbury representative, as the Sudbury Labour Council, dominated by the USWA, subsequently "voted down the idea, 68–1." Jim Turk, the co-chair of the OCSJ, said that "there was a sense we hadn't gone to any Northern Community." But Hancock, who was present at the meeting, said she "didn't know how" the decision to target Sudbury was taken and called the decision "unfortunate."[8]

Sid Ryan had earlier "downplayed" the significance of the divide in the labour movement represented by the pink paper backlash. "Yes, there are one or two unions, which we've had all along. I mean, this is nothing new. We've had this from day one. Not everybody is supportive of being able to get their members to shut down their work places."[9] But it *was* something new – a move from private discontent to public opposition, from glum disquiet to aggressive opposition to the Days of Action. Underestimating the depth of the split was perhaps a factor in the counter-intuitive selection of Sudbury as the next focus for the Days of Action. Whatever the reasons, it soon became clear that the split *would* have an impact on the scale and spirit of events in that city.

Like Hamilton, Sudbury was a USWA-dominated town. But unlike Hamilton, in the wake of the pink paper split, USWA opposition to the movement was expressed openly and aggressively. John Filo, president of the local labour council said, "February is a non-starter," not just "because of the weather" but "because the Steelworkers are not crazy about a day of protest." Wayne Fraser, president of USWA local in Sudbury said: "As far as we are concerned" Days of Action "are a waste of time and energy and are counter-productive in establishing anti-Harris support."[10]

As the dates for the Sudbury Days of Action approached – now moved to March 21 and 22 – it was clear that events on the two days would be pitched in a much lower register than any previous. There would be no workplace shutdowns.[11] Transit would operate, and schools would be open. Organizer Mick Lowe tried to put a good face on it. "We're celebrating people's resistance to the government. And we want to have fun. Because the Mike Harris government is not fun. They're creating misery."[12] But the massive protests in Hamilton and Toronto had also, in fact, *been* fun (remember Ryan's characterization of Hamilton as the Woodstock of the labour movement); at the same time, they were grimly serious events, determined to challenge the cuts that were devastating our lives, and impressive displays of the force of the Days of Action movement.

There would be no display of force at Sudbury. Lowe hoped to "pack" the 6,500-seat Sudbury Arena.[13] But on Saturday, March 22, the most optimistic figure given for the turnout was 3,000.[14] Events on the preceding Friday – which in every other city had seen strikes and picket lines – in Sudbury were limited to "demonstrations outside municipal, provincial and federal buildings as well as outside the university and some high schools."[15] Having an anti-Tory protest of 3,000 in a small city like Sudbury, in itself, was a real accomplishment. But from the standpoint of the trajectory of the Days of Action movement as a whole, it represented a very big step backward from the heady days of October in Toronto.

However, that trajectory could not be accurately plotted solely from the events in Sudbury. In CAW-dominated Windsor, a January 1997 meeting of local labour leaders and social justice groups confirmed that there would be Days of Action in that city, the 13th and 14th of June, "unless a federal election campaign is underway about the same time." There would be a federal election called, and the Windsor events would not take place until the autumn. However, the plans put forward at that January meeting focussed on a June shutdown and seemed as if from a different universe than the planning for Sudbury. Plans included the following:

> Disruption of international border traffic and a complete shutdown of unionized workplaces – including the Big Three automakers and parts suppliers ... Participation was promised by U.S. unions to give the protest a strong international flavour.
>
> Unions in Sarnia, Chatham and Tilbury are also showing interest in workplace protests to coincide with those in the Windsor area. ... Teachers' associations promised support for the event, but said they'll likely have to plan a separate protest of their own for March because of the speed with which the government is pushing ahead with changes to the educational system.[16]

Both the two souls of the Days of Action – Sudbury's reticence and Windsor's defiance – were on display on April 28 in Thunder Bay. Like Sudbury, it was a scaled-down event compared to the first Days of Actions, one day instead of two. Unlike Sudbury, the local labour council backed the protests, by a convincing nine to one vote.[17] And like Windsor, you could "feel" the power of the movement in the enthusiasm with which the call for action was answered. The press reports indicated that just 1,500 took part.[18] But that many alone were involved in a five hundred-car motorcade that "clogged the main arteries of the Northern Ontario city for about 90 minutes." The motorcade's destination was a noon-hour rally at Canadian Lakehead Exhibition grounds,[19] which involved many hundreds more than those involved in the motorcade itself. Further – as in all previous Days of Action, except for Sudbury, there were workplace actions taken by various sections of the labour movement. "Mail to most of Thunder Bay, including disability and family benefit cheques, was not delivered ... Teachers ended their classes early throughout Thunder Bay and employees from various ministries took vacation days to lend strength to the rally. Teachers' unions formed an information picket at the Ontario government building."[20] All of this makes much more plausible the CAW figure of 5,000 participating in the Day of Action.[21] If Sudbury represented a real step back for the Days of Action, Thunder Bay could rightly be considered a partial recovery.

To some extent, this partial recovery was driven by changes at the top of the national movement. In March, the Canadian Labour Congress announced a call for a National Day of Protest on Saturday, May 3, a coordinated protest in at least twenty communities across Canada, "to protest the false solutions of the Liberal government."[22] The possibility of a provincial movement against government cutbacks becoming national had a galvanizing effect.

The partial recovery was also driven by the grinding nature of the Harris cuts and the continuing anger throughout the province at these cuts. When the Tories organized a $150 a plate fundraising dinner in April in St. Catharines, more than 1,500 marched in protest to attend a rally labelled the "Mike Harris Not Welcome Party."

> Former CAW Local 199 president Gabe MacNally ... was master of ceremonies at the anti-Harris event. MacNally said the St. Catharines rally was so successful he believed the area could host one of the Days of Protest, which have shutdown numerous cities for a day including London, Hamilton, Kitchener-Waterloo, Peterborough and Toronto. "I think this area's ready to fight back on a larger scale,' said MacNally. 'We'll just have to wait our turn."[23]

One year later, MacNally's prediction would come true – the penultimate Day of Action would take place in his city. But in the intervening months, the fate of the movement would be sealed by actions taken by both the Tories and the labour leadership.

An Offensive on Two Fronts

As the Days of Action movement made its way through Sudbury and Thunder Bay, trying to find its footing after the pink paper backlash, the Tories were preparing an escalation of their offensive, an escalation on two fronts that would once more see opposition to the Tories take the form of mass activism. The first front was Bill 136, introduced the first week of June by Labour Minister Elizabeth Witmer – the "Public Sector Transition Stability Act."[24] The second was Bill 160, introduced the third week of September by Education Minister John Snobelen – the "Education Quality Improvement Act."[25] The former was a declaration of war on organized labour in the province, in particular on the public-sector union movement; the latter was a declaration of war on teachers, students, and education. The spectacle of a divided and feuding labour movement – leading to small events and a de-emphasis on strike action – had given the Tories an opening, a sense that with opposition slackening, they could push their agenda more aggressively. The two bills would together define the terrain of struggle for the summer and autumn of 1997.

Bill 136 sent a shock through the union movement. Witmer portrayed it in very mild terms, saying: "A legal and institutional framework is needed to ensure that, during this time of public sector restructuring, everyone is treated fairly and that services continue to be provided to the taxpayers."[26] But these mild words fooled no one. The late Joe Flexer quite rightly called Bill 136 "the centrepiece of the current phase of the Harris agenda."

> Bill 136, for the next four years, authorizes the government, acting through appointed boards, to decide which public-sector unions will be the bargaining agent for any particular jurisdiction, merge bargaining units and seniority lists (including non-organized workers), deny the right to strike for those who have it and impose collective agreements with appointed arbitrators for hospital workers, firefighters and police. ... The OFL leadership has correctly seen this legislation as a decisive blow aimed at virtually destroying public-sector unionism in the province of Ontario.[27]

Bill 136 was an existential threat, not just to services and jobs, but to the union movement itself. To sit by and let the bill pass without resistance would have been to severely weaken the capacity of public-sector workers to defend their interests through collective bargaining – and given the increasingly important role of public-sector workers in the workforce as a whole, this would be a blow to the entire union movement, public *and* private sector. The intensity of the threat had the effect of completely revitalizing labour's role in the Days of Action movement and putting back on the agenda the question of a province-wide general strike – an idea that had seemed to disappear after the pink paper backlash.

Within hours of the announcement of Bill 136, CUPE's Sid Ryan announced the formation of a common front including "municipal and hospital workers, firefighters and teachers." The inclusion of the latter group, teachers, was all-important. The explicit attack on teachers was not to come until September, but everyone knew that it would come.[28] The education file, after all, was managed by John Snobelen, who the year previous had been caught on tape talking of the need to "invent a crisis" in education to push forward restructuring.[29] Ryan not only announced the formation of a common front but openly talked about actions which, while he called them "political protests," would no doubt be considered illegal walkouts – and on a scale much greater than had been seen to this point. "I don't think one day is going to do with this one," said Ryan referring to the one-day strikes that to this point had characterized the movements. "We've got to promote a political climate where this government is forced to back off."[30] By July, CUPE had in the works an emergency convention, pulling together hundreds of local leaders. A province-wide general strike was on everyone's lips. Not untypical was Brian O'Keefe, CUPE secretary-treasurer. "The last thing that we want is a province-wide strike, but if this government is pig-headed enough to persist in pursuing this outrageous piece of legislation, we may not have any option."[31]

Teachers too – knowing that companion legislation would soon come to target them specifically – began to organize. John Ryrie, president of OSSTF in the Kitchener-Waterloo area, said that five teachers' unions, united in the framework of the Ontario Teachers' Federation (OTF), would hold emergency meetings within days of such legislation being introduced, and that a strike was very much on the cards.[32]

Most significantly, the OFL called its first-ever emergency convention on July 28 in advance of the second reading on Bill 136 expected in August. This, "the largest convention ever held by the OFL" according to the CAW, was to decide on the next steps.[33] Flexer said that about 1,200 delegates were expected. Double that – 2,400 – registered, reflecting the depth and breadth of the anger against the Tory attacks. "Significantly, many labour organizations not affiliated to the OFL, such as all the various teachers' unions, the Ontario Nurses Association, the Firefighters and even the Police Association, participated and took an active part in the deliberations of the convention." Tempering Flexer's enthusiasm, however, was the relative lack of participation from the private sector. His union, the CAW, was present in numbers "with a delegation of 150 members" but the other "large private-sector unions were represented by small groups of top leaders."[34] The old divisions, muted for the moment in the face of the Tory offensive, were nonetheless very much alive in the background.

The convention overwhelmingly approved an action plan entitled "The Last Straw." According to point 13, collective action in defiance of Bill 136 was a real possibility:

> These political protests will include job actions such as coordinated and complete work stoppages; the timing and duration of which will be individually determined by the affiliates and non-affiliates ... These ... may take place by sector, by city, by region, or on a province-wide basis, as the affiliates and other organizations determine.[35]

The CAW described this as "a detailed action plan which calls on union members, non-affiliate groups such as firefighters and nurses as well as social activists to develop a broad-based and province-wide response including political protests and job actions such as coordinated and complete work stoppages."[36] However, the plan avoided specifics, including the question of moving from citywide to province-wide general strikes. In the somewhat cynical coverage of one reporter, "the resolution left open whether the action will be a general protest, a series of rotating protests, or maybe no protest at all. It also authorized the OFL to launch an advertising campaign against the government."[37] A minority at the convention argued that this did not go far enough and that the plan was too vague, particularly in its careful avoidance of committing the OFL to a province-wide strike. Wilson's response reeked of sarcasm. "People I guess read 'The Charge of the Light Brigade' and decided it's not a good idea to repeat that. There are other mechanisms and ways of doing things."[38]

This new terrain – an intensification of attacks from the Tories and a new mandate to resist from the OFL's largest-ever convention – transformed the political mood in the province. It also meant that the next Days of Action, in Mike Harris's riding of North Bay September 26 and 27, would be a dramatic departure from both Sudbury's and Thunder Bay's Days of Action. In the run-up, we again saw angry local protests against the Tory agenda. In August, the OFL organized demonstrations in eight cities – Toronto, Sudbury, Thunder Bay, Windsor, London, Cambridge, Burlington, and Kingston – against Bill 99, which would reduce benefits to those on workers' compensation. These demos drew 1,000 people. "In every city unionists and injured workers disrupted the hearings demanding the right to be heard" as only 130 out of the approximately 1,300 applications to make presentations to the hearings had been accepted. In Kingston, demonstrators "took over the hearing room to conduct their own meeting. They debated and passed unanimously a resolution calling on workers to continue the fight 'on the streets, in the workplace and to build support within their communities for a just compensation system and safe and healthy workplaces.'"[39]

At the end of August, "after weeks of wrangling," the Tories and union leaders agreed to sit down and talk about alternatives to Bill 136.[40] Labour Day 1997 saw the sometimes staid Toronto parade transformed into a mass demonstration against Bill 136.[41] In North Bay, Harris's hometown, the premier was dogged by the "angry howls of nearby demonstrators" as and he his family holidayed on the waterfront's mini-train.[42] Finally, the next day, leading representatives from the government and the union movement held a first meeting, about which both sides expressed optimism. The next week, serious talks began in earnest.

Simultaneously, the union movement was preparing for a strike. CUPE Ontario used the month of September to poll its 180,000 members. In Hamilton-Wentworth, nearly 90 per cent voted in favour of strike action, on turnout that union officials said was "between 55 and 60 percent." In Oshawa later in the month, the vote was 85 per cent in favour of strike action. In some locales, support for strike action was as high as 94 per cent.[43] On September 11, in the context of this unfolding polling of the membership, 1,000 local leaders met and voted "overwhelmingly" in support of conducting a province-wide strike if talks with the Tories failed to win drastic changes to Bill 136.[44] The very next day – Friday, September 12 – talks between the OFL and the Tories collapsed. Wilson declared that it seemed clear that for the Tories, the meetings were nothing more than public relations. When on September 16 the Tories tabled a motion of closure, which meant Bill 136 could become law within two weeks, Ian Urquhart was not alone when he predicted that within days there would be rotating strikes throughout the province as the OFL initiated strike action.[45] "The employers had better batten down the hatches," said Wilson. "I'm sure by the beginning of next week there will be some (labour disruption) activity starting to develop and it will gain momentum as we go down the road."[46] Judy Darcy, president of CUPE, mapped out a plan of action linking the anti-Bill 136 protests with the Days of Action: coordinated action first by health care workers on September 24, then by teachers on September 25, culminating in two days of protest, September 26 and 27 in Harris's hometown of North Bay.[47]

And then, in the words of many – CUPE National president Judy Darcy and OFL secretary-general Ethel LaValley to name just two – the Tories "blinked."[48] One day after indicating they would be enacting closure on Bill 136, Labour Minister Elizabeth Witmer announced changes to the bill, stripping it of virtually every clause to which the OFL objected. "There will be no temporary elimination in any way, shape or form of the right to strike," said Witmer.[49] The climbdown was extraordinary. In addition to preserving the right to strike, the government would "eliminate its proposal for a Dispute Resolution Commission; allow the Ontario Labour Relations Board to handle the duties of the proposed Labour Relations Transition Commission"; and "drop proposals that would allow it to hand pick arbitrators."[50] The strikes set to begin the next week were on hold as labour leaders waited to see if these promised changes would in fact be voted into law. "While we're talking, we're not walking,"[51] said Darcy. A day later, Education Minister Snobelen said that he too would not be trying to take away the right to strike of teachers in the education sector.[52]

The calm lasted less than a week. On Monday, September 22, Snobelen released long-awaited details of his plans for the education sector. Bill 160, the Education Quality Improvement Act, might not have explicitly threatened the right to strike, but it did so implicitly, giving the province the right to "prevent disruption in the education of pupils" during the restructuring of school boards.[53] Earl Manners, president of the Ontario Secondary School Teachers Federation, called this simply a "back door for the government to limit or prevent the right to strike and put further limitations on collective bargaining."[54] The longer school year proposed in the bill would mean less prep time for teachers – because the summer break, as any teacher knows, is not just about vacation – it's about getting ready for September. The Tories claimed they could save $1 billion out of the $14 billion per year currently spent on education. Critics of the bill said this was only possible through a drastic restructuring, centralizing decision-making in the hands of the province, making it easier for them to lay off thousands of teachers. How many? Analyses by some teachers' unions put the jobs at risk because of the decrease in preparation time at between 6,000 and 10,000.[55] If the drastic changes to Bill 136 had taken off the table the threat of a province-wide strike by the OFL, the drastic attacks on education workers embodied in Bill 160 had put onto the table the prospect of a province-wide teachers' strike. When asked directly whether a strike was possible, Marshall Jarvis, president of OECTA, said simply "I don't see any alternative."[56]

On September 24, 800 officials from the five teachers' unions held a day-long strategy session in North York, accompanied by an afternoon demonstration by 1,200 at Queen's Park. Earl Manners, president of the secondary school teachers' federation, "said he was confident teachers will get support from the other public-sector unions."[57] The scale of the attacks and the atmosphere of solidarity made a strike by teachers almost inevitable.

> "The Ontario Teachers' Federation and the affiliates are putting (Education Minister) John Snobelen on notice," federation head Eileen Lennon said. "If John Snobelen does not move off his legislative agenda, every school in this province will be shut down."
>
> "If they … put me in jail for breaking the law … so be it. I would quite gladly do that," said Peter Guthrie, a staff member with the Ontario Secondary School Teachers' Federation. …
>
> "If we have to walk out we will stay out," said Earl Manners, president of the secondary school teachers' federation. "Bill 160 needs to be withdrawn or it needs to be gutted."
>
> … "We will shut down the schools if that's what's required to get this government to move," said Marshall Jarvis, president of the Ontario

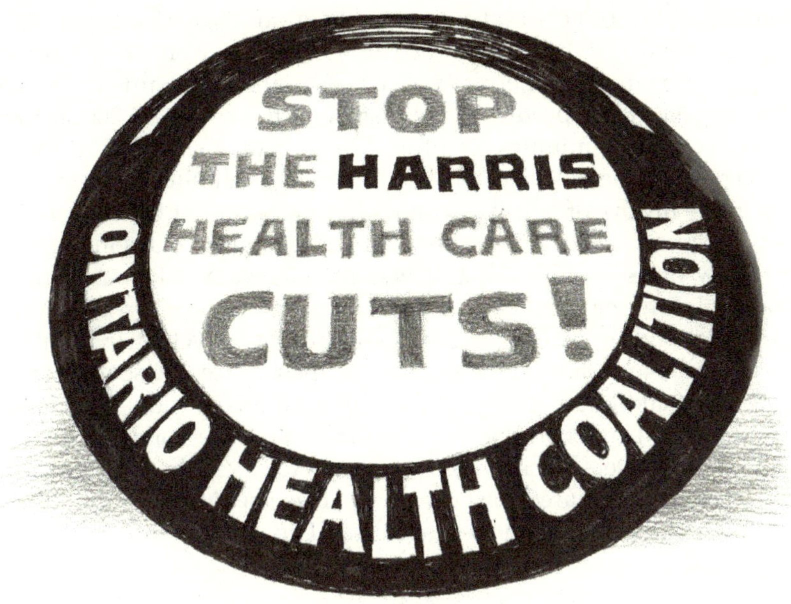

Image 9.1. "Stop the Harris Health Care Cuts."

> English Catholic Teachers Association. "I think the government is pushing this situation to a confrontation."
>
> Phyllis Benedict, president of the Ontario Public School Teachers' Federation, said the "unions will stand united until we are forced to go back and then we will make a decision whether or not we do go back."[58]

Such a strike would involve 167,000 teachers and affect 2.1 million elementary and secondary school students. Being outside of the provisions of their collective agreements, a strike would be, like stoppages during the Days of Action, illegal.

North Bay – "This Isn't Mike Harris's Town This Weekend"

All of this meant that the North Bay Days of Action, on Friday and Saturday, September 25 and 26, happened with a greater level of participation and militancy than in the preceding Day of Action in Thunder Bay – and of course far more than in Sudbury. "On Saturday between 15,000 and 20,000, including 180 busloads of protesters, marched through the streets against Harris, easily the biggest protest ever seen in the city."[59] Some estimates were higher for total participation, ranging from 25,000 to 30,000[60] – and even an enthusiastic 35,000 from one *NOW Magazine* reporter.[61] Whether 15,000 or 35,000, these were extraordinary figures for a small northern city. The CAW called the Saturday march "the biggest public protest in the history of the city of 56,000. It took approximately 40 minutes for protestors marching shoulder to shoulder to pass."[62] Glenn Wheeler called it "the biggest political demonstration in the history of North Bay, jamming the shores of Lake Nipissing and the streets of a city that's been dinged a thousand jobs in the Tory chainsaw massacre."[63] In fact, it was the largest-ever labour demonstration in any city in Northern Ontario.[64] Actions on Friday closed provincial and municipal offices, the North Bay Psychiatric Hospital, the Ontario Northland Railway, the main post office, the sewage treatment plant and liquor stores, and it impacted bus services and classes at Nipissing University. Some 3,000 rallied at Memorial Gardens.[65] "About 300 pickets blocked the main doors to city hall, turning away a few workers who dared to show up … 'This isn't Mike's town; this is our town,' Days of Action co-chairperson Lana Mitchell told a boisterous crowd."[66]

> "This is just one step along the road to the Ontario Days of Action, when the entire province is shut down and Harris is driven out," vowed John Clarke, of the Ontario Coalition Against Poverty, whose members had come up from Toronto to picket and protest … "The Tories have awakened a sleeping giant among the public-sector unions and their members," pronounced Julie Davis, Ontario director of the Canadian Union of Public Employees. "Harris has unleashed something we may not have been able to unleash on our own."[67]

"One Struggle and Two Issues"

The theme of both days was "one struggle two issues," a theme that continued in the weeks after North Bay. Sid Ryan, in a speech on the day, said "if we don't see the promised changes, in 48 hours, we'll be calling a province-wide strike."[68] *Contact* reported Hargrove saying that "the CAW will stand in solidarity with the teachers and public sector workers."[69] In an interview, Gord Wilson said that "any move by the government to legislate teachers back to work will trigger a walkout by private-sector unions … 'We'll empty out the private-sector plants and then the CEOs of the private-sector companies can call Mike Harris and ask him to solve their problem,' Mr. Wilson said."[70] At North Bay, the union leadership picked up the gauntlet thrown down by Harris and announced their refusal to be divided from the teachers. Plans were already underway for the next Day of Action, scheduled for Windsor on October 17. The Day of Action that Friday in the CAW-dominated city "could be a very important day" said Gary Parent, president of the Windsor and District Labour Council. Brian Cross reported that "the province-wide strike could start on Windsor's Day of Action and just keep going," and quoted Parent saying that "'they aren't talking about being out for just one day' … upon his return from the rally that attracted thousands of union members to the premier's home town."[71] For the third time we had a clear road map: use North Bay to build Windsor, use both to build solidarity with the teachers, and when they strike, use their momentum to strike the whole province. Again, there was everything to play for.

The pink paper pessimists had receded into the background, and it was the militant Days of Action side of the labour movement that had the wind in its sails. Again and again, the movement was told that the Bill 136 attack on labour rights in general was of a piece with the Bill 160 attack on education. Both would be approached as one attack. In October during the Windsor Days of Action, Hargrove would say "to loud applause from the massive crowd … 'We will stand shoulder to shoulder with teachers against Bill 160.'"[72] September 24, in the run-up to the North Bay Day of Action, Ryan said: "We are fed up with the bullying tactics of this government. We will not be split apart."[73]

Importantly, it was not just the left of the movement, but the central leadership of the Ontario Federation of Labour which, in the words of Ryan, had "decided to treat the labor bill and education legislation as one package."[74] Gord Wilson, president of the OFL, was very public about this solidarity strategy, maintaining that any strike by teachers would be joined by municipal and health sector workers.[75] In the early autumn of 1997, Wilson would make this point repeatedly.

- September 27 in the *Ottawa Citizen* – "We have said from Day 1 that there is one struggle and two issues … So our position is we're either all in together or all out together."[76]
- September 30 in *The Hamilton Spectator* – "We want to be very clear that Bill 160 will get the same attention and treatment from us as did Bill 136 … We've said from day one there is one struggle and two issues. We're either going to be all in together or all out together, and it's up to the government to decide."[77]
- October 2 in *NOW Magazine* – "The deal, as I understand it … is that with the exception of the essential workers, the municipal and health-care sectors would go down (on strike) if the teachers went out. We're all in together, or we're all out together."[78]

- October 22 in *The Standard* (St. Catharines) – "The labor movement in this province cannot leave the teachers to hang out to dry … We said from Day 1 when we went into this fight around health, education, and municipal services with Bill 136 … and Bill 160 that they were two bills and one fight."[79]

This message of solidarity inspired education workers, up against the full force of the Harris attack. Art Callegari, president of an OECTA local in Northern Ontario, said about the Day of Action in North Bay: "The most heartening thing I heard in North Bay was that the Ontario Federation of Labor was going to stand with us … They won't abandon us even if they get the concessions to Bill 136 – we won't be alone."[80] Events, however, were to prove Callegari mistaken.

Chapter Ten

Watershed 3: The Class (Room) Struggle

The Tories' retreat on Bill 136 was a real victory for the labour movement. However, as Glenn Wheeler pointed out in his coverage of the North Bay Days of Action, this victory might prove to be "bittersweet." The Tories' move showed "signs of cunning as well as collapse."

> Now that the garbage collectors, library staff, bus drivers and all the other public employees have been freed of the most virulent anti-union elements of Bill 136, one group remains locked in conflict with the government – teachers.
>
> Amid the joy, there's the foreboding sense that the worst may be yet to come as teachers confront Bill 160, that though the teachers plan to meet with the government again, a strike is all but inevitable, and that it will be long and bitter.[1]

For the moment, the twin blows of Bill 136 and Bill 160 had galvanized the labour movement. The speeches from the podiums at North Bay talked about solidarity, and the "one struggle, two issues" theme continued for some time after North Bay. At a very general level, the rhetoric had not changed. Joanne Lucius in the *Ottawa Citizen* reported that even though public-sector workers "appear to be winning with their battle with the Harris government," according to Gord Wilson, a strike by teachers "will be backed by 600,000 unionized public-sector workers across the province."[2] However, with the Tory concessions on Bill 136, the *content* of these expressions of solidarity was drifting away from a strong commitment on leading a province-wide walkout in the event of a teachers' strike to something much more ephemeral. This was no mystery to Marshall Jarvis, president of OECTA. "There's no expectation on my part that these (other public sector workers) will be walking with us," he told Wheeler. "We expect them to respect our picket lines and show support on the line and in our communities."[3]

On September 24 in Sault Ste. Marie, just before the North Bay Days of Action, one of what were to become increasingly common student walkouts took place – 500 students from both separate and public schools leaving their classes to protest Bill 160.[4] During their protest, Ryan said that if Ontario's 126,000 teachers went on strike, CUPE members who worked in the schools would respect their picket lines. "What we're prepared to say is if the legislation is not satisfactory to the schoolteachers, then the CUPE members in the school board sector – we've got 40,000 of them – will not be crossing the picket lines. We'll be joining those school teachers."[5] The next day at a 700-strong teacher's rally at Queen's Park in Toronto, to cheers from the crowd, he said that CUPE "will not cross your picket lines anywhere in this province" in the event of a strike.[6] At one level, this was a very fine statement of solidarity, from one section of the union movement to another. However, as I pointed out at the time, this approach restricted active solidarity within CUPE to those who worked in the school system, less than a quarter of all CUPE Ontario members. Second, it meant a very big climbdown from the strategic orientation of shutting the province down against the Tory attacks, discussions of (and votes about which) had dominated labour discussions in Ontario through the summer of 1997. "The Tories want to isolate and crush the teachers. Not mounting solidarity strikes in support of the teachers would be a huge blow to the entire labour movement and everyone who hates the Tories."[7]

The North Bay Days of Action had served as a kind of "pep rally," according to one reporter, for the coming "confrontation with the Mike Harris government." This was certainly true for teachers in the North and across the province. As the government was preparing the second reading of Bill 160, teachers in Sault Ste. Marie gathered for an information session to discuss the impact of the bill, "as well as their endorsed action plan – an illegal walkout."[8] CUPE's 180,000 members were also preparing, but not with their eyes not Bill 160, but on whether the Tories would live up to their promised changes to Bill 136. On September 28, the Tories did just that, with Witmer tabling several amendments to Bill 136, removing the bulk of its contentious items, and putting into legislative effect the changes promised on September 18.[9] This was the consolidation of an enormous victory for the labour movement. According to Reshef and Restin: "Between Mike Harris's election in 1995 and resignation in 2001, the Bill 136 modifications represented the most significant concessions the Ontario forces of neo-conservatism made to mollify the unions."[10]

Gord Wilson said that the concessions on Bill 136 were so thorough that there was "nothing left to fight about."[11] But this victory was not

Image 10.1. Teachers' Strike.

simply a retreat by the Tories. It was part of what Brian Tanguay from Wilfrid Laurier University called "the old divide and conquer strategy."[12] The general attack on public-sector unions had been blunted. But the harsh attacks on the education sector, through Bill 160, were very much still on the agenda. Taking on one sector was a much surer bet than taking on the entire public sector at once. OECTA's Marshall Jarvis indicated that the teachers' unions were going to approach Bill 160 much as the entire public-sector had approached Bill 136 – threatening a strike in order to seek concessions.[13] However, no concessions were forthcoming.

"Kill the Bill"

A new factor was soon to enter the picture. The looming confrontation between the teachers and the Tories was about to escape the realm of collective bargaining. At the end of September and through the first days of October, a social movement announced itself – a mass movement of teachers, students, and parents – all united in their opposition to Bill 160.

You couldn't miss that mass movement in Toronto on October 6. A rally at Maple Leaf Gardens packed 17,000 into the arena and onto the concrete floor that, in that era, would normally be covered in ice (Maple Leaf Gardens had not yet been transformed into a grocery store and was still the iconic home of Toronto's hockey team). Thousands who couldn't fit into the Gardens listened to the speeches on speakers set up outside. Some put the total attendance, inside the arena and out on the streets, at 24,000.[14] It was a rally that completely deserved the adjective "thunderous" given to it by one reporter.[15] Speeches done, the massive crowd spilled onto the streets for a candlelit march to Queen's Park, chanting, "we won't back down."[16] "There's never been a stronger show of solidarity among teachers before in the history of Ontario," said teacher Maurice DiGiuseppe.[17] A parallel rally was held in Peel Region, and in the afternoon before the evening march, hundreds of students demonstrated at Queen's Park.[18]

But you did not have to be in Toronto on October 6 to know that a social movement in defence of education was brewing. There were actions against the Tories throughout the province in multiple communities and on an almost daily basis. What follows is by no means a complete list. But it will give a sense of the depth and breadth of the movement that was emerging.

- Ottawa, September 29 – Some 6,000 teachers rallied at the Civic Centre. "Several times teachers were on their feet, clapping vigorously while a few waved placards reading 'Kill Bill 160' and 'Education on the Line.'"[19]
- Kingston, September 29 – About one-quarter of the students at Sydenham High School in Kingston walked out of class and staged a four-hour protest "in front of the school in the pouring rain … Some of them carried placards saying No More Cuts To Education and It's Our Future, Talk To Us."[20]
- Hamilton, September 29 – John Byers, president of the Wentworth branch of OSSTF in Hamilton-Wentworth, was preparing a rally the next week at Copps Coliseum, where 9,000 were expected on the day. "If it [the strike call] happens tomorrow, we're ready," he said.[21]

- Kingston, September 30 – Steve Durant, a student at Kingston Collegiate and Vocational Institute (KCVI) said: "They walked out. They marched. They chanted. They made some noise, got some attention, and went back to class … Finally, students in this area (Sydenham on Monday, KCVI on Tuesday, Ernestown, QECVI and Loyalist on Wednesday) have decided to organize and show some support for their education.[22]
- Odessa, October 1 – Students at Ernestown Secondary School walked out of class, crowding both sides of Highway 2 and "asking cars to honk in support … Organizer Nathan Owehand said the protest was to last all day. 'I want to end the cuts to schools,' he said." There were also walkouts at Queen Elizabeth Collegiate and Loyalist College – the latter including "Grade 7 and 8 students from Calvin Park Public School, which is housed inside Loyalist."[23]
- Durham Region, October 1 – More than 1,000 students from six high schools walked out of classes to protest Bill 160. "'I don't care if we get in trouble,' said Kattie Sutton, in Grade 9 at Father Leo J. Austin school. 'Nobody ever listens to us and if this is what it takes, this is what we'll have to do.'"[24]
- Kitchener-Waterloo, October 1 – Teachers scheduled lunch-time protests building to a rally October 2 at Kitchener Memorial Auditorium.[25] Said one student, daughter of a teacher, "if my mother is forced to go on strike, my sisters and I will be there to support her and her fellow teachers."[26]
- Kitchener-Waterloo, October 2 – Chanting "we won't back down," an after-school rally at Kitchener Memorial Auditorium drew 4,000. The rally was supported by student actions – including morning walkouts by 300 at Resurrection Catholic Secondary School and 1,000 (out of a school population of 1,100) who walked out of Listowel District Secondary School, carrying signs saying, "we support our teachers."[27]
- Oshawa, October 2 – Four thousand "angry, foot-stomping teachers" filled all the seats at the Oshawa Civic Auditorium for a rally against Bill 160. "Chanting 'We won't back down,' the angry teachers waved signs and banners proclaiming 'Durham teachers will fight for what's right.'"[28]
- Toronto, October 2 – One hundred students from Central Technical School came together with a similar number from Northern and North Toronto Collegiate Institute for a Queen's Park rally against Bill 160. "Carrying hastily made signs and chanting 'Bill 160 has to go,' the students drew bewildered stares from several busloads of tourists, some of whom joined in the chant."[29]

- Guelph, October 3 – Some 200 protesters – mostly students – "besieged the office of Guelph Tory MPP Brenda Elliot … demanding changes to education-reform legislation. 'You guys are trying to take away our machine shop and hairdressing shop,' said Brad Spurgeon, a Grade 10 vocational student at College Heights. 'That's what's going to get us a job after we finish school.'"[30]
- Halton, October 3 – One thousand teachers from both Halton school boards demonstrated outside the offices of Halton's four Members of Provincial Parliament, including 300 who "waved placards and marched peacefully outside Burlington South MPP Cam Jackson's Brant Street office."[31]
- Hamilton, October 6 – More than 8,000 teachers from Hamilton, Halton, and Wentworth[32] packed Copps Coliseum to protest Bill 160. "They cheered, yelled, booed, and stamped their feet as Eileen Lennon, president of the Ontario Teachers' Federation, told them Education Minister John Snobelen 'should learn the rules of the playground … This is the fight of our lives,' Lennon told the boisterous crowd … The teachers cheered and clapped as about 100 students from Westmount High School in Hamilton marched into Copps after having walked out of the school earlier in the day.[33]
- Blind River, October 7 – Outside École St. Joseph, 35 teachers and supporters held the first of a series of noon-hour protests, scheduled to rotate through the five schools in the city.[34]
- Toronto, October 7 – Students from six schools – three high schools in Scarborough, two in East York, and an elementary school in Oshawa – walked out of class. A former Woburn Collegiate student who helped organize the 300 who walked out at that school said: "Students will back the teachers if they strike."[35]
- Kitchener-Waterloo, October 8 – "Carrying candles and placards," 2,000 teachers and students "gathered around the clock tower in Victoria Park at 8 pm and chanted, 'We can't back down,' after a series of speeches by union officials, teachers and a school board consultant."[36]
- Prince Edward County, October 8 – One hundred and sixty teachers rallied at Pinecrest Public School against Bill 160.[37]
- East York, October 10 – One hundred students "shouting 'Kill the bill'" held a demonstration outside the East York Civic Centre.[38]

The size, breadth and determination of the movement took the Tories by surprise. It included not just teachers, students, and many parents of the students, but also principals[39] – and this movement followed them everywhere. When Snobelen arrived at a small fundraising event in Hamilton on October 6, the 25 in attendance were outnumbered by 200 teachers, students, and union supporters gathered outside "who chanted and taunted the minister with protest signs."[40] In a clear sign of panic, Harris on October 10 shuffled his cabinet three months ahead of schedule, pushing the discredited Snobelen out of the education portfolio. "Snobelen could not recover from the fact that he was a high school dropout or from a video showing him making plans to create a 'crisis' within the education system," and he was replaced by Dave Johnson. Some saw this not as panic, but as cold calculation, Johnson after all being the man who had presided over the confrontation with OPSEU. Richard Brennan quoted one Harris adviser saying: "This is the teachers' worst nightmare come true, dealing with iceman Johnson."[41] Earl Manners said Johnson had two weeks to either change Bill 160 or the teachers would go on a strike, whether or not such a strike was considered "legal." Unions across the province considered how they could support such a strike. Waterloo Regional Labour Council, for instance, passed an emergency resolution asking any affiliated union members to respect teachers' picket lines in the event of a strike. Lucy Johnson, from the social justice coalition in the region, was not alone in revisiting the idea of a general strike. "Maybe it's time to look at a general strike," she said. "Maybe it's time that teachers and everyone else rally around the people who don't have that tool of the right to strike in the first place."[42]

The Streets of Windsor

Between the emergence of the pro-education social movement and the launch of the teachers' strike, there was the Day of Action in Windsor. On the surface, it represented a powerful return to the heady days of London, Hamilton, and Toronto. Thousands demonstrated. Dozens of workplaces were picketed shut. There was unity on the streets between labour and social justice organizations. But beneath the surface, there were signs of a movement at a turning point.

The event took place on Friday, October 17, a combination of workplace shutdowns and mass demonstrations. According to the Windsor Chamber of Commerce, the closures created by strike action cost $100 million in lost production.

> The protest shut one Chrysler minivan assembly plant, five Ford engine and casting operations, and one General Motors transmission factory, which together employ about 12,000 people.
>
> Several independent parts makers that supply those auto makers and their parents across the Detroit River in Michigan closed up shop for the day.

> The shutdown at Chrysler meant the plant didn't crank out its daily total of about 1,500 minivans, which represented about $32 million in lost production. Ford estimated its lost production at about $4 million, while GM refused to provide a figure.[43]

It was difficult to quantify exactly how many participated in what was an overwhelmingly successful day. According to *The Canadian Press*: "The day-long protest, the ninth in a series of rotating actions in cities across the province, effectively shut down much of the city as organizers said 40,000 citizens took part and 200 businesses shut down ... The day culminated in a march by up to 15,000 people that wound its way through Windsor's downtown to an afternoon rally."[44] The *Toronto Star* counted 20,000 at the rally.[45] The CAW account was more enthusiastic.

> Workplace after workplace including Chrysler, GM, Ford, Peregrine, auto parts makers, the Casino and more than 170 others were closed ... Auto manufacturers, parts plants, schools, mail delivery, bus service and much of the rest of Windsor ground to a halt ... In CAW Local 195 alone about 62 workplaces went down voluntarily, recognizing our members' democratic right to demonstrate. Flag waving, noisy protestors marched and chanted as they took part in two parades that wound through city streets and converged at Dieppe Gardens. Close to 30,000 listened to speaker after speaker from labour, community, church, seniors, and anti-poverty groups take on the Harris agenda.[46]

Organizers claimed, probably accurately, that "more people were off the job in Windsor and Essex county yesterday than during any of the other protests held in six Ontario cities since 1995" and that "the Windsor Day of Action had the highest per capita participation of any of the nine days of protest held across Ontario since Harris came to power."[47] However, those of us who were there could tell that this incredible feat of workplace organizing – picketing out dozens of workplaces and pulling people onto the streets – was overwhelmingly the work of the CAW, the union that dominated labour politics in the city. Gary Parent from CAW Local 444 and labour co-chair of the event proudly reported that "160 of the 200 workplaces targeted by the union were completely shut down by noon."[48] But that meant that the vast bulk of the shutdowns had been carried by his union alone. The CAW was shouldering the lion's share of the work.

This is a tribute to the capacities of that organization – not surprising given its central role through the whole Days of Action movement.

But there was a notable absence of significant forces from other unions, unlike at Toronto or Hamilton. Further, Windsor was one day, not two. The high points of the Days of Action movement had been in Hamilton and Toronto, where Friday strikes closed the city and Saturday demonstrations pulled in tens of thousands. This was, at that level, a less ambitious undertaking – in part reflecting the strain of so much responsibility being on the shoulder of one section of the union movement. The relative absence of other forces could be seen in the parking lots. Whereas up to 1,200 busses had travelled to the great events in Hamilton and Toronto, and even little North Bay had seen 180, for the shutdown of Windsor just 40 busses came into the city.[49]

The impact of the day was far beyond the labour movement itself, with school closings impacting approximately 60,000 students. The day displayed real commitment and real solidarity. For an enthusiastic minority, events began early. Late on the 16th, picket lines went up at the GM transmission plant "hours in advance of scheduled demonstrations." Early on that day, in a rally against the Harris Tories, "teachers and their supporters waved banners and cheered as labour and education leaders delivered indictment after stinging indictment of the Conservative government's contentious education bill." The same report recording these events put forward this analysis: "The teachers' fight against Bill 160, which would reduce class preparation time for teachers and increase the number of teaching days, has become intertwined with the unionists' Days of Action protests."[50]

However, the coming battle between the teachers and the Tories was not the only issue of concern for labour organizations involved in the Windsor Day of Action. If the pink paper pessimism had retreated into the background in the wake of Bills 136 and 160 and the undeniable revival of militancy represented by North Bay and Windsor, the pink paper forces had by no means abandoned the field. In November the Ontario Federation of Labour was scheduled to have its biennial convention, Gord Wilson had indicated he would not stand for re-election, and a bitter contest had opened up, pitting the pink paper forces against the CAW, CUPE, and the other advocates of the Days of Action movement. So all-consuming was this contest that no further Days of Action were on the drawing board, let alone plans for a province-wide strike.

The Days of Action unions – in particular CAW and CUPE – were backing Paul Forder. He was the man so centrally involved in launching the movement in 1995, directing labour's organizational work for the first five extraordinarily successful citywide actions, and so unceremoniously demoted by Wilson after the Toronto events. Wilson, along with the pink paper group, would have nothing to do with Forder.

During the Windsor Day of Action, Wilson told *The Globe and Mail*'s Richard Mackie that he did not believe that Forder's candidacy "will unite the labour movement. There's very clearly a number of major unions that object to his candidacy."[51] The pink paper group did not yet have a candidate. For a few weeks, their candidate of choice had been Hamilton Centre NDP MPP Dave Christopherson. But Christopherson had two strikes against him. First, Christopherson had been in the NDP cabinet that imposed the Social Contract. Second, he was not currently a member of a union. Hargrove called him a "party person" but "not a trade unionist" and asked: "Why would we reach outside the labour movement to find a candidate?"[52] Christopherson declined to run. The pink paper group also courted Harry Hynd, director of District 6 of the United Steelworkers. But Hynd was more associated with the pink paper attack on the Days of Action movement than perhaps any other individual in the province.[53] Hynd declined to run. For many leading figures in the OFL, *this election campaign* was the preoccupation on October 17, not thinking strategically about how to use Windsor as a springboard to build solidarity with the teachers.

On the ground, the focus was on education, not union elections. Monday, October 20, no progress was made at a face-to-face meeting between new Education Minister Johnson and the presidents of the elementary and secondary school unions that were part of the 126,000-strong Ontario Teachers' Federation. The teachers' unions gave Johnson until noon the next day to seriously amend Bill 160 (as the Tories had done with Bill 136), or they would "start a 48-hour clock ticking towards a province-wide school shutdown," something that "key labour leaders say could turn into a province-wide general strike."[54] The latter, a province-wide strike, was the maximum kind of solidarity on offer. At a minimum was the pledge from Sid Ryan, reiterating what he had said in the run-up to North Bay, that the 40,000 CUPE members in the school system – custodians, maintenance staff, education assistants, and others – would respect their picket lines.[55] Ultimately the strike deadline would be pushed back to Monday, October 27 – and while the Tories refused to budge, teachers and their supporters continued to organize, a mobilization that went beyond the Day of Action in Windsor.

This was true on the day itself. Friday, October 17, the Tories were holding a conference in London. The convention was "the third major meeting of the party to be held since the Tories won the 1995 election and the third in which demonstrators protested outside, the party met inside, and police stood in between." The London Convention Centre was surrounded by 1,000 teachers and supporters, protesting

Bill 160.[56] In St. Catharines the same day, 200 teachers demonstrated outside the constituency office of MPP Tom Froese – again, protesting Bill 160. In Etobicoke, a referendum was held on Bill 160 among the 13,000 students at twelve of the Etobicoke Board of Education's fourteen high schools. Out of 5,640 who voted, 93 per cent (5,256) voted against the bill.[57]

Events after Windsor showed growing support for the teachers and increasing opposition to the Tories. Monday, October 20, public hearings on the bill began in Toronto, attended by members of the group People for Education and other opponents of the bill, some dressed in black veils "in mock mourning for the province's education system."[58] Tuesday, October 21, the local Kitchener paper brought together a group of seven high school students, all of whom criticized Bill 160 and "spoke of their high regard for teachers and the job they do."[59] Thursday, October 23, the local paper in St. Catharines interviewed students leaving classes, and while many were upset at the idea of a prolonged strike, several also blamed the situation on the Tories. "'I blame (Harris) for this,' said Sara Palmieri, a Grade 12 student ... 'He's trying to win over the parents,' she said, 'but it won't work.'"[60] The same day, in the Frontenac-Lennox and Addington County Roman Catholic School Board, all but one of twenty-four principals and one of fourteen vice-principals, resigned their positions so as "be in a position to protest Bill 160 with their fellow teachers."[61]

This support for the teachers was not always visible through a superficial reading of the polls. Friday, October 24, a poll by Oracle research showed a province evenly divided – 44 per cent supporting the teachers, 42 per cent supporting the government. However, the latent support for the teachers was huge. Only 21 per cent would choose the Harris government to set education policy, compared to an overwhelming majority – 62 per cent – who would put their trust in teachers.[62] In part, this was driven by the increasingly transparent motives behind Bill 160. While at first pitching the bill as one designed to improve the quality of education – on Thursday, October 23, both Harris and Johnson openly linked the bill to cutting the provincial budget, with Harris saying: "We do believe there is another four or five percent of savings to be achieved in the system."[63]

As the strike deadline loomed, every level of the union movement reiterated support for the teachers. OFL leadership met Thursday, October 23, and Gord Wilson vowed that organized labour would "throw its support behind teachers"[64] in the event of an illegal strike even though only two of the unions involved – the 50,000-member Ontario Secondary School Teachers Federation and the 35,000-member Ontario English

Teachers Association – were part of the OFL. The OFL leaders agreed to contribute to a strike fund to cover the cost of any fines incurred by teachers (for a strike, which after all, would be illegal), to pay for pro-union advertisements, and even to establish alternate childcare for parents who were unable to access childcare facilities located within struck schools.[65] Wilson did not rule out a province-wide strike. But this was no longer posed as part of a Days of Action plan to challenge the entire Harris agenda, but as a defensive response to be triggered if the Tories legislated teachers back to work.[66]

Ryan reiterated that he would be asking the 40,000 CUPE members within the school system to honour the picket lines. Ominously, not all within CUPE were happy with this instruction. Larry Hardman, president of CUPE Local 1344 in Hamilton, said his members would not be following Ryan's instructions, and that he had been in touch with other local presidents who felt the same. In part, this reluctance to engage in solidarity was rooted in a three-month CUPE strike in 1992, "when teachers not only crossed picket lines but were accused of doing the caretakers' work."[67]

A Fighting Strike

Monday, October 27, the strike began. On the picket lines, 126,000 teachers confronted the Harris Tories, keeping 2.1 million students from their classes. It was the largest-ever strike by teachers in Canada.[68] For the first time since the Days of Action movement, a mass action was unfolding that made Luxemburg's notion of a fighting strike extremely relevant. To date – while there had been many, many moments of impressive organization and militancy – the movement as a whole had fit within her category of "demonstration strikes," mass actions taking place within a time and place set by the leadership, with a well-structured beginning, middle, and end. While the launch of the teachers' strike was of course set by the union leadership, it was (a) illegal, outside of the bounds of any collective agreement provision; (b) without an official end date; and, most significantly, (c) accompanied by a mass explosion of solidarity and organization which, as we shall see two weeks later when the strike was called off, threatened to move beyond the control of the official union structures. It was a "fighting strike" – pitting a mobilized working class against the state, a confrontation whose timing was determined by the relative organization, determination, and willpower of the opposing sides.

The fighting nature of the strike was evidenced from the first hours of the strike, and in every community in the province. Take just two cities – Belleville and Sault Ste. Marie. Monday, October 27, on the bridge linking Prince Edward County to the city of Belleville,[69] 1,700 teachers held up traffic for two hours as they launched their strike and then marched to Tory MPP Gary Fox's constituency office. Fox's staff "pulled blinds and locked the door as the group arrived."[70] In Sault Ste. Marie, teachers from the fifty-six elementary and secondary schools on strike in the area threw up pickets outside the Water Tower Inn where Tory ministers were scheduled to speak. They surrounded the Holiday Inn where hearings on Bill 160 were ongoing and then rallied 500-strong at the Roberta Bondar Pavilion next door.[71] The next day, the Holiday Inn hosted Harris and local Sault supporters for a $150-a-plate dinner. Next door, teachers responded with a $1.50-a-plate "Common-Sense Barbecue" and made it a fundraiser for the Sault Ste. Marie Soup Kitchen, urging attendees to bring canned goods for donation.[72] The barbecue had "a party-like atmosphere" as hundreds of teachers, students, and strike supporters jammed into the pavilion, filling it to near capacity. "Organizing officials estimated a turnout of between 2,000 and 3,000 protesters for the event, based on the fact they barbecued about 3,000 sausages, hot dogs and burgers, twice running out of meat in the process, and the price of admission included one barbecued item."[73]

The response from teachers to the strike call was extraordinary. Waterloo region said that on Wednesday, October 29, only 140 public school teachers and 10 principals and vice-principals crossed the lines, just over 4 per cent of the workforce. In the separate schools, the figure was 2.6 per cent.[74] Hamilton reported that in the region, fewer than 1 per cent of teachers crossed the picket line.[75] In Bruce County on Tuesday, October 28, after picketing their workplaces, 1,000 teachers went to a solidarity rally at the CAW's Family Education Centre near Port Elgin. "The crowd included principals, secretaries, supervisors, education assistants and representatives of retired teachers and custodians who are also walking the picket lines."[76] At General Brock High School in Halton, on the first day of the strike just 3 of 520 students showed up. The next day in Halton, teachers were joined on the picket lines by high school principals and vice-principals. "Bryn Davies, principal of General Brock High School, and spokesman for the principals' association said it was a tough decision, but in the end, the 48 members representing 17 high schools felt they had to support teachers."[77]

The strike of teachers became the focal point of a social movement which went far beyond the teachers' unions themselves. Some passed resolutions. At the Ontario Institute for Studies in Education, 150 faculty met to discuss the strike and voted almost unanimously to support the teachers "while urging the Ontario government to kill Bill

160 for its 'potential negative impact on education' in the province."[78] Some wrote letters. In the first days of the strike, the Ontario Conference of Catholic Bishops wrote to parish priests supporting the actions of the teachers in the separate school board. "When all other avenues are exhausted and individuals are convinced that their cause is just, Catholic social teaching supports their right to strike and requires just treatment for them."[79] Some picketed and rallied. On day one of strike action in Hamilton, seventy-five students – led by their student council president Adam Brodie – marched from their school, closed because of the strike, to Burlington Tory MPP Cam Jackson's office, waving signs saying "Pro Education" and "End the Bill."[80] The same day in Kingston, nurses "braved high winds and blustery conditions to march alongside teachers at Confederation Park."[81] In St. Catharines, seven-year-old Casie Helie stood in Montebello Park, holding up a homemade cardboard sign saying: "Don't take money from the school." Helie was part of a 2,000-strong rally – attended by the city's mayor and local Liberal MPP – protesting Bill 160. A group of Grimsby high school students came to the two-hour long rally "with a 20-metre-long banner, signed by more than 400 students and reading; 'Support our teachers.'"[82]

It is difficult to convey just how broad and deep was the support for those on strike. On the picket lines in St. Catharines, passing motorists honked in support, and picketers received coffee and doughnuts brought to them by students and parents.[83] At the end of the first week of the strike in Kingston, a local press report said: "If there's one thing that teachers have had in abundance this week, it's food, glorious food. Since teachers took to the picket lines five days ago to protest the Ontario government's Bill 160, they've been overwhelmed by donations of home-cooked meals, urns of steaming coffee and trays of freshly baked sweet things."[84] I was at the time living in the east end of Toronto, with one fifteen-year-old attending Riverdale High School and one nine-year-old attending Wilkinson Public School. The latter, my daughter, recalls going down to Wilkinson with a neighbourhood friend to see their teachers on the picket line. One of the picketing teachers helped her with her new rollerblades. Simple moments of solidarity like that happened thousands of times outside dozens of schools. At Riverdale, I remember not knowing what to expect the first time we visited the picket line, and my astonishment at the size of the crowd, spilling off the sidewalk and onto Jones Avenue, packed not just with teachers, but parents and students, enthusiastically supporting the teachers. Just as in St. Catharines and Kingston, the coffee was ubiquitous, as were the supportive horns from passing motorists.

There were other, less positive signs. Sid Ryan's pledge that CUPE members inside the school system would respect the picket lines proved difficult to enforce. Sometimes reluctantly, CUPE members *did* cross the picket lines. On the first day of the strike in the Hamilton region, while there were delays in opening the schools, by the middle of the day "all schools were open to staff who reported for work." This caused angst for many. "'I would sooner somebody would have beaten me up on the (picket) line than have to cross,' said Jackie Robinson, a caretaker at George L. Armstrong Public School and health and safety representative for Local 1344, Canadian Union of Public Employees. 'I've never felt like a scab before in my life.'"[85] This was a very worrying sign. We had seen a gradual de-escalation of strategic plans from the key union leaders: from a province-wide shutdown to stop the Tories when Bill 136 was on the table, to promises that the teachers would not stand alone, to promises that their picket lines would be respected. Now the danger was that there would be precisely *no* strategy offered to the teachers, and that they would be left alone – as had OPSEU the year before. While the OPSEU strike occurred when the Days of Action movement was young, and there might have been some understandable trepidation about winning support for escalating actions of solidarity, by 1997 the Days of Action movement was mature and experienced – and the overwhelming support for the teachers was obvious to everyone. Despite all this, the heads of unions and the OFL had only very general words of solidarity to offer and precisely nothing in terms of a strategic plan for building solidarity.

The absence of a strategic plan from the central organizations of the labour movement put the entire burden of the strike on the teachers' union leadership. Even two days into the strike, left isolated by the rest of the union movement, the resulting strain was beginning to show. Eileen Lennon, president of the Ontario Teachers Federation, said that she and the other union leaders were "considering how to bow out of the job action if the government does not bend" on Bill 160. "'The ideal end is for the government to announce amendments to Bill 160, other exit strategies are being considered,' said Lennon. 'But today, on the second day of the political protest, that is not the day to announce the exit strategy.'"[86] On the third day, the Tories announced how they would try to end the strike – through an appeal to the courts, seeking a court order to send the teachers back to work.[87]

On the fourth day, both the unions and the Tories made offers to end the strike, each unacceptable to the other. The unions' five-point proposal, in the words of press reports, "substantially softened" the unions' demands, but retained an insistence that class size and teachers' preparation time be settled locally through bargaining with school boards rather than centrally by the provincial government. As for the Tories' offer – which included a renewed attempt to remove principals and vice-principals from the bargaining units – Lennon described herself as "disappointed and angry." Phyllis Benedict, president of the Ontario Public School Teachers Federation, used the word "bully" to describe the Tories, trying to be "bigger and meaner than anyone."[88]

Support for the teachers was reflected in polling done throughout the strike. In Waterloo region, a poll done a few days into the strike showed 34 per cent support for the teachers compared to 26 per cent for the Tories (and 23 per cent who could "see the logic on both sides").[89] On a province-wide basis, an Angus Reid poll conducted in the first week of the strike showed "'serious' growing support for the teachers' strike, fuelled by the message that Bill 160, the government's education reform package, is simply designed to take money out of education."[90] Before the strike, John Wright, vice-president of Angus Reid, said that 56 per cent of those polled opposed the looming walkout, while 42 per cent of those polled were in favour. However, soon after, within Metropolitan Toronto, "those positions were completely reversed. 'This thing has come off the rails for the government over one clear thing: their admission that they are going to cut,' says Wright. 'While the government won Round 1 in the court of public opinion, it is clear that the teachers have taken Round 2.'"[91] According to Wright: "From the court of public opinion it would appear that even if they get the injunction (forcing the teachers back to work) it would be a costly victory."[92]

And in fact, the injunction plan failed. On picket line after picket line, teachers indicated a willingness to defy any court-ordered end to the strike. Bill Dunphy, after a tour of picket lines in the Hamilton region, said that "if provincial politicians think winning an injunction today will put an end to the battle over Bill 160, they haven't been listening to teachers walking the line here." Dunphy talked to picket captain Diane Moore, a teacher at Memorial School who said: "I'm going to stand pat right here on this corner in my wheelchair ... I'm not moving."[93] A defiance of the injunction proved unnecessary. Justice James Macpherson denied the Tory request, saying that the province had asked for court intervention "two weeks too early."[94] NDP veteran Gerald Caplan said that, in the wake of the ruling, "the government looked terribly inept and terribly incompetent." The judge "went out of his way to complement the teachers on the stately way they are conducting themselves. ... The question, I agree, is: where do we go from here? And nobody knows where we go ..."[95]

Impasse, Fragmentation, and Retreat

The second week of the strike saw not only a failed injunction, but a third failed round of talks between the teachers and the Tories. The strike continued, with no further talks scheduled. In the wake of the breakdown of talks, two articles, both published November 5, both co-written by Richard Brennan and Carolyn Abraham, revealed the pressures growing within the teachers' union leadership. In the first, Earl Manners, president of the Ontario Secondary School Teachers' Federation, "said he saw no end in sight for the strike."[96] In the second, Manners telegraphed a different possibility. "As long as the government continues on this path, the political protest will continue far into the future," Manners told Brennan and Abraham. But political protest did not necessarily mean strike, with Manners saying that "the form it will take will obviously have to change."[97] Importantly, this open speculation about a return to work was working with an assumption that the five unions would act together, under the umbrella of the Ontario Teachers' Federation.[98] Events were to prove that assumption mistaken.

On the ground, the mass movement nature of the strike continued. The refusal of Judge Macpherson to grant the injunction was correctly seen as a victory by the striking teachers. Tuesday, November 4, 2,000 marched through the streets of Welland in the pouring rain. "Carrying placards and waving at passing motorists, the mass of educators from southern Niagara covered a 1.5-kilometre stretch of King Street – both sides in some areas."[99] The next day in Halton, Buzz Hargrove addressed a rally of 2,500 teachers, where "one after another, teacher union leaders spoke about the importance of 'continuing the fight for kids.'"[100] In Aurora, York Region Catholic teachers were one part of the movement whose strike was, in fact, legal, after contract talks with the York Separate School Board had broken down. Friday November 7, 2,500 of these legal strikers demonstrated outside the Aurora board office. "'We're fighting on two fronts – against our local board and against Bill 160,' said Ihor Baczynsky, the teachers' chief negotiator."[101] These impressive rallies paled in the shadow of the huge crowd that gathered at Toronto City Hall and then marched to Queen's Park on Thursday, November 6, estimated at anywhere from 15,000 to 20,000.[102] The day before, Education Minister Johnson had delivered forty-five amendments to the legislative clerk's office. Even he acknowledged that these would not be enough to satisfy the teachers, but it was the first sign of the Tories bending on Bill 160. Union leaders could feel the change. Lannon said that "public opinion continues to be on the side of the teachers" and that "the schools will continue to be closed."[103]

At the rally in Toronto, the leaders of the unions showed a united front and a determination to continue the strike.[104] The same night in Sudbury, Mike Harris spoke to 350 supporters at a Tory fundraiser, vastly outnumbered by 2,500 picketers outside, picketers "who jostled some guests, preventing their entry into the building." After the dinner, Harris had a very different message from the one delivered by union leaders to the 20,000 at Queen's Park. According to Harris, "the unions had already decided not to keep 126,000 teachers on the picket lines into next week. But the premier said the unions couldn't agree on how to announce the strike's end."[105]

And in fact, just hours following the massive November 6 Toronto rally – the "biggest protest so far against the government's new education bill"[106] – the strike, in the words of one report, "disintegrated."[107] Three of the five unions (the Franco-Ontario Teachers Association, the Ontario Public School Teachers' Federation and the Federation of Women Teachers' Associations of Ontario) broke ranks with the Ontario Teachers' Federation and announced that their 60,000 members would be returning to work on Monday, November 10, leaving the 76,000 members of the Ontario Secondary School Teachers' Federation and the Ontario English Catholic Teachers Association members to continue without them.[108] Leaders of OSSTF and OECTA announced they would be meeting on the weekend to consider their next move.[109] In fact, the strike was over. By the next week, all 126,000 teachers and 2.1 million students would be back in their classrooms.

But if it was the end of the strike, it was not the end of the story. In city after city and union after union, rank and file teachers expressed their fury at what many perceived as a sell-out. Pierre Martin, chair of the OTF in North Bay, said: "In the eyes of teachers, it's a form of capitulation."[110] In Timmins, eighty French high school teachers vowed to stay on picket lines. At a rally in Elmira, many elementary school teachers expressed the same sentiment. "In Kenora, the local president of the women teachers' federation said the provincial president's decision doesn't reflect her members' resolve."[111] Joyce Whittle, co-chair of the Hamilton Teachers' Federation, said that she and her co-chair, Sue Dunlop, were "appalled that our provincial body would split the federations and leave OSSTF to carry on alone." In an extraordinary move, they drew up a statement, offering "an apology to the teachers of Hamilton and the community they serve."

> The provincial decision that returns elementary teachers to the classroom and leaves their colleagues to continue the fight for public education is divisive. Teachers initiated their protest to make the public aware that Bill

> 160 will result in devastating cuts to the classroom and will remove parental involvement in decision making. Elementary teachers are still committed to fighting Bill 160 and the government that has attacked the poor, the sick and now the young.[112]

At a mass demonstration outside the Stoney Creek office of Conservative MPP Ed Doyle, many teachers expressed similar sentiments. "'I'm really annoyed that our unions have backed down over this,' elementary school teacher Jaime Dianda said … 'For us to go back to work with Bill 160 intact is just terrible' … Andrea McCabe, of OECTA, was so upset she scrawled the words 'sold out' on the picket signs she carried."[113] In St. Catharines, 2,000 rallied at the CAW hall and then marched to a Conservative constituency office in Merritton, the same sentiments were expressed.

> "I am very disappointed that our unions did not all stand together," said Lois Dix, a St. Catharines elementary school teacher and one of numerous teachers upset by Thursday's decision by leaders of three unions to end their involvement in the strike … "I wish they could have got their act together. There seems to be a split at the top," said St. Catharines secondary school teacher Rick Young of the leaders of the three unions." Young held a picket sign bearing the slogan We Won't Back Down. With a magic marker, he had scratched out the word We and replaced it with 40 Per Cent of Us.
>
> "It is gallows humour," said Young, adding he still feels there is a lot of unity among rank-and-file members of all five teachers' unions across Niagara.[114]

Without question, the most explosive moment of rank and file anger against the return to work occurred in Toronto on Friday, November 7. Part of the anger was directed at the Tories. When Education Minister Johnson tried to enter the Bell Canada building to "promote a computer-for-kids program" he "needed an eight-man police escort to get past a crowd of striking teachers blocking the driveway … 'Sic him! sic him!'" some yelled.[115] Part of the anger was directed at the leaders of their union. Perhaps as many as 3,000 elementary school teachers packed into the Hummingbird Centre (formerly the O'Keefe Centre, since 2019, Meridian Hall) and expressed their anger at the fragmenting of the teachers' united front.[116] "'We feel they've betrayed our secondary school colleagues,' said teacher Elizabeth Pepa. 'We went in united and we felt that we should come out united and if they were going to call it off, it should have been one voice … It's like pulling the rug out from underneath someone.'"[117] Phyllis Benedict, president of the Ontario Public School Teachers' Federation, said: "People are a little bruised. It's to be expected."[118] This was a serious understatement. At the Hummingbird Centre meeting, Benedict and Maret Sadam-Thompson, president of the Federation of Women Teachers Associations of Ontario, "left the stage under a hail of boos and to shouts of 'resign' and 'sell-out.'" When the crowd was told that there was not enough money to book a hall big enough to hold a vote on the return to work, an extraordinary scene unfolded.

> One teacher marched onto the stage and threw a $5 bill onto the table out of her pocket to help pay for the hall. The floodgates opened. Hundreds of teachers marched up to the stage and threw money out of their own pockets in front of the leadership. In short order, $5,000 had been collected.[119]

In any case, it was over. The threat of a province-wide strike had forced a humiliating retreat for the Tories on Bill 136. But when the OFL heads of unions only played lip service to solidarity – breaking the promise of "one struggle and two issues" – the magnificent social movement in defence of education was unable to win the victory that at one point had seemed so close.

Chapter Eleven

Denouement

The end of the teachers' strike left the Days of Action movement in disarray. Rather than soberly confront the problems so deeply exposed by the teachers' strike, the OFL became consumed with the looming elections for its next president after Wilson. For some months, the Days of Action unions had their candidate – CAW veteran Paul Forder. By November, the pink paper group had their standard-bearer – Wayne Samuelson, a veteran of the principal pink paper union the USWA with a long history as a union staffer.

Forder, in the running for months, had the backing of the CAW (which would have approximately a quarter of the 2,000 delegates to the convention), as well as from most of the other Days of Action unions, CUPE in particular. Samuelson, a late addition to the ballot, was implicitly backed by Wilson and was without question the candidate of the pink paper unions, with one notable exception. Leah Casselman, although president of OPSEU, which had been part of the Days of Action unions, not only supported Samuelson but would actually end up nominating him from the floor of the convention.[1] Casselman herself had been the ambivalent choice of a union that no longer supported President Fred Upshaw – "the first black person to be elected president of a major Canadian union"[2] – but which turned not to the left and David Rapaport, but rather to the career corrections officer, Casselman. She had been the face of the OPSEU strike and in that sense associated with the Days of Action movement, but in supporting Samuelson, she was indicating a return to her more conservative roots.

"A Dramatic Shift to the Right"

It was an extremely bitter contest, the first time in twenty years that there had been a contest for the presidency of the OFL.[3] Sid Ryan articulated a common critique of Samuelson, seeing him as too closely tied to the NDP and its imposition of the Social Contract when that party had been in office between 1990 and 1995, complicit in "the strategy to screw the public sector unions."[4] Forder, by contrast, was often seen as too far removed from the experience of the shopfloor, having "spent 29 of his 49 years working in union or government jobs, thus removed from the assembly line and the dues-paying membership."[5] Some of us sympathetic to Forder's candidacy made much the same point. "Forder, 49, last held a job on the shop floor three decades ago, when he was 20. He was a full-timer for the auto workers until 1975, and since then has worked full-time for the OFL."[6] By contrast, Samuelson was often portrayed as "a former tire-plant worker from Kitchener,"[7] "on the OFL staff only since 1990."[8] This was true enough, but Samuelson – who served as president of the Waterloo Regional Labour Council for five years before beginning his full-time OFL position in 1990, was like Forder years removed from the day-to-day reality of rank and filers. Most significantly, Samuelson's campaign became the focal point for the pink-paper-influenced section of the OFL, sceptical of the Days of Action – a section of the OFL now reinforced by people like Wilson and Casselman.

No one, however, could *openly* run against the Days of Action. All had to pay at least lip service to a continuation of the movement. During the teachers' strike, Wilson and the OFL had gone silent on the topic of the general strike. Once the strike was over, however, talk of a province-wide general strike was again part of the discourse. A "senior labour official" told reporters that Wilson would sponsor an emergency resolution at the convention, "calling for all unionized workers 'except for those necessary for the maintenance of life' to walk off their jobs for two days in mid-December."[9]

Wilson's was a transparently cynical move. Forder was the candidate associated with the Days of Action and who was from Wilson's home union, the CAW. Forder was supported, not just by Hargrove and Ryan, but by the key teacher union leaders fresh from the picket lines – Manners and Jarvis.[10] Yet Wilson was siding with the pink paper group, the very people who had worked so hard to prevent general strike action, as well as a conservative figure like Casselman. We had just had votes through the summer authorizing strike action, two incredibly successful Days of Action at North Bay and Windsor in the run-up to the teachers' strike, and then the magnificent two-week illegal walkout itself. It was not complicated that it was *this* moment when a strategic plan needed to be implemented, and scandalous that at precisely *this* moment the entire OFL went silent. Now that the moment had passed, we were going to get another resolution, but a resolution without resolve would again be doomed to remain just words on paper.

In the end, Samuelson squeaked out a victory – 1,251 to 1,046. "The numbers were so close, delegates sat momentarily silent when they were announced – a rare calm on the raucous convention floor."[11] Steve Farkas from the CAW quite accurately called the result "a dramatic shift to the right,"[12] in a very real sense representing the reassertion of control over the Ontario labour movement by the pro-Social Contract pink paper unions, a slap in the face to all those who had been at the centre of the Days of Action mass movement.

The same convention delegates who had rejected Forder *unanimously* voted to continue with Days of Action and for the OFL heads of unions to call for a one-day general strike sometime before the end of 1998.[13] Emergency Resolution 6, in addition to saying that it would push for an NDP government in the next provincial election, "stipulated that: 'the OFL Executive Board develop a political plan, inclusive of more Days of Action, to build the solidarity of working people and our community allies against the Harris government and its policies; The OFL Executive Board shall call a one-day province-wide political protest and strike before the end of 1998.'"[14] There would in fact be two more Days of Action – one in St. Catharines and another (final one) in Kingston. But the resolution on a province-wide strike would never be implemented.

What had we been through during the summer and fall of 1997? At the very least there was a huge disconnect between words and deeds. Perhaps we might adapt contemporary terminology and call it "bureaucratic gaslighting" – promises of general strikes and grand strategies of resistance, promises of united fronts, promises of solidarity, but when the moment came, teachers left to stand alone, the OFL staying silent. It was all a perfect example of a movement leadership that could not see beyond the "demonstration strike" described by Luxemburg – carefully sketched out plans where a key criterion was the control and containment of the movement within limits determined by a small group of leaders. When confronted with a mass movement with elements of what Luxemburg had called a "fighting strike" – the explosive uprising of teachers and students against the Tories' attack on education, culminating in a two-week illegal strike – the OFL union heads did precisely nothing.

So Samuelson was formally charged with implementing a plan culminating in a general strike, but in fact he had been put in place on the backs of that section of the union movement united by a firm opposition not just to the calling of such a strike, but to the whole Days of Action movement. Many knew precisely the contradictions of the entire situation, including John Clarke from OCAP. In the context of preparing a fightback against the Tories' attempt to "gut the province's employment standards legislation," Clarke said that "the OFL convened a series of meetings for rank-and-file activists in a number of communities."

> I attended the gathering in Toronto, which was held in the inevitable and grossly inappropriate plush hotel. Like the other meetings, it was much larger than anticipated and the mood in the room was electric. OFL President Wayne Samuelson had got only a few words into his lacklustre presentation when an older worker near the back of the hall got up and yelled, "Shut the f***ing province down!" The rest of the meeting took up this chant (without the obscenity) ... Samuelson ... looked like a deer in the headlights and you could almost hear the cogs in his head turning as he struggled for a way to diffuse such a dreadful development as an outbreak of working-class anger.[15]

From St. Kitts to Kingston

Harris was still in office, and the Tory cuts were still grinding down the lives of ordinary folk in Ontario. But now, even more so than at Windsor, it was the CAW that shouldered the bulk of the organizing work. In December CAW Council "unanimously voted in favour of a one-day, province-wide strike before the end of 1998" as well as "recommending the continuance of the Community Days of Action."[16] St. Catharines, a city with a large CAW presence, was picked as the next target, for May 1, 1998. As had been so frequently the case in the past, the labour co-chair was from the CAW – Ed Gould, president of the St. Catharines and District Labour Council – joined by Linda Rogers of the Golden Horseshoe Social Action Committee.[17] Gould was hoping that St. Catharines would witness "the biggest May Day event ever held in Canada."[18] But there were signs that the drive to build the event was not quite on that scale. The official opening of the St. Catharines Day of Action Centre was held on April 8, a mere three weeks before the event was to happen.[19]

When the day came, the event was without question, on its own terms, extremely successful. The "gates at the General Motors plants on Ontario Street, Welland Avenue and Glendale Avenue, and at Dana Canada's plant on Hayes Road in Thorold" were blocked by "human walls" of "placard-carrying protesters."[20] Bus service had to be cancelled, and "workers in most downtown government offices – provincial and municipal – arrived at work to face picket lines."[21] Press and police reports put participation at 4,000, an implausibly low figure given the fact that forty busses joined the demonstrators from Windsor, London, Oakville, Toronto, and Kingston.[22] The CAW estimated that between 8,000 and 12,000 "took part in a march through city streets," ending at Montebello Park where "thousands of flag waving and banner carrying labour and community activists gathered."[23]

These figures would not make the event the "largest May Day event ever" in Canada, but without question, they would qualify as "the largest protest in St. Catharines' history."[24] But if successful on its own terms, there was no question that something like the "protest fatigue" identified by one reporter[25] was setting in on the Days of Action movement. The anti-Days of Action pink paper group was now in control of the OFL, forced to pay lip service to the movement, but in fact, sitting back and letting the CAW in particular do all the heavy lifting.

The eleventh and final Day of Action, June 8 in Kingston, Ontario, would again have both these characteristics – the largest protest ever in the city, but part of a movement beginning to wind down. Without question, the Kingston Day of Action showed many of the signs of the depth of feeling against the Harris Tories. Both the city council of conservative Kingston and that of even more conservative Belleville voted to endorse the Day of Action.[26] Again, the labour co-chair came from the CAW – Charlie Stock, Local 1837 president and president of the Kingston and District Labour Council, along with Natalie Mehra from the Kingston Action Network.[27]

For a small city such as Kingston, June 8 was a remarkable day. My normally sedate *alma mater*, Queen's University, saw confrontations not normally part of daily life on campus. Three motorists tried to aggressively cross the picket line in front of the Queen's University underground parking lot. "They tried to run us over," said picket captain Corinne Kellar, a medical secretary at KGH [Kingston General Hospital]."[28] Press estimates put the number involved in the main demonstration at 5,000, marching from the Memorial Centre to City Park, where the crowd "cheered as fiery speakers called for a province-wide strike."[29] The CAW account called the demonstration a "three-kilometre march along city streets" that "attracted 8,000 flag waving, banner carrying participants. Bands of musicians were set up at various street corners along the parade route and a sailing ship was in the St. Lawrence flying a banner marking the Kingston Day of Action."[30] Transit was shut down, as well as city hall and other municipal buildings.[31] Pickets slowed or stopped work at the Alcan factory and various provincial offices, including the Ministry of Transportation and the Ministry of Health. The main post office on Clarence St. was picketed shut,[32] and the post office at Collins Bay was unexpectedly shut, too. "The pickets left behind anti-government graffiti and Canadian Union of Postal Workers placards in Collins Bay."[33]

The placards left behind in Kingston were to be the last Days of Action placards left behind anywhere in the province.

The Sound of Silence[34]

After Kingston, the phones stopped ringing. The intense organizing of the previous summer, when for a moment anything seemed possible, was a distant memory. As July was about to turn to August, the summer of silence was broken through articles in the press – the heads of Ontario unions met and there would be no one-day province-wide strike against the Harris Tories.[35] In Ian Urquhart's version, the heads of unions had "quietly decided to postpone the general strike indefinitely."[36] Geoff Bickerton was speaking for many in the movement who saw this "retreat from industrial action" as "a clear-cut violation of the convention mandate."[37] This author made a round of phone calls to try and piece together the whole story. Hargrove said, "my understanding is that there's no one-day" general strike. Ryan said, "apparently, the province-wide strike at this time has been cancelled." Samuelson did not return my calls.[38]

It was the end of the Days of Action movement, which had been the centrepiece of the struggle against the Tories. There had been three watershed moments. The 1996 OPSEU strike – hard on the heels of Hamilton's "Woodstock of the Labour Movement" – had forged a union but not a strategy about how to build a winning struggle against the Tories. The massive Toronto general strike of October 25, 1996, had been the high point, with one million workers staying away from work, the next day between 250,000 and 300,000 marching through the city, the chant for a province-wide strike receiving massive support. But it was followed not by a strategic vision but by a debilitating faction fight launched by the pink paper unions. Finally, in 1997, after the Tories had tabled draconian anti-labour legislation, union local after union local voted for illegal province-wide strike action. Just the threat of a province-wide strike forced the Tories to back down. But instead of using that as a springboard to generalize the struggle, the OFL left the field to the Tories, leaving the teachers isolated. Like OPSEU, the teachers' struggle forged union consciousness, but not a strategy for challenging the Tories.

Samuelson's candidacy for president of the OFL had been backed by the "pink paper unions" – Steelworkers, CEP, and others – who had tried to kill the Days of Action after the Toronto general strike. But support for strike action was so strong that Samuelson and the pink paper unions had to say that they supported a province-wide general strike. Had he said anything else, he would never have been elected head of the OFL. But it was clear now that it was just talk that he was unprepared to back up with action. The unanimous vote to authorize strike action had little meaning, coming as it did after the teachers had returned to work.

Ryan said that CUPE and CAW had demanded that the pink paper unions allow cross-picketing – the picketing of workplaces by workers in other unions – or the general strike was off. According to Ryan: "We wanted cross-picketing to be the centrepiece of any province-wide strike ... We would have liked to have gone into some of the steel plants to picket them, and some of the paper mills and so on. That way, we could all be assured that everybody was going to be closing their workplaces. A lot of the unions balked at the idea of having cross-picketing, which signalled to us that a lot of those workplaces wouldn't be closed."

There was an understandable logic behind this. Ryan's CUPE members and Hargrove's CAW members to an even greater degree had for long carried the bulk of the work for the labour side of the Days of Action movement. "By mid-1998" write Reshef and Rastin, "the CAW leaders, those staunch supporters of collective action and the engine that propelled the first DOA, felt that the events had become, to an extent, a single-union show."[39] They quoted one as telling them that "at the end, a lot of time it became really a CAW affair. An awful lot of the unions either couldn't or didn't deliver membership and people ... A lot of other unions did not shut down their workplaces. And eventually we had decided that we couldn't or won't work with just ourselves. So the idea of a province-wide shutdown kind of fizzled, which was unfortunate."[40] Ryan wanted some guarantees that there would be backup, should the Days of Action continue. That wasn't going to be forthcoming from the pink paper side of the table. Hargrove and Ryan were faced with the prospect of either going forward without them and creating new structures or retreating. They chose the latter.

The Canadian Federation of Students, in anticipation of the proposed province-wide shutdown, had called a week of protest ending October 16, and this pressure forced the heads of unions to nominally call one more Day of Action for that day in Ottawa, in solidarity with the students. Ryan emphasized this: "I wouldn't say that the Days of Action campaigns are being called off, because October 16 is part of the Days of Action." Wayne Samuelson promised an "in your face" demonstration on the 16th of October in Ottawa.[41] But when the day came, the rally outside the Tory Convention Centre was so small as to receive ridicule in the press. "The party meeting at Ottawa's downtown Congress Centre had been expected to draw mass protests. But fewer than 200 students showed up to half-heartedly wave placards outside."[42] This was, in fact, a little misleading. While the OFL did fail to mobilize for October 16, student organizations did not. Thousands marched out of their classes and participated in actions all across the country, including a demonstration of 10,000 in Ottawa on October 17.[43] But it was very much *not* an Ottawa Day of Action, nowhere near on par with the eleven previous ones. The Days of Action movement was over.

Social Movement Electoralism and a Class-in-Formation

Return to the pivotal year of 1991 when the Rae government set the stage for the politics of the coming years by standing down from its first big promise – the implementation of public automobile insurance. Thinking through that experience means that, while we need to nuance our understanding of neoliberalism, as I will suggest below, we should not abandon the concept. The Rae government was a social democratic one, and as such was inclined to consider public insurance not as an industry, but as a social service – an extension of the publicly delivered health care so central to the Canadian polity. But it was also a social democratic government in the context of the neoliberal offensive with its emphasis on a reified notion of "individual rights." Couched as a rights issue – as Peter Kormos and others certainly did – it was hard to argue against the "right to sue." However, in the real world, that "right" would be one almost exclusively wielded by a minority at the top of the social hierarchy. The majority of poor and working-class automobile users would benefit far more from reduced premiums and enhanced benefits than an individual "right" that they were unlikely ever to use.

This analysis was not front of mind when, on a bleak winter night at the end of December 1991, the remnants of the ill-fated Automobile Insurance Review gathered for a staff holiday celebration (or perhaps a wake) in a downtown Toronto restaurant. Off at a corner table of the crowded pub sat the self-named "troika" – one, a former left-wing unionist and supporter of the Waffle (a late-1960s, early-1970s left-wing caucus within the NDP);[1] another, a long-time supporter of Mao's China; and me, a former left-wing grad student, specializing in critiques of the limits of social democracy. We were, as usual, sitting together, observing proceedings, and were consumed not by the subtleties of political analysis but by despair at the unfolding trends in Ontario politics. In January and February of 1991, we three had felt

Image 12.1. Andrea Horwath (right) at a press conference with the late Peter Kormos (left).

ourselves to be on the cutting edge of policy change in the province, sitting in on meetings at the highest level of the provincial bureaucracy, confidently clearing the ground for state-run public auto. By December we sat, isolated in a corner, the room populated not with unionists, socialists, and left academics, but lawyers, insurance executives, and long-time bureaucrats. As the evening wore on, the deputy minister wandered over, our table a stop on his inevitable rounds. "What are you three up to, plotting the revolution?" "No," said the former Maoist, "we already tried, and it failed."

On that cold, bleak night of the AIR reunion, with pro-public policy analysts depressed and silent, and with a room populated with chirping, happy lawyers, insurance industry representatives, and contented anti-government-control neo-con bureaucrats, we had one omen of perhaps better days to come. There was a draw for the door prize. It was an unbelievably tasteless coffee mug in the shape of a car. But it was the only door prize. And the winner was ... me. The real door prize would come just four years later when a movement took to the streets and thrust a progressive political agenda into the realm of public discourse at a far higher level than any of our policy efforts in the Rae years.

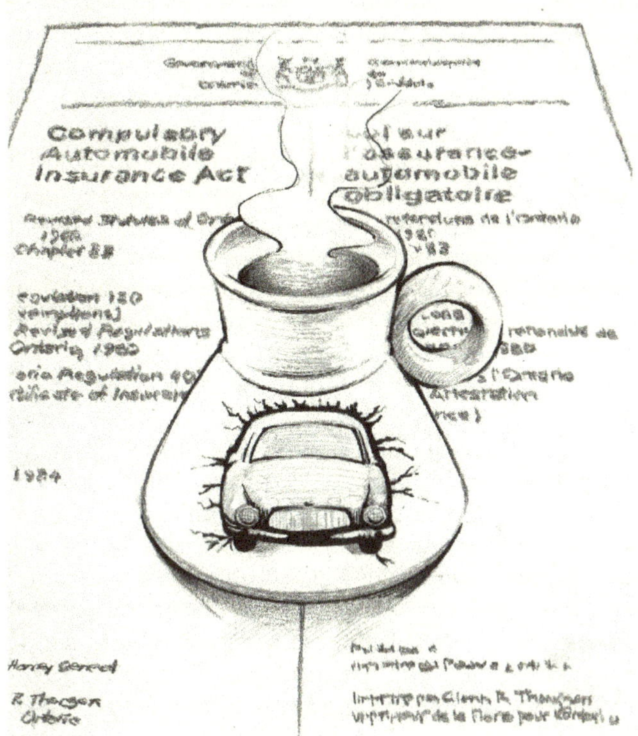

Image 12.2. Auto insurance. The first broken promise.

How to assess those almost three years of struggle we now call the Days of Action? Some were utterly dismissive. The return to work by the teachers, for instance, was greeted with derision from certain conservative quarters, few laced with as much sarcasm as that penned by Andrew Coyne.

> We won't back down? What else do you call this ragged retreat, first three unions, then a fourth, then at last the fifth? The largest teachers' strike in Canadian history began as a show of muscle by one of the most powerful organized labour groups in the province: a naked attempt to dictate education policy to an elected government, in defiance not only of democracy but of the law. And what have the teachers to show for two weeks' lost pay? Union has been set against union, strikers against anti-strikers, the membership feels betrayed by its leaders – and the government hasn't budged.[2]

Coyne's perspective is oblivious to the complex interactions between collective struggle and the evolution of mass consciousness over time. He implies that the strike was completely futile. His perspective cannot account for the fact that, a generation later, it is now taken for granted that teachers are an embedded part of the labour movement in Ontario. There is no longer astonishment when thousands show up with picket signs to protest attacks on education. In a very real sense, the teachers, like OPSEU before them, became a part of the labour movement through their bitter struggles with the Harris Tories. Those struggles were embedded within the entire Days of Action social movement against the Harris Tories, and our assessment of them must be a component of our assessment of the Days of Action as a whole.

Douglas Nesbitt has suggested that "the Days of Action do not feature in the collective political identity of Ontarians, or even, it could be argued, within the ranks of the province's much-diminished labour movement."[3] He characterizes the Days of Action experience as an enormous defeat, making a parallel with "similarly catastrophic union defeats against neoliberalism" such as the Miners' Strike of 1984–5 in the United Kingdom and the PATCO (Professional Air Traffic Controllers Organization) strike of 1981 in the United States. In the 1990s I made a similar comparison.[4] With the benefit of hindsight, I no longer think these comparisons hold. The defeat of the miners by Thatcher represented the end of a declining industry. In 1984 there were 139,000 coal miners in the UK. At the end of the second decade of the twenty-first century, there were less than 1,000.[5] Teachers by contrast – in Ontario and elsewhere – are part of an expanding industry, education being ever more important as mature economies progressively expand their reliance on mental labour. During the Days of Action, we talked about 126,000 teachers; by 2020 the number had increased to above 200,000.[6] As to PATCO, the air traffic controllers' confrontation with the Reagan administration led to the decertification of the union, a defeat so massive it has been characterized as "a turning point in the history of U.S. labor relations ... In the years after the PATCO strike, Phelps-Dodge, Hormel, and other large companies joined a growing list of private employers that simply replaced strikers."[7] The ending of the Days of Action was by no means a decertification and a defeat on this scale with these kinds of consequences. The comparison, like that with the miners, does not hold.

The Days of Action, which began with such promise, did end in a way that bitterly disillusioned thousands of activists. Throughout I have suggested aspects of how the tactics of the OFL in particular were constrained by conservative habits and histories. As to the latter, the bitter division over the Social Contract had left sections of the union movement better prepared for an internal war than a class war in the first months of the Harris election. As to the former, the habit of reducing trade unionism to the routine of bargaining and reducing activism to what Rosa Luxemburg called "demonstration strikes" made it difficult for many to rise to the challenge posed by a movement organized around political strikes. At the beginning of the movement, it wasn't until confronted by the ragtag army of anti-Harris activists who were by and large *outside* the ranks of organized labour that the Ontario union leadership began to organize against the Common Sense Revolution. At the end of the movement, when confronted by the great fighting strike of the teachers, the rhetoric of solidarity from the OFL leadership was revealed as just that – rhetoric. The teachers were left to fight on their own.

At the very least, this poses the need for what Panitch and Swartz have called "the most pressing" issue for labour as it searches for a new strategy. "At the heart of a new strategy for labour must be a strategy for reorganizing and democratizing the labour movement towards developing the new capacities that workers and their unions need to start to change the structure of power."[8] Panitch and Swartz, borrowing a term from Sam Gindin and Kim Moody, call this approach "movement unionism" – and here the Days of Action experience leaves behind a mixed legacy. The unique structure adopted after the first Day of Action in London, of sharing leadership with social justice organizations, was an important step towards this kind of movement unionism. But that willingness to share leadership was very much restricted to the local level. The OFL Executive Board kept the door firmly shut during its strategic leadership meetings – a missed opportunity if there ever was one – and a sign of how the leadership of the Ontario union movement found it difficult to change old habits to meet new challenges.

Larry Savage argues that the "OFL's decision to pull the plug on the Days of Action had the effect of pushing unions back into the electoral arena" – one section looking to give the NDP a "second chance," another section who "came together under the umbrella of the Ontario Election Network (OEN) in an effort to promote strategic voting."[9] Attempting a synthetic analysis that appreciates both the realm of social movements and the realm of electoral politics is, I think, critical. Those realms, while distinct, are quite closely related. They each impact the other in complex and important ways.

In an analysis of the 2015 defeat of Stephen Harper at the federal level and the election of Justin Trudeau to his first term as prime minister, I suggested the concept of social movement electoralism as "an extension of insights developed by Rosa Luxemburg." Writing from a prison cell in 1918, "Luxemburg argued that even in flawed democracies, 'the living fluid of the popular mood continuously flows around the representative bodies, penetrates them, guides them'" and she said that even the "cumbersome mechanism" of the democracies typical of her day "possesses a powerful corrective – namely, the living movement of the masses, their unending pressure,"[10] an understanding I suggested could be called "social movement electoralism."

> Social movements and elections are often seen as existing in separate and distinct fields. When we think of social movements, we think of events outside the electoral arena – with leaders, membership, mass meetings, and so on. When we think of electoralism, we think of parties, leaders, platforms, and so on within the electoral arena. The concept *social movement electoralism* suggests a synthetic approach to the two phenomena, as an alternative to the binary approach of "social movements" versus "electoralism."[11]

The Days of Action movement, I would argue, exactly fits this framework of social movement electoralism – a mass movement which helped shape the political environment in Ontario for a generation. What it failed to find was a political vehicle that could give consistent expression to the needs of the movement. But this is not so much a limitation of the movement itself, but a limitation of the political organizing throughout the entire province.

When the Harris Tories ended up winning re-election in 1999, Reshef and Rastin answered the question first posed by the pink paper unions – who would benefit from the Days of Action movement – saying, "the final score ... favours the Harris government. In the 1995 election, the Tories won 82 seats in a 130-seat legislature with 44.9 percent of the popular vote. In the 1999 election, they won 59 seats in a 103-seat legislature with 45.1 percent of the popular vote."[12] This fear of the electoral inefficacy of the Days of Action movement was behind the pink paper pessimism. In this, they were echoing other dismissive analyses of the Days of Action. Typical was an article by Lee Prokaska who, one year after the Hamilton Days of Action, asked rhetorically, "a year later, what has come of it?"

> A public opinion poll last month suggested support for the government is at 47 percent, more than it enjoyed when it came to power in 1995. Change has proceeded apace. And there is a sense in some quarters that labour's protest efforts may not have been a public relations success.

Figure 12.1. Support for the Harris Tories and the Days of Action, 1995–9.[13]

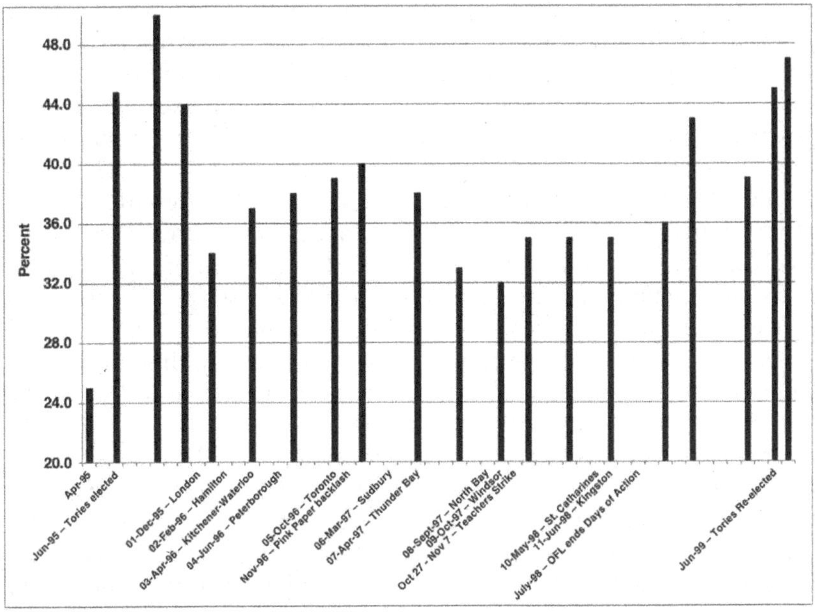

Author's calculations from multiple sources.[14]

"They may have pulled union memberships together, but by and large the demonstrations did the labour movement harm in terms of public opinion," says John Crispo, emeritus professor of political economics at the University of Toronto and a self-described right winger.

"I think (labour leaders are) slow learners when it comes to these demonstrations," said Crispo. "The people they hurt the most, especially in Toronto, were the people with low incomes who had to use public transit to get to their jobs. The wealthy went to play golf or ski – it was the poor workers who were hardest hit."[15]

But on its own terms, this kind of analysis of the inefficacy of the Days of Action is simply incorrect. Figure 12.1 provides some arithmetic with which to challenge the counterposing of social movement activism to electoralism. The figure sketches out an x-axis listing the eleven one-city general strikes and other key moments in the Days of Action movement – in particular the fall 1997 two-week teachers' strike – and a y-axis charting the downs and ups of support for the Mike Harris Conservatives in that process.

On the general question of the relationship between militancy and support for the Tories, there is *no* evidence of increasing militancy being associated with electoral gains for the Mike Harris Conservatives. The opposite seems to be the case. At the moment of the pink paper backlash, support for the Tories was at 40 per cent. The backlash slowed down but failed to stop the movement, and support for the Tories dropped steadily to just 32 per cent at the moment of the widely popular illegal teachers' walkout in 1997. It stayed low through the summer of 1998 when the OFL Executive Board called off the movement. In the weeks and months after that decision – after the end of an organized mass movement on the streets against the Tories – support for the Conservatives steadily increased, culminating in their re-election in June 1999. It was, at least in the case of Ontario, extremely short-sighted to counterpose mobilizations on the streets and in the workplace to the arithmetic calculations of electoral politics.

Greg Albo and Bryan Evans argue that the "Mike Harris-led 'Common Sense Revolution' ... firmly embedded the neoliberal project within the Ontario state and political economy."[16] The Ontario Tories, subsequently under the leadership of Ernie Eves, were finally voted out of office in 2003, with the Liberal Party under first Dalton McGuinty and then Kathleen Wynne (from 2013) governing the province for the next fifteen years. Albo and Evans suggest that with the victory of the provincial Liberals in 2003, "the rather crude and aggressive variant of neoliberalism expressed by the Common Sense Revolutionaries may have been defeated" but that "neoliberalism itself endured. Indeed, this project was deepened and advanced by the Liberals as a more politically sustainable endeavour under their leadership, including over the premiership of Kathleen Wynne after 2013."[17] Tom McDowell has developed this argument at length, saying that the Liberal years of rule in Ontario were years of a "*consolidation* – both of the policies of the CSR and in its approach to parliamentary governance." Citing Bryan Evans, he says that "the legacy of the Harris government 'lives on' in Ontario, 'having been politically embedded in policy and structures.'"[18]

The refusal for fifteen years to undo the cuts to social assistance is certainly compatible with this analysis. Larry Savage points out that the "Liberals also refused to restore the right of farm workers to unionize and flat out rejected calls to bring back the NDP's anti-scab law, which had been repealed by the Harris government."[19] However, Savage also documents the very real labour law reforms passed in the first Liberal administration of McGuinty. "Passed in 2005, Bill 144, the Labour Relations Statute Law Amendment Act, returned remedial certification authority and other powers to the OLRB [Ontario Labour Relations Board] and repealed the Harris government's law requiring employers to post notices explaining how to decertify their unions."[20] Bradley Walchuk adds that "a card-based certification system for the construction sector was re-established."[21] There were other policies introduced by McGuinty, clearly very different from Harris and the Common Sense Revolution. Among other reforms, the McGuinty government:

- raised the minimum wage in the province to $8 an hour by the end of its first term in 2007[22]
- in 2008, in the context of the Great Recession, made the decision "to bail out the Ontario auto sector,"[23] promising "$500 million in strategic investments to both create and retain jobs"[24]
- in the education sector so seriously damaged by Harris and the CSR, "announced plans to invest an additional $1.6 billion in education by 2006," and in their budget, "increased pupil grants by 6 percent ($8,325), allowed for a 2 percent raise in teachers' salaries, and came with added reporting requirements to ensure local compliance with government priorities (e.g., class size reduction and help for students at risk)"[25]
- created "a hard cap of just 20 students in public school classrooms from Junior Kindergarten to Grade 3" (later adjusted upward to 23)
- in what Anna Esselment calls "the key piece" of their education reforms, introduced and implemented "full-day, every-day junior and senior kindergarten in Ontario schools"
- in the health care sector, similarly seriously damaged by Harris and the CSR, "set about to hire more nurses, reduce wait times in key areas, ensure more families had family doctors … and improve the nature of home care in the province"[26]

As for Kathleen Wynne, McGuinty's successor, her sell-off of 60 per cent of the Hydro One transmission utility (along with the sale of Hydro One Brampton and Hydro One Networks' distribution arm) can be seen to fit within a "Common Sense Revolution" neoliberal framework. Many of her other policies simply do not.[27] Among other reforms, Wynne's government:

- oversaw a $29 billion expansion of mass transit in the Greater Toronto and Hamilton Area, in part funded by the sale of the province's Hydro assets[28]
- raised the minimum wage in Ontario to $14 an hour, January 1, 2018, with a promise to increase it again to $15 by January 1, 2019[29]

- made post-secondary tuition free for students whose family income was $50,000 or less, or mature students earning less than $30,000
- increased the number of licensed childcare spaces to 427,000
- made 4,400 prescription drugs free for those under 25[30]
- promised to make prescription drugs free for seniors from August 1, 2019, should the Liberals be re-elected[31]

The Hydro One issue is the one policy on this list that might seem to fit with the neoliberal framework. However, it strains credibility to hang the label "neoliberal" on Wynne based on this one policy. First, it was a partial privatization, Ontario retaining a 40 per cent stake in Hydro One and minority shareholders "limited to a 10 per cent ownership."[32] Second, it is not nothing that Wynne linked the Hydro One sale to a mass expansion of public transit, with a focus on the GO system. "Over 10 years, we aim to phase in electric train service every 15 minutes on all GO lines we own," Wynne said one year prior to the Hydro One sale.[33] Of course, this ambitious plan has not been entirely realized, but that does not mean that *nothing* resulted from Wynne's policy choices. We have yet to see electric GO Train service. There have been many implementation challenges associated with the public-private approach chosen by the Liberals, but in the end, there *has been* a major expansion of the transit system in Toronto (and Mississauga and elsewhere). Any regular riders of the GO Train will have noticed the expansion of service that has made commuting by rail much more practical than before the investments made by the Wynne government, an expansion not typically associated with neoliberal rule.

Neither the election of the Liberals nor the reforms they introduced were unrelated to the social movement struggles against the Tories, of which the Days of Action were the most prominent. "In the run-up to the 2003 provincial election, under the banner of the newly formed Working Families Coalition [WFC], the CAW joined forces with building and construction trades, nurses' and teachers' unions to launch a major third-party anti-Conservative advertising blitz."[34] The CAW as we know, was central to the Days of Action, and among their allies in the WFC were two unions central to the Days of Action era teachers' strike – the OECTA and the OSSTF.[35] It was the Liberals, not the NDP, who benefitted from this intervention, the Liberals winning that election "with 46.4 percent of the vote, doubling their seat total from thirty-six at the time of dissolution to seventy-two after the election. The Conservatives, meanwhile, lost thirty-two seats and saw their share of the vote drop to just below 35 percent."[36]

Certainly, the WFC initiative would not please many social movement activists deeply suspicious of the Liberal Party, given the very severe cuts to transfer payments that were a foundational part of the 1990s attacks on health care, education, and social assistance. Nor would the WFC please the pro-NDP section of the union movement. Savage says that the coalition "has created a lasting fissure in the politics of the province's labour movement, which has helped to forestall a resurgence of union support for the traditionally pro-labour NDP."[37] But the Tories *were* defeated, and important reforms *were* granted by the Liberals over the next fifteen years. There is no easy way to prove the extent to which the WFC had an electoral impact. But interestingly, the reforms listed above are in sectors – education, health care, and auto – that coincide precisely with the union sectors that backstopped the WFC. In terms of the Liberals' labour law reforms, Walchuk maintains that "perhaps the greatest beneficiaries of the new Liberal government were the construction and building trades unions" following the reintroduction of "card check certification for the construction industry."[38]

All of these Liberal reforms are important to Ontario's working people, and none of them would have been implemented under a Tory government. It suggests that we should be careful about collapsing the experience of the provincial administrations of the early twenty-first century into the experience of the Harris Common Sense Revolution under the heading of "neoliberal." Such a move runs the risk of making the definition of the term so broad as to lose its meaning.

Add one more piece to the puzzle. In chapter 3, I offered a figure (3.1) to dramatize one critically important aspect of the federal contribution to the attack on the social wage and the introduction of neoliberal policies into the Canadian mainstream – the systematic reduction of transfer payments from the federal treasury to sustain social programs at the provincial level. It is in fact, a partial picture. Figure 12.2 extends the lens into the twenty-first century, and we see something very different.

The federal cuts to transfer payments bottomed out in fiscal year 1997–8 (where figure 3.1 ended) at just under $1,200 per capita ($1,190). From this low-point until 2003–4 per capita transfer payments increased only slightly. However, in 2004–5 under Liberal Prime Minister Paul Martin, this changed dramatically, with per capita transfer payments jumping to $1,933, their highest level to that point. The trend since has been steadily upward, stagnating in the last years of Conservative rule under Stephen Harper, but steadily increasing under the Liberals and Justin Trudeau. Visible in 2020 is the extraordinary impact of the pandemic – per capita transfer payments jumping to $3,202. Even discounting that one-time emergency increase, we can see an almost

Figure 12.2. Major Transfers to Other Levels of Government, 1967–2024 (per capita, 2025 dollars).

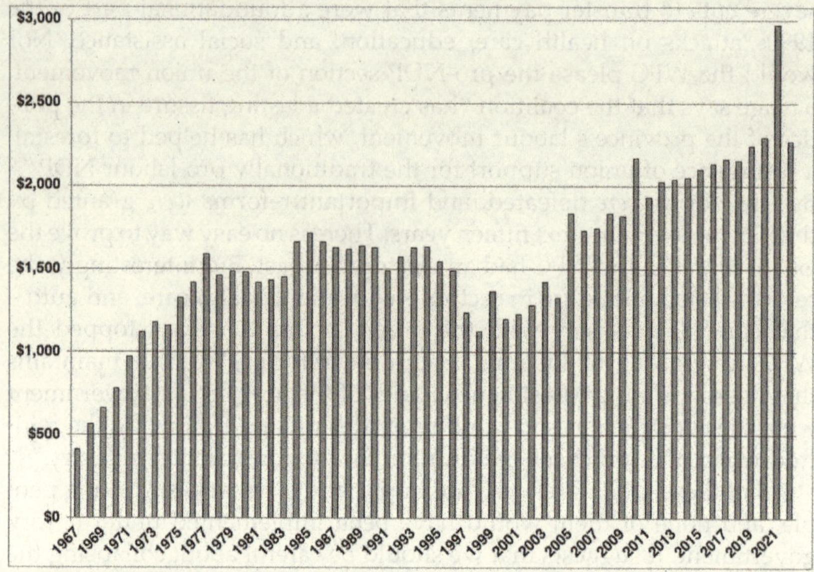

Author's compilation from official figures for Federal Transfers, CPI, Current Population, and Population.[39]

quarter-century history of increases in per capita transfer payments from the federal government to other levels of government, backstopping health care, education, and social assistance. In the last fiscal year for which we have complete figures, 2023–4, per-capita transfers stood at $2,453 – double what they had been in 1997–8. This suggests that we have to nuance our understanding of neoliberalism at the federal level as well as the provincial, a very big project and outside the scope of this book. Relevant to this book, it also helps explain the more "muted" approach to austerity by Ford compared to Harris, Ford every year receiving vastly more transfers from the central government than happened in the Harris years.

Nuancing our understanding of the neoliberal is not the only issue left unresolved by this book. There is much, much more from the Harris era that this book has not even touched. There was a campaign within Toronto against the imposition of the megacity. There was horror in the province at the murder of Dudley George. There was anger and disgust at the price of restructuring paid by the people of Walkerton, 2,000 of whom fell sick and 7 died resulting from contaminated water. The last two might well have been the last straws, forcing Harris to leave the political stage. All these topics will have to be part of other assessments of the 1990s. This book has been more narrowly focussed on the question of agency. In my conversation with Hargrove after news of the cancellation of the Days of Action began to circulate, he said that the Days of Action were "not a rank and file driven thing, this was a leadership driven debate at the OFL."[40] This book has tried to make the opposite case. The Harris Tories, immediately upon their election, were confronted by a divided and demoralized union movement, only revitalized by social movements organized *outside* the labour movement, a leadership only galvanized into action when those social movements connected with the Labour Council of Metro Toronto and York Region for the 10,000-strong march on Queen's Park September 27, 1995. Without that months-long process of organizing, the "leadership-driven debate" was going nowhere.

The Days of Action movement has to be seen as a moment in the complex process of class formation. In a quite different context,[41] I have suggested the importance of revisiting how E.P. Thompson and G.E.M. de Ste. Croix understood class formation – something that they both insisted could only be done through a concrete analysis and history of the evolution of its *subjective* self-understanding.

> Thompson chose to use "making" in his title because his book is "a study in an active process, which owes as much to agency as to conditioning. The working class did not rise like the sun at an appointed time. It was present at its own making." As he goes on to explain, "I do not see class as a 'structure,' nor even as a 'category,' but as something which in fact happens (and can be shown to have happened) in human relationships." Writing about class in the context of ancient Greece, G. E. M. de Ste. Croix put it this way: "I am not going to pretend that class is an entity existing objectively in its own right like a Platonic 'Form.'" Rather, with Thompson, he understood class as "essentially a relationship" – as an expression of the social relations into which human beings enter in the process of production.[42]

This understanding is true both for minority or ruling classes, as well as majoritarian or working classes. All classes are shaped in relation to other classes – struggle shapes consciousness, both for the elite and for the popular classes. In Doug Ford's Ontario, we have again been in the midst of a series of bitter confrontations between a Tory government and its education unions. In these twenty-first-century disputes, both sides are operating under the shadow of the last big confrontation a quarter century ago. As a result of that awareness, we all know that Tory attacks on education, if they go too far, can spark outrage among teachers, students, and the wider public. We all know now that teachers have a reservoir of support, just below the surface, because of their frontline role in assisting us in raising and educating our children. As a result of that awareness, the struggle this century is taking a different shape – more a fencing match between a government probing to see how far it can go and the teachers wielding a rotating strike strategy as their weapon of choice in 2020, then threatening a general strike in 2022, in the face of which the government decided to retreat. But that fencing match would have taken a very different shape without the way in which the events a quarter of a century ago have become embedded into both elite and mass consciousness.

For the people of Ontario, the Days of Action from 1995 to 1998 remain a very big experience, one that shaped a generation of workers, students, and social movement activists. Our movements against austerity today stand on the shoulders of the organizing and struggles of this earlier era. Those struggles – with all the problems, missteps, and mistakes – helped build a foundation without which we would all be weaker today.

Appendix 1

Submissions to Bill 26 Hearings, Samples by Levels of Support

Chapter 5 covered the circumstances which led to 476 individuals and organizations, in late 1995 and early 1996, making submissions to the hearings on the implications of Bill 26 – the infamous "omnibus bill." A content analysis of these submissions revealed sixteen sectors and four categories: (2a) Strong support – submissions that expressed their support for the omnibus bill without reservations. (2b) Some concerns – submissions that clearly indicated support for the bill but asked for amendments or indicated some reservations. (2c) Serious concerns – submissions that did not always explicitly say they were opposed to the omnibus bill but indicated very strong opposition to or reservations about key aspects of the legislation. (2d) Strong opposition – submissions that unequivocally came out against the omnibus bill.

Appendix 1 provides further examples from these transcripts in addition to the four illustrative ones used in chapter 5. There are more selections here from those strongly opposed to the bill than those strongly in support of the bill, in line with the information from table 5.1, which documents that there were almost four times as many who voiced strong opposition compared to those who voiced strong support. The net effect, hopefully, is to provide a clear window into the struggle that was unfolding inside the province. Appendix 2 provides a complete list of all the submissions, with their sector identified, and categorized by level of support or opposition to the bill. On occasion, an organization appears more than once. This occurs if representatives from the organization delivered presentations at more than one of the hearings.

Sources for Appendices 1 and 2: Ontario, "Committee Transcripts," Bill 26, Savings and Restructuring Act, 1995 (Toronto: Legislative Assembly of Ontario. Standing Committee on General Government. 36th Parliament, 1st Session, December 14, 1995).

Strong Support – "Government Restructuring Is Long Overdue"

Paul Pagnuelo – Ontario Taxpayers Federation

December 18, 1995, Toronto – "There are those in this province who see the government's economic statement of November 29 as nothing but doom and gloom. They claim the so-called social fabric of Ontario will be ripped apart by the government's spending reductions. Because of these reductions, the government, in their eyes, stands accused of being mean-spirited and uncaring. However, I would like to suggest that critics of the government's economic reforms are in fact a vocal minority. They're out to protect their slice of the pie from the Ontario treasury ... the Harris government's economic statement is a sobering cure for taxpayers left with a bad hangover by tax-and-spend politicians."

Jim Montag – London-Middlesex Taxpayers' Coalition

January 9, London – "Our present government was elected with promises to cut the deficit, among other things. To this time, this government has kept its election promises, and I think this is really wonderful. This is a radical departure from previous administrations. It is our hope that this refreshing display of integrity will continue without falter, despite massive protests and confrontations from some of the groups affected. The ones most responsible for the deficit are now the biggest whiners."

Allan Faux – Whitby Chamber of Commerce

January 19, 1996, Peterborough – "In 1995 Ontarians overwhelmingly voted for change, a change where the will for restructuring is larger today than it ever has been. The people of this province have given the government a mandate to pursue this change, and the promise we have been given is that government will get out of the business of competing with the private sector. The pith and substance of Bill 26 captures that promise."

Author's note: While throughout I have presented the submissions in chronological order, below I group together several Chamber of Commerce submissions and *put key sections in italics*, to draw attention to a certain extraordinary repetition, some of the submissions being identical in content, formulation, and style.

Ian Cunningham – Ontario Chamber of Commerce

December 18, 1995, Toronto – *"It is clear that government restructuring is long overdue. With deficits averaging near $10 billion annually over the past four years and an accumulated debt of more than $90 billion, it is imperative that the Ontario government take strong measures to reduce spending and to get its finances under control."*

Larry Sandre – Windsor and District Chamber of Commerce

January 8, 1996, Windsor – *"It is clear that government restructuring is long overdue. With deficits averaging near $10 billion annually over the past four years and an accumulated debt of more than $90 billion, it is imperative that the Ontario government take strong measures to reduce spending and get its finances under control."*

Darla Scott – Sudbury and District Chamber of Commerce

January 16, 1996, Sudbury – *"With deficits averaging nearly $10 billion annually over the past four years and an accumulated debt of more than $90 billion, it is imperative that the Ontario government take aggressive measures to reduce spending and get its fiscal house in order."*

Frank Varga – Chamber of Commerce of Kitchener and Waterloo

January 10, Kitchener – "The chambers [of Commerce of Kitchener and Waterloo, and of Cambridge] strongly support, *in principle, the stated purpose of Bill 26, which is to reduce government spending, to promote economic prosperity through public sector restructuring and to create a climate which will attract investment, create jobs and encourage businesses to grow."*

Ron Carther – Chamber of Commerce of Kitchener and Waterloo

January 17, Kitchener – "The chamber supports *in principle the stated purpose of Bill 26, which is to reduce government spending, to promote economic prosperity through public sector restructuring and to create a climate which will attract investment, create jobs and encourage businesses to grow."*

Some Concerns – "There Is No More Money Available to Be Spent Frivolously"

Shelly Jamieson – Ontario Nursing Home Association

December 19, 1995, Toronto – "Frankly, we believe our health care system is broken. We believe that anyone defending the status quo in health in Ontario is a dinosaur. While the June election might have introduced a new style of government, it did not introduce this serious problem in health care. In fact, we would hope that the definition of the problem would be an area where there is three-party unanimity."

Tom Wright – Office of the Information and Privacy Commissioner

December 21, 1995, Toronto – "I realize that reducing health care fraud is necessary, and I understand this is one of the major goals of these amendments. However, I also believe that in order to achieve this goal, it is not necessary to introduce measures which put the privacy of Ontarians at risk."

Elizabeth Margles

December 21, 1995, Toronto – "I probably represent the silent majority of Ontarians. I agree with some of the policies of the Liberals, some of the NDP and even some of the Conservatives, though with regard to Bill 26, I'm not convinced that you're at all progressive. I'm here today to demonstrate to you how an all-encompassing bill like Bill 26 has much wider-reaching implications than the government has considered, how it is vacuous in some parts, how the government definitions are faulty and how, in the government's efforts for a short-sighted power and control grab, Bill 26 can lead to the disintegration of societal contribution and professional demoralization."

David Town – London Chamber of Commerce

January 9, 1996, London – "Some provisions maintained with the Ontario government do run counter to what we see as the government's stated intent of empowering municipalities to better manage their own affairs ... Under user fees, the chamber is on record as supporting the greater use of user fees in the funding of municipal services ... Some suggest that user fees for municipal services unnecessarily penalize lower-income users of these services. We do not believe that a modest entry fee for the use of a municipal facility like a swimming pool or an ice rink is a prohibitive expense. Maintaining such services free for all is an expensive way of helping those truly in need."

Ken Ferguson – Manitoulin-Sudbury District Health Council

January 9, Sudbury – "We offer qualified support for amendments to other legislation intended to achieve restructuring and savings ... Our qualification stems from our commitment to the broad determinants of health. It should be possible to amend the legislation to achieve these fiscal objectives while ensuring that a healthy physical environment and healthy communities are also achievable."

David Kresky – Waterloo Region Tax Watch

January 10, 1996, Kitchener – "We support what the current government is doing in its intent. We support the need to reduce spending, the need to eliminate the deficit and the debt, the need to bring back to reality the fact that there is no more money available to be spent frivolously and that priorities must be set so that the province of Ontario and its people will be able to prosper in the coming years. However, having said that, I have to say that Tax Watch has some concerns about this particular bill. One of our concerns is the process by which this omnibus bill is being put through the government."

Brenda Drinkwalter – Canadian Drug Manufacturers Association

January 11, 1996, Ottawa – "The total lack of consultation in crafting Bill 26 and the absence of interpretive regulations has resulted in legislation that puts at risk the delicate balance that must be maintained between the interests of the province's consumers, governments and employers who pay for drugs and the province's pharmaceutical industry that makes an important contribution to the economy of this province. These changes should be suspended pending a thorough regulatory impact analysis and a comprehensive consultation process on the effect of this bill on all parties."

Lyn MacMillan – Federation of Ontario Naturalists

January 12, Hamilton – "We all understand that deep cuts are necessary all across the province, if our deficit is to be reduced ... Those of us who remember the hard years of the war – now I'm really going back – will know what it's like to face austerity; we certainly faced it then. We also know that it brings out the very best in people. Volunteerism was never stronger than during those times; also people took on new and demanding jobs that they never thought of doing in peacetime. The same urgency exists now, and people will rally to achieve our financial balance if you give them a chance. Do not get rid of such historically important agencies as the conservation authorities. Let them regroup. Let them find other solutions to their budgetary problems."

Robert Metz – London-Middlesex Taxpayers' Coalition

January 16, London – "The London-Middlesex Taxpayers' Coalition supports a totally private medical system, with government assistance directed only to those in demonstrable need. However, our preceding comments and suggestions acknowledge that this final and ideal option is not within the purview of Bill 26, nor within the mandate of this government. Nevertheless, we urge you to avoid painting yourselves into a funding corner with no options by preparing yourselves for the inevitable future."

Serious Concerns – "Hand-Woven with Threads of Dictatorship"

Michel Labelle

January 8, 1996, Timmins – "There is a blue blanket that covers our province today. We have felt it smothering us under unworkable labour legislation. This blanket is hand-woven, and it's hand-woven with threads of dictatorship."

Paul Ham – Access AIDS Committee of Sudbury

January 9, 1996, Sudbury – "We who are living with HIV rely on confidentiality with our care team, and build trusting relationships with them so that our health is of number one concern. Why would a minister of health and members of cabinet need to see my personal medical files? The proposed changes to the Health Insurance Act, the Ontario Drug Benefit Act, the Independent Health Facilities Act and the Public Hospitals Act would be a violation of my fundamental human rights."

Mark Parsons – Canadian Mental Health Association, Ottawa-Carleton Branch

January 11, 1996, Ottawa – "The changes you have already introduced, and those you introduced in your budget statement and through Bill 26, do in fact penalize people who are disabled. Most individuals who have a psychiatric disability are on some form of social assistance. Individuals who have been formally diagnosed by a doctor may be receiving family benefits allowance. There are many people who have a psychiatric illness who are only receiving general welfare assistance because they do not want the label of being permanently disabled, for example, and their application for FBA [Family Benefits Allowance] has not been processed, or for other individual reasons."

Margaret Cahoon – Hastings and Prince Edward Council on Aging

January 12, 1996, Kingston – "Bill 26 seems to be declaring war on the medical profession. The proposed legislation threatens the ability of physicians to provide care by setting fees for services, paying variable rates for the same services, and ordering repayments by the doctor for services considered retrospectively to be unnecessary. The power to decide which doctors can have hospital appointments and to revoke their privileges without recourse or compensation is almost unbelievable."

Paul Leger – Peterborough Community Physicians

January 12, 1996, Peterborough – "The right to physician-patient confidentiality has to be protected. The power of inspectors to remove patient information from a place of storage and the right of the minister to publish personal information should be stricken ... The goal of this legislation was reputed to be cost saving in health care delivery. The size of the bureaucracy required to police and administer it alone would preclude this goal. The inefficiencies of bureaucratic micromanagement are going to increase cost and decrease service provision."

Anne Marie Delorey – National Action Committee on the Status of Women

January 18, 1996, Ottawa – "Our concern about the wiping out of the proxy system in pay equity is that you take the jobs that have been the lowest-paid women's jobs, the women's ghetto jobs – the libraries, the day care workers – and you say that's going to be capped, the money you give them. But you've already determined that they're actually owed a lot of money. It's completely inappropriate in our view to say, 'You're owed a lot of money,' and then pay them 3 per cent."

Strong Opposition – "It Scares the Hell Out of Me"

Katerina Makovec – Pay Equity Advocacy and Legal Services

December 18, 1995, Toronto – "It is, politically, morally, fiscally and gender-equity-related, simply wrong to phase out [the] proxy method ... The proxy method is a very slow process. It's a generational process of change and it's aiming to finally bring pay equity to workers in jobs that were historically undervalued and underpaid ... the Conservative government is taking away even this minimum and abolishing the trend that brings wage justice to jobs historically discriminated against. This action dramatically hurts both working women and communities."

Kerry McCuaig – Ontario Coalition for Better Childcare

December 18, 1995, Toronto – "This bill will undermine, if not destroy, early education and care programs for young children in the province. We estimate that neither Ontario's 25-year-old junior kindergarten program nor quality, non-profit child care programs can survive the cuts when they are coupled with the downloading on to local governments ... with each one of these cuts, the quality and accessibility of early childhood education and care programs was diminished. It took about 15 years to build the child care budget up to what it was, and many of those gains were stripped away in the first 15 weeks of the government."

Ramani Nadarajah – Canadian Environmental Law Association

December 18, 1995, Toronto – "Bill 26 will allow mining corporations to file closure plans as opposed to obtaining the director's acceptance of the plan. Essentially the amendments are a move towards self-regulation by the mining industry. It's our submission that these proposed amendments will undermine environmental protection ... It's only through rigorous environmental standards incorporated in closure plans that we will be able to ensure against environmental catastrophes such as the 1990 tailings spill which occurred at the Matachewan Consolidated Mines, Ltd site ... That tailings spill was the largest in Ontario's history, causing the disruption of the drinking water supply for at least three communities and resulting in the evacuation of homeowners. The spill cost the provincial government over $2 million in cleanup, although the final figures have yet to be tabulated."

James Turk – Ontario Coalition for Social Justice

December 18, 1995, Toronto – "We see this bill as nothing short of an assault on democracy. Powers are granted to cabinet and to the ministers without statutory limitations or conditions usually provided to ensure political accountability and effective recourse to the courts."

Sid Ryan – Canadian Union of Public Employees

December 18, 1995, Toronto – "The Savings and Restructuring Act represents an enormous fraud and breach of promise perpetrated against the people of Ontario by the Harris government. … Bill 26 is not about reform or even saving money; it is about slashing programs, privatizing our social support system and, at a more fundamental level, dismantling the democratic structures that give the citizens of Ontario control over the future of their province."

Tim McCaskell – AIDS Action Now

December 18, 1995, Toronto – "People with AIDS and HIV often find themselves dependent on the Ontario drug benefit plan to pay for prescriptions. Unable to work, we often find ourselves on or below the poverty line. A $2 prescription fee may not seem like a great deal, but where we're talking about people who routinely may have to submit 10 or more prescriptions per month, 12 months a year, we're talking about whittling down an already meagre existence to levels where such basics as nutrition will be seriously put into jeopardy, and where nutrition is undermined, health is undermined."

Warren Thomas – Ontario Public Service Employees Union

December 18, 1995, Toronto – "Every single part of this bill introduces fundamental changes. Every single schedule should have received individual attention, consideration and consultation in an open, democratic process. Bill 26 proposes changes which will destroy government accountability in many areas where it needs to be most accountable."

Avvy Go – Metro Toronto Chinese and Southeast Asian Legal Clinic

December 19, 1995, Toronto – "Like many marginalized communities, the immigrant community is aware of the deficit problem, but like many other conscientious Ontarians, we are also concerned about the speed and the way in which the deficit is being reduced. We are affected, if not more severely, by the series of cutbacks we are seeing everywhere we turn."

Frances Gladstone – Toronto Teachers' Federation

December 19, 1995, Toronto – "The bill confers such broad powers on ministers that decisions could be made through their direction or administrative order, by regulation and without debate, public scrutiny or local input. This is not democracy. This is no Common Sense Revolution. It is a massive, unprecedented intrusion by government, by one swift, shocking movement, into all our lives."

Jack Layton

December 20, 1995, Toronto – "I think this bill in one fell swoop is going to do more to undo democratic governance in this province than any measure ever taken by any government, with the possible exception of the War Measures Act, because it takes into the cabinet minister's office absolute power on many, many different fronts. This has never happened before. I think it needs to be rejected."

Daina Green – Equal Pay Coalition / Coalition pour un salaire égal

December 20, 1995, Toronto – "The problem with the omnibus Bill 26 is that it shuts the door on women who are still owed wage adjustments under pay equity using what's known as the proxy method. These women who are being left out in the cold are women who work in child care centres, nursing homes, treatment centres and other organizations, and those who provide services in the community and in people's homes. These are very important services."

Katheryne Schulz – Metro Toronto Coalition for Better Child Care

December 21, 1995, Toronto – "In 1996, Metro could lose almost half of its subsidized system – that's the total, 11,000 – and there is no doubt that child care in Metro will be devastated. A cut of 47% to municipalities will force even supportive local governments to amputate child care services."

Ken Lewenza – Canadian Auto Workers, Local 444

January 8, 1996, Windsor – "It scares the hell out of me, as a father of two and recently a proud grandfather, that there's going to be a point in life where we're going to charge people for having the initiative to read, to go to a library and read and educate themselves and become more knowledgeable about the future we have. It scares the hell out of me when we talk about the possibility – it's not a possibility any more; I guess I'm talking to the government – of the strong potential of user fees, excluding people from society on basic needs of health care, education, those types of issues ... If the government seeks to eliminate all obstacles to the market, then clearly the legal, civil and societal rights of Ontario workers and their families are under assault. This elevates the debate out of the conventional political arena and into the realm of the overt class war. We do not find this prospect surprising or frightening. In objective terms, it may be the most honest and forthright element in the government's agenda."

David Winninger

January 9, 1996, London – "Trickle-down economics have not worked in New Zealand, in Thatcher's England and in Ronald Reagan's America. The impossible combination of tax cuts and the promise of balanced budgets that Newt Gingrich promised to win a Republican majority in Congress will devastate urban life, striking the hardest at the old, the very young, the poor and the sick. How can such economics possibly succeed in Ontario when, if there ever were mega-deficits, Ronald Reagan created them?"

Jules Tupker – Canadian Union of Public Employees, Local 1409

January 10, 1996, Thunder Bay – "This bill, disguised as a money-saving venture for all of Ontario's citizens, is going to lead to unprecedented hardships for all the citizens of Ontario who are least able to fight back – the sick, elderly, poor, disabled and unemployed. The implementation of Bill 26 is a major step for the Harris government towards the creation of a totalitarian state."

Jack Drewes – Service Employees International Union, Local 268

January 10, 1996, Thunder Bay – "I say to you, go back to the big business backroom boys and tell them that the people of Ontario will not stand for this type of leadership. If you do not stop this right-wing behaviour, the province will be split into two warring camps: the haves and the have-nots. I think you've already woken up the sleeping giant known as the Ontario worker."

Gabe MacNally – St. Catharines and District Labour Council

January 11, 1996, Niagara Falls – "Bill 26 is nothing short of a naked power grab by an extremist government. It does nothing to address the real needs of the people of this province, which are jobs."

Wayne Marston – Hamilton and District Labour Council

January 12, 1996, Hamilton – "This government clearly has an agenda which includes the dismantling and laying to waste of many of the gains provided by the more progressive pieces of legislation over the past 50 years."

Thomas Veitch – Peterborough and District Labour Council

January 12, 1996, Peterborough – "Peterborough has an aging population. Health care is important to them as it is to the rest of this community. This bill gives the Minister of Health the right to close hospitals. This is something we find abhorrent."

Gwen Hewitt – Canadian Union of Public Employees, Durham, Northumberland, Kawartha, and Haliburton Regions

January 12, 1996, Peterborough – "If this is a new ideology, then we submit it is one that even traditional Tories will emphatically reject. It will be the first explosion in a chain reaction that will lead the provincial Conservatives to the same destruction that Brian Mulroney bestowed upon their federal counterparts."

Gerry Philion – Canadian Union of Public Employees, Local 210

January 15, 1996, Timmins – "We, like all members of the Canadian Union of Public Employees, say scrap this bill. Otherwise, public services, programs and infrastructure will be irrevocably dismantled, democratic institutions and standards will be destroyed and Ontarians will suffer incalculable harm. This is anti-democratic legislation which turns a blind eye to the traditions, values and institutions of our province."

Michel Labelle

January 15, 1996, Timmins – "All Ontarians will soon know that when Mike Harris says, 'Ontario is open for business,' he really means, 'Big business, come and join us in the exploitation of Ontario.'"

Peggy Nash – Canadian Auto Workers – Canada

January 15, 1996, Windsor – "The dramatic policy changes contained in Bill 26 constitute a major and disturbing threat to working and poor people in this province. This bill aims to undo social advances that working people have achieved throughout the 1960s and 1970s. At stake are the living standards and the basic security of our members along with those of thousands of other working people in this province."

Julie Lee – London Battered Women's Advocacy Centre

January 16, 1996, London – "Is this government completely unaware of the ongoing national crisis with respect to the disclosure of abused women's private counselling records? It appears so, because you fail to take into consideration the full complexity of the matters at hand. You cannot continue to proceed in creating fiscally convenient policies without a full consideration of the interaction between legal and social issues."

Bonnie Quesnel – Persons United for Self Help London

January 16, 1996, London – "This bill increases vulnerability and hostility towards people with disabilities – those without lifejackets. It will encourage the health care system to identify people with disabilities as an expensive burden, a stereotype used extensively in the past. It simplifies the route for politicians and bureaucrats – some of them with the lifejackets – to forget about our humanness and our contributions, to see our rights as vexatious irritations, just like the wild white water. This easily adopted perspective will lead to the loss of our vital rights."

Bill Kuehnbaum – Ontario Public Service Employees Union, Sudbury Region

January 16, 1996, Sudbury – "Bill 26 will cut into the pensions of laid-off government employees by hundreds of thousands of dollars. We expected this government to put many civil servants out to pasture. But we did not expect it to tear up the grass, poison the water and chop down the shade trees before they got there. Bill 26 turns the pasture into a wasteland."

John Cunningham – United Steelworkers of America, Local 677

January 17, 1996, Kitchener – "These hearings became a reality only after the rightful sit-in of the Legislature. You have hijacked due process."

Chris Mather – Thunder Bay Coalition Against Poverty

January 17, 1996, Thunder Bay – "T-CAP's analysis is that, when taken as a whole, the schedules of Bill 26 have a tendency to look after the wellbeing of the rich and powerful and either to passively ignore or actively decrease the wellbeing of the poor."

Mike Poleck – Thunder Bay and District Labour Council

January 17, 1996, Thunder Bay – "This bill will destroy the distinctive Canadian society that we've come to experience in Ontario. We will move towards a have-versus-have-not society … It would appear that this government intends to move Ontario towards the American style of government where different classes of people receive different levels of public service. The former Conservative prime minister of Canada, Brian Mulroney, once said Canada doesn't have enough millionaires. What he didn't make clear is that the Conservative plan was to increase the number of poor people to allow for this creation."

Lesley Penwarden – Ontario Network of Injured Workers Groups

January 18, 1996, Niagara Falls – "In the name of all that is decent, holy, just or whatever turns your ethical crank, scrap Bill 26."

Buzz Hargrove – Canadian Auto Workers

January 19, 1996, Kingston – "If General Motors were to present this kind of change to our collective agreement, which is impacting a lot less people and is dealt with by 30 members of a bargaining committee, and give us 300 hours to study it, you would be guaranteed there would be a strike. If we were to submit, as a union, the kind of changes you're proposing here and give General Motors 300 hours to study it, you could guarantee there would be a lockout."

Gord Wilson – Ontario Federation of Labour

January 19, 1996, Kingston – "Ontario's deficits are the creation of deliberate, wrongheaded government policy by successive federal governments, first the Mulroney government and now of Paul Martin's Liberals. They are the right-wing policies of the corporate agenda, the policies of neoconservative economics and of monetarism. For more than 10 years now, they have inflicted upon us insanely high interest rates, creating a state of permanent recession, low growth and high unemployment. Combined with the free trade deal which decimated Ontario's manufacturing sector, these policies have been catastrophic for our province."

Appendix 2

Submissions to Bill 26 Hearings, Complete List by Level of Support and Sector

No Opinion	2 out of 476 (0 per cent)
Sector	**Name**
Individual Businesses	Mytec Technologies Inc.
Individuals	James Rourke

Strong Support	52 out of 476 (11 per cent)
Sector	**Name**
Provincial Government	Management Board of Cabinet Ministry of Health Ministry of Municipal Affairs and Housing Ministry of Natural Resources Ministry of Northern Development and Mines
Business Associations	Board of Trade of Metropolitan Toronto Brampton Board of Trade Burlington Chamber of Commerce City of Burlington Canadian Federation of Independent Business Chamber of Commerce of Kitchener and Waterloo Chamber of Commerce of Kitchener and Waterloo Hamilton and District Chamber of Commerce Mississauga Board of Trade Ontario Chamber of Commerce Ontario Home Builders' Association Ontario Mining Association Pharmaceutical Manufacturers Association of Canada Richmond Hill Chamber of Commerce Sudbury and District Chamber of Commerce Whitby Chamber of Commerce Windsor and District Chamber of Commerce

Strong Support	52 out of 476 (11 per cent)
Sector	**Name**
Taxpayer Associations	Canadian Taxpayers' Federation London and District Citizens for Responsible Budget London-Middlesex Taxpayers' Coalition Ontario Taxpayers' Federation Taxpayers Alliance Taxpayers' Coalition Niagara
Municipal Government	Association of Municipalities of Ontario City of Mississauga Town of Penetanguishene
Professional Associations	North-eastern Ontario Pharmacists' Association
Individual Businesses	Boehringer Ingelheim (Canada) Ltd. Glaxo Wellcome Inc. Smithkline Beecham Pharma
Health Care Sector	Association of Ontario Health Centres Canadian Mental Health Association, St. Catharines and Niagara South Branches Hôtel-Dieu Grace Hospital Ontario Chiropractic Association Ontario Nursing Home Association
Education	Lakehead Board of Education
Individuals	David Sharpe Don Cousens Duncan Macdonell George Aregers Gerard Charette Howard Greig Joseph Fox Kathy Bugeja Mitchell Day Paul Holliday Phil Cumming Robert Kernerman

Some Concerns	135 out of 476 (28 per cent)
Sector	**Name**
Provincial Government	Office of the Information and Privacy Commissioner Information and Privacy Commissioner of Ontario
Business Associations	Canadian Association of Chain Drug Stores Canadian Drug Manufacturers Association Chamber of Commerce of Niagara Falls Employer Committee on Health Care in Ontario Greater Peterborough Chamber of Commerce London Chamber of Commerce Municipal Electric Association Oakville Chamber of Commerce Ontario Prospectors' Association Ontario Restaurant Association Ottawa-Carleton Board of Trade Prospectors and Developers' Association of Canada Thunder Bay Chamber of Commerce Timmins Chamber of Commerce
Taxpayer Associations	London-Middlesex Taxpayers' Coalition Taxpayers Coalition Burlington Waterloo Region Tax Watch
Municipal Government	City of Kingston City of London City of Nepean City of Niagara Falls City of Ottawa City of Owen Sound City of Peterborough City of Timmins City of Toronto City of York County of Essex County of Kent – Thomas Storey County of Peterborough Howard Township Municipality of Metropolitan Toronto Northwestern Ontario Municipal Association Regional Municipality of Ottawa-Carleton Regional Municipality of York Town of Huntsville Township of Black River-Matheson Township of Kingston Township of Red Lake

Some Concerns	135 out of 476 (28 per cent)
Sector	**Name**
Professional Associations	Association of Ontario Physicians and Dentists in Public Service
	Canadian Bar Association – Ontario
	Ontario Association of Nephrologists OMA Section on Nephrology
	Ontario Association of Speech-Language Pathologists and Audiologists
	Ontario Pharmacists' Association
	Ottawa-Carleton Pharmacists' Association
	Registered Nurses' Association of Ontario
	Sudbury District Pharmacists' Association
Individual Businesses	Eli Lilly Canada
	Inco Ltd.
	London Life Insurance Co.
	Merck Frosst
	Rx Plus Inc.
Health Care	Association of District Health Councils of Ontario
	Association of General Hospital Psychiatric Services
	Canadian Mental Health Association Ontario Division
	Canadian Mental Health Association, Elgin Branch
	Canadian Mental Health Association, Timmins Branch
	Canadian Mental Health Association, Windsor-Essex County Branch
	Catholic Health Association of Ontario
	Centre de santé communautaire de Sudbury
	College of Physicians and Surgeons of Ontario
	Council of Medical Imaging (Ontario)
	Drug Quality and Therapeutics Committee
	Essex County District Health Council
	Essex County Pharmacists' Association
	Hamilton-Wentworth District Health Council
	Hospital for Sick Children
	Humber Memorial Hospital
	Lake Nipigon Region Hospital Association
	Manitoulin-Sudbury District Health Council
	Medical Imaging Clinics of Ontario Inc.
	Norfolk General Hospital
	North Kingston Community Health Centre
	Oakville-Trafalgar Memorial Hospital
	Ogden-East End Community Health Centre
	Ontario Association of Radiologists
	Ontario Hospital Association

Some Concerns	135 out of 476 (28 per cent)
Sector	**Name**
	Ontario Hospital Association Regional Council 4
	Ontario Hospital Association, Region 1
	Ontario Medical Association
	Ontario Medical Association Section on Psychiatry
	Ontario Medical Association, District 11
	Ontario Medical Association, Section on Diagnostic Imaging
	Ontario Psychiatric Association
	Ottawa General Hospital / Hôpital général d'Ottawa
	Peterborough City Radiologists
	Porcupine District Medical Society
	Providence Continuing Care Centre
	Royal Ottawa Health Care Group
	Salvation Army and Jewish Hospitals
	Southeastern Ontario Health Sciences Centre
	St. Joseph's Health Care System
	St. Joseph's Hospital
	St. Joseph's Hospital, Hamilton
	Sudbury General Hospital
	Sunnybrook Health Science Centre
	Thunder Bay Regional Hospital
	Victoria University Hospital
Education	Ontario Separate School Trustees' Association
Police Services	London Police Services
	Metropolitan Toronto Police Services Board
	Ontario Association of Police Services Boards
Service Providers	Davenport-Perth Neighbourhood Centre
	Dixon Hall Neighbourhood Centre
	Kitchener Public Library Board
	N'swakamok Native Friendship Centre
	Ontario Association of Non-Profit Homes and Services for Seniors
	Path Employment Services
	Strategic Directions Council, Ontario Public Libraries
	Windsor Public Library
Environment	Association of Conservation Authorities of Ontario
	Big Rideau Lake Association
	Eastern Ontario Wardens' Conference
	Federation of Ontario Naturalists
	Hamilton Region Conservation Authority

Some Concerns	135 out of 476 (28 per cent)
Sector	**Name**
Faith	Sisters of St. Joseph of Sault Ste. Marie
Advocacy Groups	Citizens for Public Justice International Freedom in Health Niagara Mental Health Survivors Network Ontario Advocacy Coalition Ontario Federation of Anglers and Hunters Organization for Quality Education
Individuals	Anne Khan Craig McNaughton Dave Wilson Derek Paul Dorothy Sit Dr. Randy Zettle Elizabeth Margles Graham Corke Richard Pentney Shirley Farlinger Ted Krasowski

Serious Concerns	98 out of 476 (21 per cent)
Sector	**Name**
Municipal Government	City of Guelph Township of Dymond
Professional Associations	Professional Association of Interns and Residents of Ontario Region of Waterloo Pharmacists' Association
Health Care Sector	Academy of Medicine, Ottawa Association for Persons with Physical Disabilities of Windsor and Essex County Bedford Medical Associates Canadian Cancer Society, Ontario Division Canadian Mental Health Association, Ottawa-Carleton Branch Community Health Centres: Ottawa and Eastern Ontario Department of Obstetrics, St. Catharines General Hospital

Serious Concerns	98 out of 476 (21 per cent)
Sector	**Name**
	Essex County Medical Society Hamilton Academy of Medicine Hastings and Prince Edward Council on Aging Kitchener-Waterloo Academy of Medicine Liberty Health Lincoln County Academy of Medicine London and District Academy of Medicine London Intercommunity Health Centre Medical Reform Group of Ontario Nurse Practitioners' Association of Ontario, Southwestern Region Ontario Association of Optometrists Ontario College of Family Physicians Ontario Dental Association Ontario Health Records Association Ontario Medical Association, Section of Obstetrics and Gynaecology Ontario Society of Obstetricians and Gynaecologists Peterborough Community Physicians Peterborough County Medical Society Sandwich Community Health Centre Inc. Sudbury and District Medical Society Toronto Birth Centre
Education	Ottawa-Carleton Headstart Association for Preschools
Police Services	Police Association of Ontario Sudbury Regional Police Association
Service Providers	Children's Aid Society of Ottawa-Carleton Ontario Library Association Parkdale Community Legal Services Pens Project Share Rockview Seniors Co-operative
Environment	Essex Region Conservation Authority Lakehead Region Conservation Authority Niagara-on-the-Lake Conservancy Society Northwatch Wildlands League
Faith	Toronto Christian Resource Centre

Serious Concerns	98 out of 476 (21 per cent)
Sector	**Name**
Advocacy Groups	Access AIDS Committee of Sudbury
	Building a Stronger Involved Community
	Chiefs of Ontario
	Community Action Programmes, Niagara
	Halton Region Coalition for Social Justice
	Income Maintenance Group
	Iroquois Falls Heritage Coalition
	Kitchener-Waterloo Association for Community Living
	Mississauga Professional Networking
	Niagara South Social Safety Network
	Ontario Social Development Council
	Patient Action
	Persons United for Self Help, London
	Peterborough Child Care Forum
	Peterborough Coalition for Social Justice
	Poverty Action Committee
	Social Assistance Recipients' Council
	United Senior Citizens of Ontario
	Waterloo Public Interest Research Group
Fire Services	Kingston Professional Fire Fighters' Association
	London Professional Fire Fighters' Association
	Ontario Professional Fire Fighters' Association
	Ontario Professional Fire Fighters' Association
	Ontario Professional Fire Fighters' Association, District 7
	Windsor Professional Fire Fighters' Association
Labour Organizations	London and Middlesex Ontario English Catholic Teachers' Association
	Ontario Secondary School Teachers' Federation, Porcupine Division
	Steelworkers Organization of Active Retirees
	Waterloo County Women Teachers' Association
Individuals	Ada Lo
	Art Kidd
	Barbara Sullivan
	Caroline Andrew
	Charles Shaver
	David Calvin
	Deborah Kent
	Fred Netherton
	Jane Hughes
	Jaroslav Kotalik

Serious Concerns	98 out of 476 (21 per cent)
Sector	**Name**
	Joe Swan John Dawson Larry Edwards Linda Kemp Megan Walker Michel Labelle Miguel Bonin Robert Richards Rosemary Christinck Shalom Schacter Sheila Davenport Sheila Richardson

Strong Opposition	189 out of 476 (40 per cent)
Sector	**Name**
Municipal Government	South Neebing Community Organization
Individual Businesses	Peter Cassidy Consulting Ski Telemark Ltd.
Health Care Sector	Halton Medical Society Health System Labour Advisory Committee K.N. Reddy – Greater Niagara Medical Society Lakeshore Area Multi-Service Project Niagara Coalition of Registered Nurses Ontario Medical Association Ontario Physiotherapy Association Parkdale Community Health Centre Psychiatry Residents' Association of Toronto Residents of the Clarke Institute South Riverdale Community Health Centre Thunder Bay Medical Society Toronto Mayor's Committee on Aging Toronto Psychoanalytic Society Waterloo Region District Health Council West Central Community Health Centres
Education	Faculty of Social Work, University of Toronto
Police Services	Police Association of Ontario

Strong Opposition	189 out of 476 (40 per cent)
Sector	**Name**
Service Providers	Community Resource Centre of Scarborough Legal Assistance of Windsor Metro Toronto Chinese and Southeast Asian Legal Clinic Parkdale Community Legal Services
Environment	Canadian Environmental Defence Fund Canadian Environmental Law Association Canadian Institute for Environmental Law and Policy Cataraqui Conservation Foundation Pollution Probe Storrington Committee Against Trash
Faith	Interfaith Social Assistance Reform Coalition Scarborough Presbytery United Church of Canada Sisters of Providence of St. Vincent de Paul Toronto Conference of the United Church of Canada United Church of Canada, London Conference
Fire Services	Ontario Professional Fire Fighters' Association Ottawa Professional Fire Fighters' Association Provincial Federation of Ontario Fire Fighters St. Catharines Professional Fire Fighters' Association Sudbury Professional Fire Fighters' Association
Advocacy Groups	Action League of Physically Handicapped Adults AIDS Action Now AIDS Committee of Thunder Bay AIDS Committee of Toronto Alliance of Seniors to Protect Canada's Social Programs Canadian Association of Retired Persons Canadian Grey Panthers Canadian Pensioners Concerned, Ontario Division Child Care Action Network of Ottawa-Carleton Chinese Canadian National Council Coalition of Health Care Workers Communist Party of Ontario Equal Pay Coalition / Coalition pour un salaire égal Feminist Alliance on New Reproductive and Genetic Technologies Grey Association for Better Planning Guelph/Wellington Coalition for Social Justice Halton Region Coalition for Social Justice Kingston AIDS Project

Strong Opposition	189 out of 476 (40 per cent)
Sector	**Name**
	Life*Spin
	London Battered Women's Advocacy Centre
	London Social Planning Council
	Metro Toronto Coalition for Better Child Care
	National Action Committee on the Status of Women
	Northumberland Coalition Against Poverty
	Older Women's Network – Toronto
	Older Women's Network – Ottawa
	Ontario Association for Interval and Transition Houses
	Ontario Coalition for Better Child Care
	Ontario Coalition for Social Justice
	Ontario Coalition of Senior Citizens' Organizations
	Ontario Health Coalition
	Ontario Network of Injured Workers Groups
	Pay Equity Advocacy and Legal Services
	Persons United for Self Help London
	Perth County Coalition for Social Justice
	Peterborough Social Planning Council
	Resistance Against Psychiatry
	Seniors on Guard for Medicare
	Survivors of Medical Abuse
	Thunder Bay Coalition Against Poverty
	Toronto Injured Workers' Advocacy Group
	Toronto People with AIDS Foundation
	Union of Injured Workers
	Waterloo Public Interest Research Group
	Waterloo Regional Coalition for Social Justice
	Waterloo Regional Council of Retirees
	Women Against Bill 26
	York Region Coalition for Social Justice
Labour Organizations	Amalgamated Transit Union
	Canadian Auto Workers
	Canadian Auto Workers Regional Political Action Committee
	Canadian Auto Workers – Canada
	Canadian Auto Workers, Local 1451
	Canadian Auto Workers, Local 1451
	Canadian Auto Workers, Local 1986
	Canadian Auto Workers, Local 444
	Canadian Auto Workers, Locals 1973 and 195
	Canadian Labour Congress
	Canadian Union of Public Employees
	Canadian Union of Public Employees, North Bay
	Canadian Union of Public Employees, Local 1140
	Canadian Union of Public Employees, Local 1214

Strong Opposition	189 out of 476 (40 per cent)
Sector	**Name**
	Canadian Union of Public Employees, Local 870
	Canadian Union of Public Employees, Ontario Division
	Canadian Union of Public Employees, Local 1097
	Canadian Union of Public Employees, Local 1409
	Canadian Union of Public Employees, Local 210
	Canadian Union of Public Employees, Local 369
	Canadian Union of Public Employees, Local 3906
	Canadian Union of Public Employees, Sudbury and Area
	Cdn Union of Public Employees, Durham, Northumberland Kawartha and Haliburton Reg's
	Chatham and District Labour Council
	Communications, Energy and Paperworkers Union, Local 914
	Federation of Women Teachers' Associations of Ontario
	Hamilton and District Labour Council
	Hamilton Steelworkers' Area Council
	International Brotherhood of Electrical Workers, Local 636
	Kingston and District Labour Council
	London and District Labour Council
	Niagara Falls and District Labour Council
	Niagara South Ontario Public School Teachers' Federation
	Northwestern Ontario Steelworkers Area Council
	Ontario English Catholic Teachers' Association
	Ontario Federation of Labour
	Ontario Public Service Employees' Union
	Ontario Public Service Employees' Union Northeast Area Council
	Ontario Public Service Employees' Union, Ambulance Division, Local 264
	Ontario Public Service Employees' Union, Local 645
	Ontario Public Service Employees' Union, Region 3
	Ontario Public Service Employees' Union, Region 3 – Local 345
	Ontario Public Service Employees' Union, Sudbury Region
	Ontario Secondary School Teachers' Federation
	Ontario Secondary School Teachers' Federation, District 30
	Ontario Secondary School Teachers' Federation, District 31
	Ontario Secondary School Teachers' Federation, District 8

Strong Opposition	189 out of 476 (40 per cent)
Sector	**Name**
	Ontario Teachers' Federation / Fédération des enseignantes et des enseignants de l'Ontario
	Ottawa and District Labour Council
	Oxford Regional Labour Council
	Port Colborne and District Labour Council
	Public Service Alliance of Canada
	Queen's University Faculty Association
	Renfrew and District Labour Council
	Sarnia and District Labour Council
	Service Employees' International Union, Local 268
	Service Employees' Union, Local 210
	St. Catharines and District Labour Council
	St. Catharines Labour Council
	Sudbury and District Labour Council
	Thunder Bay and District Labour Council – Health Committee
	Thunder Bay and District Labour Council
	Timmins Women Teachers' Association
	Toronto Teachers' Federation
	United Food and Commercial Workers International Union
	United Steelworkers of America
	United Steelworkers of America District 6 (Ontario)
	United Steelworkers of America, District 6
	United Steelworkers of America, Local 6500
	United Steelworkers of America, Local 677
	Port Colborne and District Labour Council
	Public Service Alliance of Canada
	Queen's University Faculty Association
Individuals	Albert Schumacher
	Bob Callahan
	Chris Archer
	David Winninger
	Doris Grinspun
	Elizabeth Hill
	Elizabeth Rowley
	Eva Gede
	Hanoch Bordan
	Jack Layton
	Jenny Carter
	John Dawson
	Ken Rubin
	Marc Grushcow
	Michael Rachlis
	Michael Weinstock
	Michel Labelle

Strong Opposition	189 out of 476 (40 per cent)
Sector	**Name**
	Monty Mazin
	Pam McConnell
	Peter Tabuns
	Philip Berger
	Raffaele Filice
	Ray Wilson – Niagara Falls Seniors
	Ron Wexler
	Ruth Lunel

Notes

Preface

1 Kristin Rushowy, Robert Benzie, and Rob Ferguson, "Ford Slammed amid U-Turn," *Toronto Star*, September 26, 2023, A3.
2 Isabel Teotonio, "'Scared to Death to Go to School': York Memorial Students Stage Mass Walkout amid Concerns over Violence and Teacher Shortage," *Toronto Star*, December 3, 2022, A6.
3 Joanne Laucius, "Repeal of Bill 28 Fails to Quell Labour Woes," *Ottawa Citizen*, November 17, 2022, A1.
4 Martin Regg Cohn, "Ford Will Pay Price for Overplaying Hand," *Toronto Star*, December 3, 2022, A4.
5 Kellogg, "Workers Versus Austerity," 116–40.
6 Kellogg, "Labour Against Austerity"; "Ontario's Days of Action"; "Sitting-In and Speaking Out"; "Political Economy of Austerity"; "Social Movements"; "Workers Against Austerity."
7 Using this archive had its own complications. *Socialist Worker*, the paper referred to above and which I edited (1995–2006) while it was bi-weekly, and co-edited (1987–94) when it was published monthly, was a paper published within a specific political framework. Aspects of this framework I now find limited, in particular, a tendency to reduce the problems of the era to the absence of a political left modelled on the early years of the Russian Revolution – see Kellogg, "Voice of Iulii Martov," 1–32; *"Truth Behind Bars."* That said, the specific coverage of the Days of Action does, I think, stand the test of time. For reasons not relevant to the narrative being developed here, I and a few others ended our association with that paper in 2013. See Bakan and Kellogg, "Sexism and the Left."
8 Christopher Reynolds, "Métro Média to Declare Bankruptcy as Local Journalism Takes Another Hit," *Canadian Press*, September 17, 2023, https://toronto.citynews.ca/2023/09/17/metro-media-to-declare-bankruptcy-as-local-journalism-takes-another-hit/.

9 Kellogg, *Escape from the Staple Trap*, xxiii.
10 Sam Gindin, "Peterborough and Beyond," *Contact* 26, no. 25 (July 7, 1996).

Introduction

1 James Rusk, "Major Unions Withdraw from Protests," *Globe and Mail*, November 8, 1996, A8.
2 Henry Hess, "Ontario Unions Set Out Plan to Unseat Tories," *Globe and Mail*, November 27, 1997, A6.
3 Richard Mackie, "Pickets Put Aside to Launch Campaign," *Globe and Mail*, July 28, 1998, A3.
4 Paul Kellogg, "Heads of Unions Cancel General Strike," *PolEconJournal*, August 3, 1998, https://poleconjournal.com/heads-of-unions/.
5 Kellogg, "Workers Versus Austerity," 134; cf. Paul Kellogg, "Can Mike Harris Win?," *PolEconJournal*, May 10, 1999, https://poleconjournal.com/can-mike-harris-win/.
6 Ian Urquhart, "OFL's Wilson Bows Out with a Bang," *Toronto Star*, November 22, 1997, C5.
7 Luxemburg, "The Mass Strike," 192.
8 Luxemburg, "The Mass Strike," 191.
9 Luxemburg, "The Mass Strike," 192.
10 Hyman, *Sociology of Trade Unionism*.
11 Hyman, "Workplace Trade Unionism," 54.
12 Hyman, "Workplace Trade Unionism," 64 n4.
13 Schwarz, *Lénine et le mouvement syndical*, 82–5; Tosstorff, *Red International of Labour Unions*.

Chapter 1

1 Elections Ontario, "Election Results."
2 Aikenhead, "The End of an Accord."
3 Steve Paikin, "Thirty Years Later, a Look Back at the Biggest Ontario Majority Government Ever," TVO Today, September 11, 2017, https://www.tvo.org/article/thirty-years-later-a-look-back-at-the-biggest-ontario-majority-government-ever.
4 Denise Harrington and Alan Christie, "Peterson Takes Over as Premier of Ontario," *Toronto Star*, June 26, 1985, A1.
5 Gerald Caplan, "Ontario NDP Comes of Age at Convocation Hall," *Toronto Star*, October 7, 1990, B3.
6 Elections Ontario, "Election Results."
7 Rachlis and Wolfe, "Insiders' View," 335.
8 Statistics Canada, "Unemployment Rate (Rate); Both Sexes."

9 Rachlis and Wolfe, "An Insiders' View," 336.
10 Rachlis and Wolfe, "An Insiders' View," 335–6.
11 Tanguay, "'Not in Ontario!'" 24; Rachlis and Wolfe, "An Insiders' View," 338.
12 Statistics Canada, "Canada; Unemployment Rate (Rate); Both Sexes."
13 Rachlis and Wolfe, "An Insiders' View," 340.
14 Donaldson, "Ontario Insurance Crisis," 376.
15 Gene Allen, "Ontario Pushes Through Car Insurance Bill," *Globe and Mail*, May 29, 1990, A1.
16 Elizabeth Payne, "Ont. to Get No-Fault Insurance," *Ottawa Citizen*, September 16, 1989, A1.
17 Tony Van Alphen, "Keep No-Fault Plan, Auto Insurers Urge," *Toronto Star*, September 8, 1990, C1.
18 Thomas Parry, "Critics Attack No-Fault Automobile Insurance Plan," *Globe and Mail*, September 18, 1989, A13. For a thoughtful survey of Kormos's career, see Savage, *Socialist Cowboy*.
19 Lawrence Welsh, "Report on Insurance: Industry Decries Lack of Discussion on Auto Plan," *Globe and Mail*, August 20, 1991, C1.
20 George Brett, "5,000 Protest Insurance Plans," *Toronto Star*, August 16, 1991, C1.
21 Rachlis and Wolfe, "An Insiders' View," 341.
22 Reshef and Rastin, *Unions in the Time of Revolution*, 12.
23 Tanguay, "'Not in Ontario!'" 25.
24 Walkom, *Rae Days*, 136.
25 Leslie Papp, "Rae Given a Rough Ride at Emotional Convention," *Toronto Star*, December 1, 1991, B4.
26 Virginia Galt, "Public Servants Walk Out on Rae," *Globe and Mail*, November 27, 1991, A4; Ron DeRuyter, "Union Members Stage Walkout on Rae Speech," *Kitchener-Waterloo Record*, November 27, 1991, A1; Papp, "Rae Given a Rough Ride."
27 Galt, "Public Servants Walk Out."
28 Rapaport, *No Justice, No Peace*, 68.
29 DeRuyter, "Union Members Stage Walkout."
30 Galt, "Public Servants Walk out on Rae."
31 Ron DeRuyter, "Kitchener Labor Leader Criticizes Walkout at OFL," *Kitchener-Waterloo Record*, November 28, 1991, A4.
32 Papp, "Rae Given a Rough Ride."
33 Joe Friesen, "Faculty Groups Seek Legal Aid in Response to Ontario Plan to Cut Salaries of Elderly Professors Drawing Pensions," *Globe and Mail*, May 15, 2019, A6.
34 Rapaport, *No Justice, No Peace*, 68.
35 Walkom, *Rae Days*, 131.

36 Ryan, *A Grander Vision*, 150.
37 The database from which these figures come includes the entire provincial government workforce, not simply OPSEU members. However, it gives a good sense of the scale of the job losses because, according to Rapaport, OPSEU at the time represented about three-quarters of the Ontario Public Sector workforce. Rapaport, *No Justice, No Peace*, 43.
38 Statistics Canada, "Public Sector Employment."
39 Quoted in David McNally, "Union leaders dither but activists continue the fight," *Socialist Worker* (Toronto), no. 188 (June 1993): 2. From 1987 until 1994, David and I co-edited *Socialist Worker*.
40 Ryan, *A Grander Vision*, 150–1.
41 This according to both myself and Abbie Bakan, present at the November 5, 1993 panel entitled "After the Election: What Way Forward for the Left," in which Layton spoke together with Carolyn Egan. "Build the Socialist Alternative," *Socialist Worker* (Toronto), no. 193 (November 1993): 14.
42 Emilia Casella, "OFL Splits Over Support for NDP," *Ottawa Citizen*, November 23, 1993, A3.
43 Ontario Federation of Labour, "Political Action"; Quoted in Reshef and Rastin, "Sins of Commission," 137–8.
44 Ziedenberg, "Labour's Dirty Secret," 16–21.
45 Hugh Winsor, "Did the New Democrats and Berlin Wall Fall Together?," *Globe and Mail*, April 29, 1994, A7.
46 Virginia Galt, "Leaders Fight to Unite Unions: 'Pink-Paper Crowd' Works to Elect NDP," *Globe and Mail*, May 7, 1994, A6.
47 "Rethinking Our Mission in Ontario," 12–13, quoted in Paolone, "NDP-Labour Relations," 83.
48 Lisa Wright, "Labor's Love Not Totally Lost NDP Insists," *Toronto Star*, April 15, 1995, B5.
49 Paul Kellogg, "How Bob Rae Destroyed His Base," *PolEconJournal*, May 15, 1995, https://poleconjournal.com/how-bob-rae/.

Chapter 2

1 Murray Campbell, "Tory Spending Revelations a Bitter Pill from Harris Era," *Globe and Mail*, March 27, 2004, A8.
2 Walkom, "The Harris Government," 412.
3 Walkom, "The Harris Government," 403.
4 Walkom, "The Harris Government," 402–4.
5 Reshef and Rastin, *Unions in the Time of Revolution*, 17.
6 Walkom, "The Harris Government," 404.
7 Paul Kellogg, "Mike Harris as Brian Mulroney – Return of the Living Dead," *PolEconJournal*, June 12, 1995, https://poleconjournal.com/mike-harris/.

8 See in particular Hall, "Great Moving Right Show," 14–20; Harvey, *Brief History of Neoliberalism*; and Duménil and Lévy, *Capital Resurgent*.
9 Miliband, "Class War Conservatism," 278–80.
10 Camfield, "Assessing Resistance," 307.
11 Nesbitt, "Days of Action," ii.
12 Bakan and Kobayashi, "Affirmative Action," 147.
13 Bouie, "How Trump Happened"; Morrison, "Mourning for Whiteness"; Kellogg, "Psychological Wage," 50–61.
14 Cranston-Reimer, "Homophobia, Misogyny & Race"; Judith Timson, "Wynne Is Crushingly Unpopular – Why?," *Toronto Star*, April 6, 2018; Rob Salerno, "Is Homophobia What's Sinking Kathleen Wynne?," *Xtra*, May 25, 2018, https://www.dailyxtra.com/is-homophobia-whats-sinking-kathleen-wynne-86870; Bob Hepburn, "Is Wynne So Hated Because She's a Woman?," *Toronto Star*, January 11, 2018, A13; Kellogg, "'Backlash,'" 21–5.
15 Angus Reid, "Premiers' Performance."
16 David Shum, "Kathleen Wynne Remains Most Unpopular Premier in Canada: Poll," *Global News*, March 22, 2018, https://globalnews.ca/news/4099335/kathleen-wynne-unpopular-premier-poll/.
17 CBC News, "Ontario Votes 2018: Results," *CBC News*, June 7, 2018, https://newsinteractives.cbc.ca/onvotes/results.
18 Rob Ferguson, "Cloud of Suspicion Lifted off Liberals," *Toronto Star*, October 25, 2017, A10.
19 Enzo DiMatteo, "Scandals Reveal Conflict, Corruption and Cult of Personality Surrounding Doug Ford," *NOW Magazine* (Toronto), December 5, 2018, https://web.archive.org/web/20190330051604/https://nowtoronto.com/news/doug-ford-opp-hydro/.
20 Graefe and Hudson, "Poverty and Policy," 320.
21 Tanguay, "'Not in Ontario!'" 28.
22 Galabuzi, "Unequal Futures," 479.
23 Dyck, "Context of Ontario Politics," 50.
24 Bakan and Kobayashi, "Affirmative Action," 156.
25 Tanguay, "'Not in Ontario!'" 29.
26 Bakan and Kobayashi, "Affirmative Action," 160.
27 Walkom, "The Harris Government," 404.
28 Bakan and Kobayashi, "Ontario: Lessons," 9.
29 York University, "F0225 - Reg Whitaker Fonds."
30 Ontario, "Employment Equity Act."
31 Reg Whitaker, "The Cutting Edge of Ontario's Bad Law," *Globe and Mail*, January 6, 1994, A19.
32 Whitaker, "The Cutting Edge," A19.
33 "CAW Refuses to Join in 'Inequity' Hearings," *Contact* 25, no. 42 (December 3, 1995).

34 Cole et al., *Commission on Systemic Racism*.
35 Morgan, "Populism and Racism," 28.
36 Morgan, "Populism and Racism," 29.
37 Anderson, *White Rage*, 3.
38 Bakan and Kobayashi, "Ontario: Lessons," 13.
39 Quoted in Michael Den Tandt, "Mike Harris Thrashes New Democrats, Invites Reformers Back into PC Fold," *Kingston Whig-Standard*, June 22, 1991, 3.
40 Rosemary Speirs, "Ontario Lurches to the Right," *Toronto Star*, June 10, 1995, B1; Paul Arnold, "Mike Harris Follows Reform Agenda," *Financial Post*, June 15, 1995, 14.
41 James Walker, "Mike Harris's 'Alliance' with Manning Makes Little Sense," *Financial Post*, September 2, 1995, 16.
42 Parliament of Canada, "Elections and Candidates."
43 Canadian Press, "Manning Ad Takes Shot at Pro-Quebecers," *Record* (Kitchener), May 24, 1997, A4.
44 Elsewhere I have developed this analysis in detail. Kellogg, "'Backlash.'"
45 Munro, "Ontario's 'Days of Action,'" 137.
46 Martin Mittelstaedt, "Ontario Election 1995 – Tories Get a Boost from Bay Street," *Globe and Mail*, May 27, 1995, A5.
47 Elections Ontario, "Election Results."
48 Turk, "Days of Action," 166.
49 Ziedenberg, "Great Day in Hamilton," 17, 19.
50 Ziedenberg, "Great Day in Hamilton," 20.
51 Ziedenberg, "Labour's Dirty Secret," 18.
52 Quoted in Ziedenberg, "Labour's Dirty Secret," 16–17.
53 Quoted in Ziedenberg, "Labour's Dirty Secret," 18.
54 Quoted in Ziedenberg, "Labour's Dirty Secret," 19.
55 Quoted in Ziedenberg, "Labour's Dirty Secret," 19.
56 Quoted in Don Lajoie and Star Wire Services, "Disgruntled Members Urge CAW to Break Ties to NDP," *The Windsor Star*, February 6, 1993, A7.
57 Brian Cross, "Anti-NDP Petitions Gain Steam," *The Windsor Star*, March 15, 1993, A3.
58 Lajoie and Star Wire Services, "Disgruntled Members."
59 Canadian Press, "Manning Woos Local That Dumped NDP," *The Windsor Star*, May 28, 1993, A11.
60 Quoted in DeRuyter, "Kitchener Labor Leader."
61 Carolyn Egan, "Ontario Labour and the NDP: The End of the Truce," *Socialist Worker* (Toronto), no. 172 (December 1991): 3.
62 Lorne Slotnick, "Welfare Worker Squeaks in to Head Civil Service Union," *Globe and Mail*, November 5, 1984, M3.

63 Jessa Sultan, "Jail Will Close Doors in February," *Standard-Freeholder* (Cornwall), October 6, 2001, 3; Glen Nott, "Angry Union Protesters Greet MPPs," *Hamilton Spectator*, March 31, 1993, B4.
64 David Vienneau, "Ontario Police Poised for Anti-NDP Campaign," *Toronto Star*, August 11, 1992, A2.
65 Alan Fotheringham, "Police Chief Leads Civil Disobedience Campaign," *Financial Post*, October 15, 1994, S3.
66 Morgan, "Populism and Racism," 28.
67 Gittens et al., *Racism Behind Bars*, 15.
68 Gittens et al., *Racism Behind Bars*, 17.
69 Gittens et al., *Racism Behind Bars*, 17.
70 Virginia Galt, "Upshaw Beats Racism to Reach Top," *Globe and Mail*, May 4, 1991, A5.
71 Quoted in Galt, "Upshaw Beats Racism," A5.
72 Virginia Galt, "Public Servants Re-Elect Upshaw to Lead 'Fight,'" *Globe and Mail*, April 17, 1993, A5.
73 Tony Van Alphen, "Upset Win for New OPSEU Leader," *Toronto Star*, April 29, 1995, A21.
74 Kelly Toughill, "Rae Blames Gays for Same-Sex Rights Bill Loss," *Toronto Star*, March 14, 1995, A14.
75 Rayside, *On the Fringe*, 144.
76 Quoted in Rayside, *On the Fringe*, 146.
77 Elections Ontario, "Election Results."
78 Quoted in Toughill, "Rae Blames Gays."
79 "How MPPs Voted on Controversial Legislation," *Globe and Mail*, June 10, 1994, A10.
80 Kelly Grant, "Ford, Mammoliti Bury the Hatchet," *Globe and Mail*, September 22, 2010, A14.

Chapter 3

1 Laurie Monsebraaten, "Protesters, Police Clash at Queen's Park," *Toronto Star*, September 28, 1995, A16.
2 James Rusk, "Ontario Unions Target London for Shutdown," *Globe and Mail*, November 14, 1995, A3; Paul Kellogg, "Make London a Beginning," *PolEconJournal*, December 5, 1995, https://poleconjournal.com/make-london-a-beginning/.
3 Peter Small, "Crackdown on Welfare Fraud Called Pre-Election Gimmick," *Toronto Star*, March 30, 1994, A10.
4 Quoted in Small, "Crackdown on Welfare Fraud," A10.
5 Department of Finance Canada, "Table 45: Adjusted Budget Balances."

6 Oliver et al., "UK Prepares 'Doomsday' Cuts Plan"; White, "Taking an Axe," 8.
7 Lavigne, *Building the Orange Wave*, 78.
8 Department of Finance Canada. "Table 11: Major Transfers"; Statistics Canada, "Consumer Price Index, Monthly"; Statistics Canada, "Population Estimates"; Statistics Canada, "Estimates of Population, by Age Group and Sex."
9 Senate of Canada, "The Health of Canadians," 9.
10 Senate of Canada, "The Health of Canadians," 15.
11 Quoted in Martin Mittelstaedt, "Harris Supports Cutting Federal Transfer Payments," *Globe and Mail*, June 29, 1995, A1; See also Dare, "Harris's First Year," 20.
12 Quoted in Daniel Girard, "Premier Wants $6 Billion Restored; Demands Ottawa Hand Back Cuts in Transfer Payments," *Toronto Star*, January 13, 1999, A1.
13 Oliver et al., "UK Prepares 'Doomsday' Cuts Plan."
14 "January 25 – Magnificent!" *Socialist Worker* (Toronto), no. 208 (February 8, 1995): 4.
15 "Canadian Students Rally Against Federal Cuts," *Contact* 25, no. 4 (January 27, 1995).
16 Stan Josey, "At General Motors, Many Were Called, None Chosen," *Ottawa Citizen*, January 9, 1996, A4. An iconic photograph of thousands lining up for jobs at GM in 1995 is available here – https://www.communitystories.ca/v2/oshawa-automotive-community_communaute-automobile/gallery/gm-job-applicants-1995/.
17 Carolyn Egan, "A Shot of Adrenalin," *Socialist Worker* (Toronto), March 8, 1995.
18 Canadian Press, "Harris Hit List Names Photo Radar, Bureaucrats and Public Housing," *Canadian Press Newswire*, June 28, 1995, http://search.proquest.com.
19 Daniel Girard and Vicki White, "385 Housing Projects Dropped," *Toronto Star*, July 26, 1995, A1; Peter Small, "Closing Bill on Eglinton $42 Million, TTC Figures," *Toronto Star*, August 3, 1995, A3.
20 William Walker, "The Axe Falls 3 Weeks in Power, Tories Chop $1.9 Billion in Spending," *Toronto Star*, July 22, 1995, A1.
21 Small, "Closing Bill on Eglinton."
22 Ibbitson, *Promised Land*, 140.
23 "The Harris Government Budget: A Summary," *Contact* 25, no. 42 (December 3, 1995).
24 MacDermid and Albo, "Divided Province, Growing Protests," 163–202.
25 Martin Mittelstaedt, "Ontario Launches Workfare amid Jeers," *Globe and Mail*, June 13, 1996, A10.

26 Statistics Canada, "Labour Force Survey Estimates."
27 David Israelson, "'We'll Be Back,' Gays Warn," *Toronto Star*, June 3, 1995, A22.
28 "Build the Resistance," *Socialist Worker* (Toronto), no. 217 (June 14, 1995): 3.
29 Laurie Monsebraaten, "Social Activists Disappointed by Lack of Women in Cabinet," *Toronto Star*, June 27, 1995, A9.
30 "Interview with Kam Rao."
31 Monsebraaten, "Social Activists Disappointed."
32 Richard Brennan and John Ibbitson, "Protesters Call for His Political Head as Harris Is Sworn In," *Hamilton Spectator*, June 27, 1995, A2.
33 Monsebraaten, "Social Activists Disappointed."
34 Tony Van Alphen, "Labor to Stand Fast on Legislated Gains," *Toronto Star*, June 10, 1995, A12.
35 Van Alphen, "Labor to Stand Fast," A12.
36 Tony Van Alphen, "Unions Predict 'Struggle in the Streets,'" *Toronto Star*, June 21, 1995, A21.
37 Phyllis Waugh, "Relaunch the Fight," *Socialist Worker* (Toronto), no. 218 (July 5, 1995): 10.
38 John Sewell, "New Tack, Not More Demos, Needed in Welfare Fight," *NOW Magazine* (Toronto), no. 708 (August 17, 1995): 21.
39 Jane Gadd, "Metro Gives Day-Care Centres Reprieve from Provincial Cuts," *Globe and Mail*, August 18, 1995, A3.
40 Kelly Toughill, "Pay Equity for 80,000 Likely to Be Killed," *Toronto Star*, July 19, 1995; Laurie Monsebraaten, "Day-Care Cuts Called an Attack on Children," *Toronto Star*, July 21, 1995, A6; Paul Kellogg, "Solidarity Against the Cuts," *PolEconJournal*, July 24, 1995, https://poleconjournal.com/solidarity/.
41 "Protesters Attack Tories' Plan for Cuts," *Toronto Star*, July 20, 1995, A8.
42 Gadd, "Metro Gives Day-Care Centres Reprieve."
43 Canadian Press, "Lesbians and Gays Target Harris During Toronto Parade," *Canadian Press NewsWire*, July 2, 1995, http://search.proquest.com.
44 Laurie Monsebraaten and Paul Moloney, "Needy Left with $6.50 a Day," *Toronto Star*, July 22, 1995, A10..
45 Ziedenberg, "The Counter Revolution," 6–8.
46 Paul Kellogg, "A Demo a Week Keeps the Tories at Bay," *PolEconJournal*, August 7, 1995, https://poleconjournal.com/a-demo-a-week/.
47 Tracey Tyler, "500 Protest 'Shameful' Harris Cuts," *Toronto Star*, July 30, 1995, A2.
48 Denise Lachance, "Opposition to Workfare Grows," *Socialist Worker* (Toronto), no. 220 (August 9, 1995): 10.
49 Kellogg, "A Demo a Week."

50 Rob Andrus, "Protesters Pitch Tents to Oppose Co-Op Cuts," *Toronto Star*, August 6, 1995, A11.
51 John Clarke, "OCAP Marks Its First 20 Years," rabble.ca, December 3, 2010, http://rabble.ca/news/2010/12/ocap-marks-its-first-20-years; Paul Kellogg, "They Profit, We Suffer," *PolEconJournal*, September 4, 1995, https://poleconjournal.com/they-profit-we-suffer/.
52 Ziedenberg, "The Counter Revolution," 6–7.
53 "Marchers Pitch Camp Harrisville to Protest Cuts," *Contact* 25, no. 36 (October 22, 1995).
54 "Feed Tories Bologna," *Contact* 25, no. 37 (October 29, 1995).
55 "Anti-Harris Campaign," *Contact* 25, no. 37 (October 29, 1995).
56 Monsebraaten, "Day-Care Cuts."
57 Laurie Monsebraaten, "Critics Condemn Plan to Change Day-Care Funding," *Toronto Star*, November 3, 1995, A12.
58 Heather Greenwood, "Day-Care Children Speak Out on Cuts," *Toronto Star*, November 8, 1995, A6.
59 Laurie Monsebraaten, "Kids Hurt by Drastic Cuts, Say Protesters," *Toronto Star*, November 14, 1995, A10.
60 "Ontario Day-Care Workers Organize One Day Strike," *Contact* 25, no. 41 (November 26, 1995).
61 John Ibbitson, "Ontario's Budget Battle: Day-Care Centres Shut Their Doors to Protest Cuts," *Ottawa Citizen*, November 25, 1995, A1.
62 Jane Gadd, "Thousands Rally to Support Day Care," *Globe and Mail*, November 25, 1995, A10.
63 Kellogg, "Solidarity Against the Cuts." The story of the remarkable 1981 hospital strike is best told in a short pamphlet written by my friend Ron Rosenthal, a rank-and-file CUPE participant in the strike. Just thirty-two years old, Ron tragically passed away in 1982. Rosenthal, *Where Is CUPE Going?*

Chapter 4

1 Apologies to The Clash, *London Calling*.
2 "Rising Anger Sparks Major Protest Against Harris Government," *Contact* 25, no. 34 (October 1, 1995).
3 Paul Kellogg, "All out Sept. 27," *PolEconJournal*, September 17, 1995, https://poleconjournal.com/all-out-sept-27/.
4 Monsebraaten, "Protesters, Police Clash."
5 "Ontario – Strike Action Can Stop the Tories," *Socialist Worker* (Toronto), no. 226 (November 1, 1995): 12.
6 Ziedenberg, "The Counter Revolution," 6; Monsebraaten, "Protesters, Police Clash"; Rapaport, *No Justice, No Peace*, 57; "Rising Anger."

7 Jane Gadd, "Police Push Back Demonstrators," *Globe and Mail*, September 28, 1995, A1; Martin Mittelstaedt, "Protests Mark Throne Speech," *Globe and Mail*, September 28, 1995, A1.
8 Turk, "Days of Action," 165.
9 Turk, "Days of Action," 165.
10 Rapaport, *No Justice, No Peace*, 57.
11 Martin Mittelstaedt, "Harris Eyes $9-Billion Budget Chop," *Globe and Mail*, September 26, 1995, A1.
12 Carolyn Egan, "The OFL Must Give a Lead," *Socialist Worker* (Toronto), no. 224 (October 4, 1995): 10.
13 Watson, "Ontario Workers," 138.
14 Watson, "Ontario Workers," 136.
15 Greg Crone, "Repeal Bill 40 and Jobs Will Come, Witmer Says," *Record* (Kitchener), August 26, 1995, A1.
16 Rapaport, *No Justice, No Peace*, 46.
17 Richard Brennan, "Civil Servants' Union Rights Threatened," *Hamilton Spectator*, October 14, 1995, A3.
18 Steve Cannon, "Unions Plan General Strike," *Record* (Kitchener), November 2, 1995, A3.
19 "CAW Top Leadership Endorsed Workplace Action to Challenge Bill 7," *Contact* 25, no. 38 (November 5, 1995).
20 Ted Shaw, "Big 3 Auto Makers Brace for Walkouts in Possible General Strike Action," *Hamilton Spectator*, October 31, 1995, E7.
21 Quoted in Shaw, "Big 3 Auto Makers," E7.
22 International Socialists, "Ontario Branches."
23 Cannon, "Unions Plan General Strike," A3.
24 Shaw, "Big 3 Auto Makers," E7.
25 Gindin, *Canadian Auto Workers*, 254–82.
26 Theresa Boyle, "Labor Vows Storm over Bill 7," *Toronto Star*, November 17, 1995, 3.
27 Quoted in Paul Kellogg, "We Can Strike, We Can Win," *PolEconJournal*, November 14, 1995, https://poleconjournal.com/we-can-strike-we-can-win/.
28 Quoted in La Botz, "Ontario's 'Days of Action.'"
29 Quoted in La Botz, "Ontario's 'Days of Action.'"
30 Quoted in "Chrysler and CAW Ask Harris to Reconsider Labour Law Changes," *Contact* 25, no. 34 (October 1, 1995).
31 Quoted in "Chrysler and CAW."
32 Quoted in Reshef and Rastin, *Unions in the Time of Revolution*, 139.
33 Quoted in Reshef and Rastin, *Unions in the Time of Revolution*, 139.
34 Kellogg, "Make London a Beginning."
35 Munro, "Ontario's 'Days of Action,'" 125.
36 "CAW Council, December 8–10," *Contact* 25, no. 44 (December 18, 1995).

37 Black Rose Books Editorial Collective, *Quebec Labour*, 197–209.
38 Canadian Labour Congress, "Largest Labour Protest."
39 "A Time to Build, Not Divide in Ontario," *Contact* 25, no. 32 (September 18, 1995).
40 "OFL Convention Delegates Support London Protest," *Contact* 25, no. 41 (November 26, 1995).
41 Jack Lakey and Edwards, "Mass Action Slows City Life to Trickle," *Toronto Star*, December 12, 1995, A1.
42 Paul Kellogg, "Ontario – Stop the Cuts, Stop the Victimizations," *PolEconJournal*, January 8, 1996, https://poleconjournal.com/ontario-stop-the-cuts/.
43 Richard Brennan, "Next Strike to Hit Hamilton during Tory Convention," *Ottawa Citizen*, January 18, 1996, A3.
44 Randall Scotland, "GM, Ford Hit by Protest," *Financial Post*, December 12, 1995, 8.
45 Lakey and Edwards, "Mass Action Slows City Life," A1.
46 Turk, "Days of Action," 167.
47 "There Will Be Another City and Another and Another …," *Contact* 25, no. 44 (December 18, 1995).
48 Scotland, "GM, Ford Hit by Protest."
49 Lakey and Edwards, "Mass Action Slows City Life," A1.
50 Lakey and Edwards, "Mass Action Slows City Life," A1.
51 "From Paris to London," *Contact* 25, no. 44 (December 18, 1995).
52 Ground Zero Productions, "London Calling." Evans was not alone in this. Many of us at the time – including *NOW Magazine*'s Enzo Di Matteo, could not resist referencing the famous album by The Clash when referring to this first Day of Action. Enzo Di Matteo, "Strike One! Is the Successful London Shutdown a Prelude to More Robust Actions across the Province?," *NOW Magazine* (Toronto), December 14, 1995, 18.
53 Statistics Canada, "Population Estimates"; Statistics Canada, "Person-Days Not Worked"; Statistics Canada, "Estimates of Population"; Statistics Canada, "Estimates of Population, by Age Group and Sex"; Employment and Social Development Canada, "Work Stoppages."
54 Crenshaw, "Mapping the Margins," 1241–99; Crenshaw, "Demarginalizing the Intersection," 139–67.
55 Sam Gindin, "London, December 11, 1995 What Does It Mean, What Does It Change?," *Contact* 25, no. 44 (December 18, 1995).

Chapter 5

1 Ibbitson, *Promised Land*, 131.
2 Ibbitson, *Promised Land*, 135.
3 Ibbitson, *Promised Land*, 141.

4 Ibbitson, *Promised Land*, 136, 140.
5 Ontario, "Committee Transcripts," Bill 26.
6 Paul Kellogg, "Omnibus Bill – an Attack on Democracy, Jobs and Services," *PolEconJournal*, January 21, 1996, https://poleconjournal.com/omnibus-bill/.
7 "Fight over Omnibus Bill Brings Legislature to a Halt. Liberals Link Arms to Protect Colleague in Legislature," *Canadian Press NewsWire*, December 6, 1995, http://search.proquest.com.
8 Greg Crone and Richard Brennan, "Opposition Protest Brings Legislature to Standstill," *Record* (Kitchener), December 7, 1995, A1.
9 Ibbitson, *Promised Land*, 144.
10 Ontario, "Committee Transcripts - 1996-Jan-22 [Debate]."
11 Ibbitson, *Promised Land*, 147.
12 Martin Mittelstaedt, "Hearings on Omnibus Bill Turn Stormy Outside Toronto," *Globe and Mail*, January 9, 1996, A7.
13 Ontario, "Committee Transcripts."
14 Rapaport, *No Justice, No Peace*, 60.
15 Samantha Beattie, "Holocaust Lessons Lead to Life of Protest," *Toronto Star*, September 14, 2018, A8.

Chapter 6

1 Title borrowed from the late John Bell, "Steeltown Shutdown," *Socialist Worker* (Toronto), no. 233 (March 6, 1996): 9. John and I together covered many of the Days of Action protests. After a long illness, he tragically passed away in 2024. Paul Kellogg, "John Arthur Bell: 1955–2024," *PolEconJournal*, February 9, 2025, https://poleconjournal.com/john-arthur-bell-1955-2024/.
2 Environics Research Group, "It's a Horse Race."
3 Quoted in Jennifer Lewington, "Ontario Teachers Gear Up to Fight Tory Funding Cuts," *Globe and Mail*, January 11, 1996, A6.
4 The lowest estimate for turnout, 20,000, came from OECTA president Marilies Rettig. The police estimate was 25,000 Canadian Press, "Angry Teachers Descend on Queen's Park for Huge Protest," *Canadian Press NewsWire*, January 13, 1996, http://search.proquest.com. The highest estimate was 37,000 Michael Redfearn, "News That Bleeds Sells," *Record* (Kitchener), January 20, 1996, A8; Jennifer Lewington, "Teachers Union Urges Members to Join PC Party Infiltrating Tories," *Globe and Mail*, April 17, 1996, A7.
5 Kellogg, "Omnibus Bill – an Attack."
6 Daniel Girard, "Hamilton Picked for Next Labor Protest," *Toronto Star*, January 18, 1996, A8.
7 La Botz, "Ontario's 'Days of Action.'"

8 Rapaport, *No Justice, No Peace*, 58.
9 NDP.ca, "Wayne Marston"; Lee Prokaska, "A Year After the Marches: What Good Did They Do?," *Hamilton Spectator*, February 22, 1997, A3; Turk, "Days of Action," 170.
10 Carol Goodwin, "Day-of-Protest Leaders Denied Office Space," *Record* (Kitchener), March 19, 1996, A1; "Rally to Feature Range of Speakers," *Record* (Kitchener), April 17, 1996, B2; Ontario, "Committee Transcript 1997-Aug-12."
11 "Hargrove Urges Full Participation in Peterborough Community Day of Action," *Contact* 26, no. 21 (June 2, 1996).
12 Jack Lakey, "Open & Shut City Labor Says," *Toronto Star*, October 19, 1996, E1; Rapaport, *No Justice, No Peace*, 28.
13 LUFA, "LUFA's Chronology Since 1979"; Cora-Lee Skanes, "CUPE Involved in Sudbury March," *Sault Star*, April 2, 1997, A4.
14 CURC, "Thunder Bay"; Ontario, "Committee Transcripts - 1997-08-06"; Pan, "Judith Mongrain."
15 Kinsman, "Open Letter in Support"; Jim Rankin, "Protesters Take Over 'Mike's Town,'" *Toronto Star*, September 27, 1997, A12; John Tollefsrud, "Rising Tide Buoys Ontario Budget," *North Bay Nugget*, May 3, 2000, A1.
16 Heather Greenwood, "30,000 Likely to March in Windsor's Protest," *Toronto Star*, October 16, 1997, A10; Ontario, "Committee Transcripts - 1996-Jan-8 [Windsor 1]."
17 "St. Catharines: The Next Day of Protest Against Harris," *Contact* 28, no. 7 (March 1, 1998).
18 "Kingston Day of Action: June 8," *Contact* 28, no. 14 (April 19, 1998); Ontario, "Committee Transcript 1992-Aug-27."
19 Rapaport, *No Justice, No Peace*, 59.
20 Turk, "Days of Action," 168–9.
21 Munro, "Ontario's 'Days of Action,'" 129.
22 Reshef and Rastin, *Unions in the Time of Revolution*, 140–1.
23 Reshef and Rastin, *Unions in the Time of Revolution*, 140–1.
24 Turk, "Days of Action," 170.
25 Turk, "Days of Action," 173.
26 Turk, "Days of Action," 174.
27 Munro, "Ontario's 'Days of Action,'" 128.
28 Reshef and Rastin, *Unions in the Time of Revolution*, 141.
29 Rapaport, *No Justice, No Peace*, 85.
30 Rapaport, *No Justice, No Peace*, 27.
31 Quoted in Rapaport, *No Justice, No Peace*, 92.
32 Quoted in Rapaport, *No Justice, No Peace*, 59.
33 Rapaport, *No Justice, No Peace*, 92.

34 Rapaport, *No Justice, No Peace*, 61–2.
35 Rapaport, *No Justice, No Peace*, 9.
36 Ibbitson, *Promised Land*, 159.
37 Ibbitson, *Promised Land*, 154.
38 Ibbitson, *Promised Land*, 155.
39 Kelly Toughill, "Public Servants Vote 66% for Strike," *Toronto Star*, February 19, 1996, A1.
40 Ministry of Labour Ontario, "Table VI".
41 Bell, "Steeltown Shutdown."
42 Sid Ryan, quoted by Prokaska, "A Year After the Marches."
43 Rob Andrus, "Hamilton Prepares for Labor Shutdown," *Toronto Star*, February 22, 1996, A10; Gary Rennie, "25,000 Take Message to 'Harris Dinosaurs,'" *The Windsor Star*, February 24, 1996.
44 Andrus, "Hamilton Prepares."
45 Canadian Press, "Protest Against Ontario Tories Draws Estimated 100,000 (Hamilton)," *Canadian Press NewsWire*, February 24, 1996, http://search.proquest.com.
46 Bob White, "The Strike," *Globe and Mail*, March 1, 1996, A14.
47 Paul Kellogg, "Hamilton Days of Action – One Hundred Thousand Strong," *PolEconJournal*, March 4, 1996, https://poleconjournal.com/hamilton-days-of-action/.
48 "Hamilton Days of Protest: Democracy in Action," *Contact* 26, no. 9 (March 3, 1996).
49 Ibbitson, *Promised Land*, 214.
50 James Rusk, "First Day of Protest Closes Steel City," *Globe and Mail*, February 24, 1996, A1.
51 John Ibbitson, "Public Servants Begin Walkout; 55,300 People Set to Picket in Ontario's Largest-Ever Strike," *Ottawa Citizen*, February 26, 1996.
52 Rapaport, *No Justice, No Peace*, 102–3.
53 Ibbitson, *Promised Land*, 162.
54 Richard Brennan, "Few Support Civil-Service Strike Plan in Ontario," *Vancouver Sun*, February 23, 1996, A3.
55 Mike Davison, "'No Justice, No Peace' Says It All - Be It a Strike or Closing," *Hamilton Spectator*, March 8, 1996, A6.
56 John Ibbitson, "Defiant OPSEU Locals Eager to Turn Strike into Complete Walkout," *Ottawa Citizen*, February 24, 1996, A1.
57 Ibbitson, *Promised Land*, 167.
58 Rapaport, *No Justice, No Peace*, 6.
59 Ibbitson, *Promised Land*, 168.
60 Rapaport, *No Justice, No Peace*, 7.
61 Ibbitson, *Promised Land*, 171.

62 Watson, "Ontario Workers," 140.
63 Ralph and Régimbald, *Open for Business*, 202.
64 Rapaport, *No Justice, No Peace*, 167.
65 Andrew Duffy, "OPSEU Workers Back on the Job," *Toronto Star*, April 1, 1996, A1.
66 Quoted in Ibbitson, *Promised Land*, 176–7.
67 Quoted in Rapaport, *No Justice, No Peace*, 167.
68 Watson, "Ontario Workers," 140.
69 Paul Kellogg, "The Union the Tories Could Not Break," *PolEconJournal*, April 1, 1996, https://poleconjournal.com/union-tories-could-not-break/.
70 Kellogg, "Tories Could Not Break."
71 Kellogg, "Tories Could Not Break."
72 John Ibbitson, "Tory Cuts Mean Less Red Tape, More User Fees," *Ottawa Citizen*, April 12, 1996, A1.
73 Christine Baker, "On the Line with OPSEU: A Union Is Born," *Socialist Worker* (Toronto), no. 234 (March 20, 1996): 2.
74 "Pass These Resolutions," *Socialist Worker* (Toronto), no. 233 (March 6, 1996): 9.
75 Phyllis Waugh, "Why Are OFL Leaders Dithering?," *Socialist Worker* (Toronto), March 20, 1996, 12.
76 Munro, "Ontario's 'Days of Action,'" 127.
77 Munro, "Ontario's 'Days of Action,'" 132–3.
78 "CAW Sets Up Strike Support Committees," *Contact* 26, no. 9 (March 3, 1996).
79 Ibbitson, "Tory Cuts."
80 Eric Beauchesne, "Harris Government to Launch Controversial Workfare Plan," *Ottawa Citizen*, April 12, 1996, A3.
81 Martin O'Hanlon, "Leaders Hail Protest Day: But Critics Say Tories Will Go On with Cuts," *Hamilton Spectator*, April 20, 1996, A1.
82 Luxemburg, "The Mass Strike," 196.
83 Department of Labour Canada, "Table VI (March)"; "Table VII (January)."
84 Brennan, "Next Strike to Hit Hamilton."
85 Department of Labour Canada, "Table VI (July-August)"; "Table IX (March)."
86 Paul Kellogg, "How the Press Turned 25,000 into 50,000," *PolEconJournal*, November 27, 1996, https://poleconjournal.com/how-the-press/.
87 Turk, "Days of Action," 171.
88 Jack Lakey, "Labor Socks Steel City," *Toronto Star*, February 24, 1996, A1.
89 "CAW Shuts Down Hamilton Plants," *Contact* 26, no. 9 (March 3, 1996).

Chapter 7

1 "Kitchener-Waterloo, Cambridge Next Stop in Harris Fightback," *Contact* 26, no. 11 (March 17, 1996).

2 "Waterloo Region Protest: An Anti-Harris Success," *Contact* 26, no. 16 (April 28, 1996); Chris Aagaard, "Mass Protest: Action Day Draws Thousands," *Record* (Kitchener), April 20, 1996, A1; Ron DeRuyter, "Pickets Set Up at 70 Workplaces," *Waterloo Region Record*, April 20, 1996, B1.

3 Quoted in Pauline Finch-Durichen, "Pre-Rally Faith Service Shows Depth of Community Support," *Record* (Kitchener), April 20, 1996, B3.

4 Finch-Durichen, "Pre-Rally Faith Service," B3.

5 Turk, "Days of Action," 172.

6 Quoted in Peter Lee, "Protest by Anti-Poverty Activists Targets Rich," *Times-Colonist* (Victoria), April 19, 1996, 1.

7 Simone Rose, "Teacher Joins Protest to Demonstrate Beliefs," *Record* (Kitchener), April 20, 1996, B2.

8 Quoted in "Pre-Rally Lesson on Local Labor," *Record* (Kitchener), April 20, 1996.

9 Carol Goodwin, "Cheers, Jeers from Upbeat Crowd," *Record* (Kitchener), April 20, 1996, A3; Aagaard, "Mass Protest"; Carolyn Egan, "What Next?," *Socialist Worker* (Toronto), no. 237 (May 1, 1996): 10.

10 Goodwin, "Cheers, Jeers."

11 Richard Brennan, "Head Counters Disagree on Numbers," *Record* (Kitchener), April 20, 1996, A1; Turk, "Days of Action," 172; Prokaska, "A Year After the Marches."

12 "Waterloo Region Protest."

13 Finch-Durichen, "Pre-Rally Faith Service."

14 Royal Commission on Labour, "Report on the Labour Question," 8.

15 Scheinberg, "Tessie the Textile Worker," 175, 182.

16 Elections Ontario, "Election Results."

17 Elections Ontario, "Election Results."

18 Daniel J. Christie, "It's Time to Take Action If It Is 'Our Hospital,'" *Evening Guide* (Port Hope), January 14, 2002, 4.

19 This was same legion hall that would host the funeral reception for the uncle of mine whom I visited in the Mike Harris years when he passed away in 2005. Selena Forsyth, "Remembering Lloyd Kellogg," *Evening Guide* (Port Hope), March 23, 2005, 16.

20 Wilf Day, "Hospital Rift Began with 1997 Meeting," *Evening Guide* (Port Hope), February 9, 2001, 4.

21 Jim Poling, "Hospital Cutbacks Can Damage Harris Opposition Says," *Hamilton Spectator*, October 2, 1996, B3.

22 Gary Rennie, "Peterborough Named for Next Protest Day," *Windsor Star*, May 3, 1996, A5.
23 Elections Ontario, "Election Results."
24 William Walker, "Lavish Dinner Fails to Mend Labor-Tory Rift," *Toronto Star*, May 28, 1996, A10.
25 Martin Mittelstaedt, "Ontario to Ease Employer Rules," *Globe and Mail*, May 14, 1996, B1.
26 Walker, "Lavish Dinner."
27 "1996 Collective Bargaining and Political Action Convention," *Contact* 26, no. 22 (June 9, 1996).
28 "Peterborough – Day of Action," *Contact* 26, no. 25 (July 7, 1996).
29 Prokaska, "A Year after the Marches."
30 Gindin, "Peterborough and Beyond."
31 Barbara Shecter, "Ontario's Roving Labor Protest Stalls Peterborough for a Day," *Financial Post*, June 25, 1996, 22.
32 Wendy McCann, "Peterborough Protest Packs Little Punch," *Ottawa Citizen*, June 25, 1996, A4.
33 Turk, "Days of Action," 174.
34 Jack Lakey, "Anti-Tory Labor Rally Causes Barely a Ripple," *Toronto Star*, June 25, 1996, A2.
35 Canadian Press, "Labour Protest Call Falls on Deaf Ears in Tory City," *Hamilton Spectator*, June 25, 1996, A9.
36 "Peterborough – Day of Action."
37 Gindin, "Peterborough and Beyond."
38 Eaton, "Jockeying for Survival," 10.
39 Patrick Brethour, "Hotel Strike Ends with 3-Year Deal," *Globe and Mail, Report on Business*, August 6, 1996, B2.
40 "Westin Hotel Workers Win," *Socialist Worker* (Toronto), no. 242 (August 10, 1996): 12.
41 Kuya Gwaan, "Westin Workers Fight for Survival," *Socialist Worker* (Toronto), no. 242 (August 10, 1996): 10.

Chapter 8

1 Quoted in James Rusk, Michael Grange, and Martin Mittelstaedt, "Rally Leaders Elated by New Coalition," *Globe and Mail*, October 28, 1996, A10.
2 "CAW Gears Up For Toronto Protest on October 25 and 26," *Contact* 26, no. 30 (September 8, 1996).
3 Quoted in Reshef and Rastin, *Unions in the Time of Revolution*, 139.
4 Ziedenberg, "Metro Toronto Days of Action," 9.
5 Quoted in La Botz, "Ontario's 'Days of Action.'"

6 "CAW Front and Centre on Labour Day," *Contact* 26, no. 30 (September 8, 1996).
7 Quoted in Christine Cox, "Labour Targets Harris: Workers Remember the Past and Unite for the Future," *Hamilton Spectator*, September 3, 1996, B1.
8 "CAW Front and Centre."
9 Maude Barlow, "Where Was The Globe?," *Globe and Mail, Letter to the Editor*, September 5, 1996, A16.
10 Paul Kellogg, "After Peterborough … Toronto," *PolEconJournal*, June 18, 1996, https://poleconjournal.com/after-peterborough/.
11 Paul Kellogg, "The Time to Strike Is Now," *PolEconJournal*, October 2, 1996, https://poleconjournal.com/time-to-strike/.
12 Tony Van Alphen and Donovan Vincent, "Head-on Collision," *Toronto Star*, November 2, 1996, C1.
13 Van Alphen and Vincent, "Head-on Collision," C1.
14 "CAW On Strike Against General Motors of Canada," *Contact* 26, no. 33 (October 16, 1996).
15 Haglund, "CAW's Actions," A12.
16 Quoted in Heather Greenwood, "U.S. Unions Offer Boost to Pickets in Windsor," *Toronto Star*, October 15, 1996, A11.
17 Tony Van Alphen and Donovan Vincent, "Strikers Steaming over GM Profits," *Toronto Star*, October 16, 1996, A4.
18 Quoted in Paul Kellogg, "CAW - 'We're Occupying to Save Our Jobs,'" *PolEconJournal*, October 16, 1996, https://poleconjournal.com/caw-occupation/.
19 Hargrove and Skene, *Labour of Love*, 166.
20 Tony Van Alphen, "Storming the Gates," *Toronto Star*, October 19, 1996, D1.
21 Ian Jack, "GM, CAW Set Deadline for Deal," *Financial Post*, October 17, 1996, 1.
22 "The GM Strike [Transcript]," *CTV National News* (CTV, October 16, 1996), http://search.proquest.com.
23 Quoted in Kellogg, "Occupying to Save Our Jobs.'"
24 "CAW Delegates Approve Special Dues Assessment If GM Strike Continues," *Contact* 26, no. 34 (October 22, 1996).
25 "CAW Membership at General Motors Vote Overwhelmingly in Favour of New Agreement," *Contact* 26, no. 35 (October 27, 1996).
26 Quoted in La Botz, "Ontario's 'Days of Action.'"
27 Nicolaas van Rijn, "Harris Rejects Victory Claim by Protesters," *Toronto Star*, October 26, 1996, A1.
28 Murray Campbell, "'Quite a Party' Puts Brake on Toronto," *Globe and Mail*, October 26, 1996, A1.
29 La Botz, "Ontario's 'Days of Action'"; Ziedenberg, "Metro Toronto Days of Action," 8; Campbell, "'Quite a Party.'"

30 "Toronto: Days Of Action, Days Of Hope," *Contact* 26, no. 36 (November 3, 1996).
31 John Ibbitson and Jim Poling, "Crippling Shutdown: Labour's Day of Protest Empties Toronto Offices, Factories," *Hamilton Spectator*, October 26, 1996, D1.
32 Ziedenberg, "Metro Toronto Days of Action," 8.
33 Van Rijn, "Harris Rejects Victory Claim."
34 Quoted in La Botz, "Ontario's 'Days of Action.'"
35 Van Rijn, "Harris Rejects Victory Claim."
36 Ibbitson and Poling, "Crippling Shutdown."
37 "Teachers Move Outside to Air Complaints Against Tories," *Toronto Star*, October 26, 1996, A6.
38 Ziedenberg, "Metro Toronto Days of Action," 8.
39 Phinjo Gombu, "Parade, Rallies Expected to Jam City Tomorrow," *Toronto Star*, October 26, 1996, A6.
40 Kuitenbrouwer, "Days of Factions," 14.
41 Phinjo Gombu and Nicolaas van Rijn, "Thousands March to Protest Harris But Premier Remains Committed to Cutbacks," *Toronto Star*, October 27, 1996, A1.
42 Scott Kraft, "General Strike Paralyzes France: Millions Protest Against Chirac's Austerity Plans," *Gazette* (Montreal), November 25, 1995, A22. I was privy to the untold story of the coining of this now iconic chant. In the run-up to the 1995 London one-day strike, my partner Abbie Bakan was in her basement study, preparing a "chant sheet" for the day. General strikes were rocking Paris, France, and I remember her coming up the stairs saying, "Paris rhymes with Harris – I think I have a chant." She did indeed.
43 Reuter, "1-Day French Strike Protests Job Cuts," *Toronto Star*, October 18, 1996, A3.
44 Munro, "Ontario's 'Days of Action,'" 137.
45 Quoted in Canadian Press, "'Unprecedented' Demonstration: Toronto Has Never Seen a Protest Quite like Today's, Experts Say," *Record* (Kitchener), October 25, 1996, A2.
46 Quoted in Campbell, "'Quite a Party.'"
47 Quoted in Martin Mittelstaedt and James Rusk, "Plans for Fledgling Social Movement Getting Bigger," *Globe and Mail*, October 26, 1996, A6.
48 Thomas Walkom, "It Was a Good Day but What Is Next?," *Toronto Star*, October 26, 1996, A26.
49 Heron, *Workers' Revolt in Canada*, 3; Brian Dexter, "Nurses Plan Weekend Rally to Protest Health Cuts," *Toronto Star*, September 25, 1996, A6.
50 Nicolaas van Rijn, "Day of Protest in Metro Being Run as Local Affair," *Toronto Star*, October 13, 1996, A3.

51 Greg Crone, "Labor Protest Widens Divisions," *Record* (Kitchener), October 29, 1996, A3.
52 Quoted in Ziedenberg, "Metro Toronto Days of Action," 10.
53 Kuitenbrouwer, "Days of Factions," 17.
54 Crone, "Labor Protest Widens Divisions"; Greg Crone, "Labour Leaders Take New Approach: Will Focus Efforts on Specific Issues Not Days of Action," *Hamilton Spectator*, November 8, 1996, C3.
55 Virginia Galt, "CAW's Hard-Line Stand Grates on Rivals," *Globe and Mail*, May 16, 1994, A4; Galt, "Leaders Fight to Unite Unions."
56 Kuitenbrouwer, "Days of Factions," 15; Reshef and Rastin, "Sins of Commission," 137. Kuitenbrower lists the Allied Food and Commercial Workers but is in fact referring to the United Food and Commercial Workers (UFCW).
57 Quoted in Dale Anne Freed, "Unions Buck Bid to Shut Cities," *Toronto Star*, November 8, 1996, A8.
58 "Toward the Renewal"; Paul Kellogg, "The Pink Paper Problem," *PolEconJournal*, May 14, 1996, https://poleconjournal.com/pink-paper-problem/.
59 Quoted in Crone, "Labour Leaders Take New Approach."
60 Lee Prokaska, "Steelworkers Send Aid to Strikers," *Hamilton Spectator*, October 1, 1996, A6.
61 Quoted in John Ibbitson, "Labor Vows to Fight 'Scab' Plants," *Ottawa Citizen*, November 23, 1996, E1.
62 Turk, "Days of Action," 173.
63 Ibbitson, *Promised Land*, 213.
64 Quoted in Carol Goodwin, "Labor Supports 1-Day Strike: Fiery Debate over OFL Election Stance Opens Old Wounds at Labor Council Meeting," *Record* (Kitchener), November 15, 1995, C4.
65 Ziedenberg, "The Counter Revolution," 1996.
66 Quoted in Kuitenbrouwer, "Days of Factions," 17–18.
67 Department of Labour Canada, "Table IX (November)."
68 Gombu and Van Rijn, "Thousands March to Protest Harris."
69 Ziedenberg, "Metro Toronto Days of Action," 9.
70 Nicolaas van Rijn, "Down for the Count over Rally Numbers," *Toronto Star*, October 29, 1996, A1.
71 Gombu and Van Rijn, "Thousands March to Protest Harris."
72 Van Rijn, "Down for the Count."
73 Nicolaas van Rijn and Theresa Boyle, "Police Say 'Simple Math' Confirms 75,000 at Rally but Organizers Insist Attendance at Queen's Park Topped 250,000," *Toronto Star*, October 28, 1996, A6.
74 Ziedenberg, "Metro Toronto Days of Action," 9.
75 Rusk et al., "Rally Leaders Elated."

76 Walter Podilchak, "Counting Real People, Not Images, Puts Rally Total at about 180,000," *Toronto Star*, November 2, 1996, B3.
77 Vicki Hargreaves, "Here's Another Estimate That Says 180,000," *Toronto Star*, November 2, 1996, B3.

Chapter 9

1 Apologies to Dream Academy, *Life in a Northern Town*.
2 John Ibbitson, "Unions: Labor Federation Urged to Heal Rift," *The Windsor Star*, December 11, 1996, A9.
3 Ibbitson, *Promised Land*, 205–6; Prokaska, "A Year After the Marches."
4 Ziedenberg, "Metro Toronto Days of Action," 10.
5 Quoted in Kuitenbrouwer, "Days of Factions," 17.
6 Quoted in Kuitenbrouwer, "Days of Factions," 16.
7 Adapted from Draper, "Two Souls of Socialism," 2–33.
8 Kuitenbrouwer, "Days of Factions," 18.
9 Quoted in Crone, "Labour Leaders Take New Approach."
10 Quoted in Canadian Press, "Labor Groups Oppose Sudbury Protest Plan," *Toronto Star*, November 30, 1996, A6.
11 Canadian Press, "Protest Crowds Small but Vocal," *Record* (Kitchener), March 22, 1997, A3.
12 Quoted in Gloria Galloway, "Demonstration Against Government Promises Party, Not Protest," *Canadian Press NewsWire*, March 20, 1997, http://search.proquest.com.
13 Brendan O'Hallarn, "Broad Says Protest Is Way to Share Support," *Sault Star*, March 19, 1997, B1.
14 Gloria Galloway, "Numbers Drop at Northern Protest," *Hamilton Spectator*, March 24, 1997, B3.
15 "Sudbury Fightback Builds Links," *Contact* 27, no. 12 (March 30, 1997).
16 "Planning Starts for Anti-Harris Protest," *Record* (Kitchener), January 24, 1997, A3.
17 "Thunder Bay Day of Action," *Contact* 27, no. 15 (April 20, 1997).
18 Canadian Press, "Anti-Tory Protesters March in Thunder Bay," *Canadian Press NewsWire*, April 28, 1997, http://search.proquest.com.
19 Canadian Press, "Latest 'Day of Action' Protest Blocks Mail Delivery," *Record* (Kitchener), April 29, 1997, A3.
20 Canadian Press, "Latest 'Day of Action,'" A3.
21 "Thunder Bay Day of Action."
22 "National Day of Protest - May 3," *Contact* 27, no. 9 (March 9, 1997).
23 "Massive St. Catharines' Rally Against Harris Government," *Contact* 27, no. 15 (April 20, 1997).

24 Ian Urquhart, "Labor Boiling at Tory Anti-Strike Bill," *Toronto Star*, June 5, 1997, A27.

25 Richard Brennan, "Students to Go to School Longer: Snobelen Proposes Smaller Classes, More Teaching Time," *Ottawa Citizen*, September 22, 1997, A5.

26 Quoted in Urquhart, "Labor Boiling at Tory Anti-Strike Bill."

27 Flexer, "Fightback Movement in Crisis," 10. Flexer passed away in 2000. Paul Kellogg, "Three Hundred Meet to Remember Joe Flexer," *PolEconJournal*, August 7, 2000, https://poleconjournal.com/joe-flexer/.

28 Urquhart, "Labor Boiling."

29 Richard Brennan, "'Invent a Crisis,' Minister Urged Education Staff," *Ottawa Citizen*, September 13, 1995, A1.

30 Urquhart, "Labor Boiling."

31 Quoted in Greg Crone, "Province-Wide Strike Possible: Unions Prepare to Battle Labour Bill," *Hamilton Spectator*, July 5, 1997, A13.

32 Margaret Mironowicz, "Teachers Consider Illegal Walkout," *Record* (Kitchener), July 16, 1997, A1.

33 "CAW Takes Part in Massive OFL Fightback," *Contact* 27, no. 28 (August 3, 1997).

34 Flexer, "Fightback Movement in Crisis."

35 Quoted in Reshef and Rastin, *Unions in the Time of Revolution*, 93.

36 "CAW Takes Part."

37 Greg Crone, "Labour Keeps Its Powder Dry: Unions Give Harris One Last Chance to Back down on Arbitration Bill 136," *Hamilton Spectator*, July 29, 1997, B3.

38 Quoted in Crone, "Labour Keeps Its Powder Dry," B3.

39 "Demonstrations Against Harris Government Cuts To Workers' Compensation," *Contact* 27, no. 30 (September 1, 1997).

40 Caroline Mallan, "Union Leaders Preparing for Difficult Days," *Toronto Star*, September 1, 1997, A4.

41 Jennifer Quinn, "Labor Day Marchers Aim to Send Message to Harris," *Toronto Star*, September 2, 1997, A3.

42 "Harris Unruffled by Labor Day Protest," *Kingston Whig-Standard*, September 2, 1997, 6.

43 Nicolaas van Rijn, "Public Unions Gear Up for Protests," *Toronto Star*, September 23, 1997.

44 Nancy Dehart, "CUPE Locals Vote to Strike If Necessary," *Hamilton Spectator*, September 12, 1997, A6.

45 Ian Urquhart, "Tories Muscled Their Way into Labour Mess," *Toronto Star*, September 18, 1997, A25.

46 Quoted in Richard Brennan, "Unions to Hit Tories with Rotating Strikes: Teachers Discuss Joining Health-Care and Municipal Workers," *Record* (Kitchener), September 18, 1997, A1.
47 Brennan, "Unions to Hit Tories," A1.
48 Quoted in Richard Brennan, "More Reversals on Labor Front: Public-Sector Strikes Put on Hold," *Record* (Kitchener), September 20, 1997, A1; Richard Mackie, "Unions Rule Out General Strike," *Globe and Mail*, September 30, 1997, A1.
49 Quoted in Carolyn Abraham and Richard Brennan, "Tories Back Down: Sudden Retreat on Bill 136 Stuns Labour," *Hamilton Spectator*, September 19, 1997, A1.
50 "Harris Government Drops Assault on Public Sector Unions," *Contact* 27, no. 32 (September 21, 1997).
51 Quoted in Brennan, "More Reversals on Labor Front."
52 Greg Crone, "More Reversals on Labor Front: Teachers Not Satisfied Yet," *Record* (Kitchener), September 20, 1997, A1.
53 Richard Brennan, "Education Bill Still Grants Power to Prevent Strikes, Critics Say," *Ottawa Citizen*, September 24, 1997, A6.
54 Quoted in Brennan, "Education Bill," A6.
55 Joanne Laucius, "Ontario Teachers Poised to Strike," *Ottawa Citizen*, September 25, 1997, A5.
56 Quoted in Richard Brennan, "School Bill Risks Strike, Teachers Say," *Record* (Kitchener), September 23, 1997, A1.
57 Richard Brennan, "Teachers Threaten Total Shutdown: 'If They Put Me in Jail … So Be It,'" *Ottawa Citizen*, September 26, 1997, A1.
58 Brennan, "Teachers Threaten Total Shutdown," A1.
59 Paul Kellogg, "Don't Let the Teachers Fight Alone," *PolEconJournal*, October 8, 1997, https://poleconjournal.com/dont-let-teachers-fight-alone/.
60 "Thousands Protest Harris Government in North Bay," *Contact* 27, no. 34 (October 5, 1997); Brian Cross, "Province-Wide Strike Could Kick Off Here," *The Windsor Star*, September 29, 1997, A3.
61 Carl Warren, "Hanging with Mike's Pals," *NOW Magazine* (Toronto), no. 819 (October 2, 1997): 19, 29.
62 "Thousands Protest Harris."
63 Glenn Wheeler, "A Taste of Victory in North Bay," *NOW Magazine* (Toronto), no. 819 (October 2, 1997): 18–19.
64 Sault Star Staff, "Sault, Algoma Public Sector Workers Put on Strike Alert," *Sault Star*, September 29, 1997, A1.
65 Kellogg, "Don't Let the Teachers Fight Alone"; John Ibbitson, "Labor Defying Harris in His Own Back Yard," *Sault Star*, September 27, 1997, A1; Rankin, "Protesters Take Over 'Mike's Town.'"

66 Rankin, "Protesters Take over 'Mike's Town.'"
67 Ibbitson, "Labor Defying Harris."
68 Quoted in John Tollefsrud, "Ontario Labor Groups Threaten General Strike," *Vancouver Sun*, September 29, 1997, A7.
69 "North Bay Days of Protest – Harris' Home Base Shuts Down," *Contact* 27, no. 33 (September 28, 1997).
70 Greg Crone, "Unions Vow to Support Teachers: Private, Public Sector Workers Ready to Join Strike, OFL Says," *Ottawa Citizen*, September 27, 1997, A3.
71 Cross, "Provincewide Strike."
72 "Day of Action Closes Windsor," *Contact* 27, no. 36 (October 26, 1997).
73 Quoted in Laucius, "Ontario Teachers Poised."
74 *Record* News Services, "Labor Will Back Fight by Teachers," *Record* (Kitchener), September 25, 1997, A1.
75 Crone, "Unions Vow to Support Teachers."
76 Quoted in Crone, "Unions Vow to Support Teachers.".
77 Quoted in Greg Crone, "Public Sector Unions Back Educators," *Hamilton Spectator*, September 30, 1997, C1.
78 Quoted in Wheeler, "A Taste of Victory."
79 Quoted in Richard Brennan, "Labor Backing Teachers," *Standard* (St. Catharines), October 23, 1997, A1.
80 Sault Star Staff, "Sault, Algoma Public Sector."

Chapter 10

1 Wheeler, "A Taste of Victory."
2 Laucius, "Ontario Teachers Poised."
3 Quoted in Wheeler, "A Taste of Victory."
4 Sault Star Staff, "Local Students Protest Education Changes," *Sault Star*, September 25, 1997, A1.
5 Quoted in Sault Star Staff, "Local Students Protest," A1.
6 Quoted in Peter Edwards, "CUPE Vows Support for Teacher Strike," *Toronto Star*, September 26, 1997, A7.
7 Kellogg, "Don't Let the Teachers Fight Alone."
8 Sault Star Staff, "Sault, Algoma Public Sector."
9 Richard Brennan, "Ontario Amends Labour Bill: Meeting Union Demands Expected to Avert Massive Strike," *Ottawa Citizen*, September 29, 1997, A3.
10 Reshef and Rastin, *Unions in the Time of Revolution*, 94.
11 Quoted in Crone, "Public Sector Unions Back Educators."
12 Quoted in Wendy McCann, "Harris Offers Teachers a Crab Apple," *Canadian Press NewsWire*, September 30, 1997, http://search.proquest.com.
13 Mackie, "Unions Rule Out General Strike."

14 Peter Small and Vincent Donovan, "24,000 Rally to Back Protesting Teachers," *Toronto Star*, October 7, 1997, A1.
15 Deborah McDougall, "Teachers Rally Against Education Reform," *Canadian Press NewsWire*, October 6, 1997, http://search.proquest.com.
16 Gay Abbate, Richard Mackie, and with a report from Jennifer Lewington, "We'll Walk, Teachers Shout," *Globe and Mail*, October 7, 1997, A1.
17 Quoted in McDougall, "Teachers Rally Against Education Reform."
18 Abbate et al., "We'll Walk, Teachers Shout."
19 Pat Bell and Julia Elliott, "Teachers: 'United We Stand' Teachers: More Than 6,000 Rally, Vow to Strike Against Education Legislation," *Ottawa Citizen*, September 30, 1997, A1.
20 Gary Lupton, "Students Stage Protest Against Bill 160 Cuts," *Kingston Whig-Standard*, September 30, 1997, 1.
21 Agnes Bongers, "Teachers Wait for 'the Call': Parents Told Strike Could Come Any Day," *Hamilton Spectator*, September 30, 1997, A3.
22 Steve Durant, "At Last, Students Defend Education," *Kingston Whig-Standard*, October 4, 1997, 9.
23 Ian MacAlpine, Jeff Outhit, and Whig-Standard Staff Writers, "Student Protests Hit Area Schools," *Kingston Whig-Standard*, October 2, 1997, 1.
24 "Hundreds Protest Cuts to Education," *Toronto Star*, October 2, 1997, A2.
25 Liz Monteiro, "Region's Teachers Plan Protests, Rally as Lesson for Tories," *Record* (Kitchener), September 30, 1997, A1.
26 Erin Cook, "Student Supports Teachers," *Record* (Kitchener), October 2, 1997, A12.
27 Liz Monteiro and Margaret Mironowicz, "4,000 Local Teachers Vow to Stand Firm," *Record* (Kitchener), October 3, 1997, A1.
28 Nick Pron, "Teachers, Students Protest Bill: Rallies Denounce Planned Changes in Education," *Toronto Star*, October 3, 1997, B3.
29 Pron, "Teachers, Students Protest Bill," B3.
30 Eric Johnson, "Students Demand Answers from MPP: Crowd of Young Protesters Marches in Support of Teachers' Stand on School Reforms," *Record* (Kitchener), October 4, 1997, B2.
31 Craig Sumi, "'Back Off' on Changes, Tories Told: 300 Education Protesters March Outside Jackson's Brant St. Office," *Hamilton Spectator*, October 4, 1997, N1.
32 Agnes Bongers, "Strike Could Close Elementary Schools: Teachers Can Walk Out as Early as Oct. 22," *Hamilton Spectator*, October 7, 1997, A1.
33 Ken Kilpatrick, "Hamilton Teachers Rally: 8,000 Pack Copps Coliseum to Protest Education Reforms," *Toronto Star*, October 8, 1997, A21.
34 Norlyn Purych, "Blind River Teachers Plan Rotating Protests," *Sault Star*, October 8, 1997, B4.

35 Quoted in Peter Small, "Students Take to Streets: Six Schools Stage Walkouts to Protest Cuts in Education," *Toronto Star*, October 8, 1997, B1.
36 Tony Reinhart and Liz Monteiro, "Teachers Rally, Students March Against Reforms," *Record* (Kitchener), October 9, 1997, A1.
37 Sylvia Graham, "Prince Edward County Teachers Rally Against Bill 160," *Kingston Whig-Standard*, October 10, 1997, 5.
38 Donovan Vincent, "East York Students Protest Education Bill," *Toronto Star*, October 11, 1997, A31.
39 Agnes Bongers, "Principals Ready to Join Teachers in Illegal Strike," *Hamilton Spectator*, October 10, 1997, A3.
40 Agnes Bongers, "Angry Crowd Swarms Snobelen: Minister Also Faces Heckler at Fundraiser," *Hamilton Spectator*, October 9, 1997, A1.
41 Quoted in Richard Brennan, "Harris Pressured by Political Fires: Premier Hit 'Panic Button,'" *Hamilton Spectator*, October 11, 1997, B6.
42 Quoted in Richard Brennan and Rose Simone, "Union Gives Ultimatum to Johnson: Back Down on Reforms or Face Illegal Walkouts, Teachers Warn," *Record* (Kitchener), October 15, 1997, A1.
43 James Rusk, "Protests Target Ontario Conservatives," *Globe and Mail*, October 18, 1997, A3.
44 Chris Hornsey, "Thousands March in Day of Protest," *Canadian Press NewsWire*, October 17, 1997, http://search.proquest.com.
45 Heather Greenwood, "Protest Shuts Down Windsor," *Toronto Star*, October 18, 1997, A8.
46 "Day of Action Closes Windsor."
47 "Day of Action Closes Windsor."
48 Greenwood, "Protest Shuts Down Windsor."
49 Greenwood, "Protest Shuts Down Windsor."
50 Canadian Press, "Day of Protest Gets Started a Day Early," *Canadian Press NewsWire*, October 16, 1997, http://search.proquest.com.
51 Quoted in Richard Mackie, "Ontario Labour Movement Racked by Internal Strife," *Globe and Mail*, October 20, 1997, A3.
52 Lee Prokaska, "Ontario Labour to Pick a Leader," *Hamilton Spectator*, September 4, 1997, A6.
53 Nesbitt records that when the pink paper group announced its opposition to the Days of Action movement, Hynd had "called the protests 'counterproductive', a 'mistake' and even 'suicide' for organized labour." Nesbitt, "Days of Action," 240. In fact, those comments were made by John Murphy from the Power Workers' Union. Freed, "Unions Buck Bid."
54 Carolyn Abraham and Bill Dunphy, "Teachers Give Noon Ultimatum: Kill Contentious Bill 160 Sections or Strike Starts in 48 Hours: Unions," *Hamilton Spectator*, October 21, 1997, A1.

55 Richard Brennan, "Ryan Says CUPE Will Join Strike," *Hamilton Spectator*, October 21, 1997, B2.
56 Rusk, "Protests Target Ontario Conservatives."
57 Donovan Vincent, "Etobicoke Students 'Vote' Against Education Bill. 'Referendum' Has Youth Talking About Legislation," *Toronto Star*, October 18, 1997, A16.
58 Tom Blackwell, "Hearings into Education Bill Begin," *Canadian Press NewsWire*, October 20, 1997, http://search.proquest.com.
59 Liz Monteiro, "Many Students Support Teachers: 'I'm a Success Because of My School,' Says One," *Record* (Kitchener), October 21, 1997, A4.
60 Doug Draper, "Harris Villain to Most Students Who Fear a Prolonged Strike," *Standard* (St. Catharines), October 24, 1997, A3.
61 Christine Brousseau, "Principals Resign in Support," *Kingston Whig-Standard*, October 24, 1997, 1.
62 Dan Nolan, "Johnson Dismisses Poll Results," *Kingston Whig-Standard*, October 24, 1997, 13.
63 Quoted in Richard Brennan, "Chalk It Up to Money," *Hamilton Spectator*, October 24, 1997, A1.
64 Brennan, "Labor Backing Teachers."
65 Southam Newspapers, "Unions Pledge Cash, Support for Striking School Teachers," *Record* (Kitchener), October 24, 1997, A4.
66 Brennan, "Labor Backing Teachers."
67 Adrian Humphreys, "Local CUPE School Workers Say They're Forced to Cross Lines," *Hamilton Spectator*, October 24, 1997, A3.
68 John Ibbitson, "Ontario's 126,000 Teachers Walk Off the Job," *CanWest News*, October 27, 1997, http://search.proquest.com.
69 A bridge I knew well as a teenager, being the link for gatherings at the "Mad Mechanic" pub and connecting those who lived in the city and those who lived in the county.
70 Sylvia Graham, "Teachers Unite: Teachers March to MPP's Offices," *Kingston Whig-Standard*, October 28, 1997, 1.
71 Sault Star Staff, "Local Teachers, NDP Leader Hampton Get Set to Greet Premier at Rally Today," *Sault Star*, October 28, 1997, A1.
72 Sault Star Staff, "Teachers Sponsor Common-Sense Barbecue Tuesday," *Sault Star*, October 25, 1997, B1.
73 Sault Star Staff, "Protesters Dine on Defiance at Sault Rally," *Sault Star*, October 29, 1997, A1.
74 Liz Monteiro, "Lone WCI Teacher Crosses Picket Line and He's Proud," *Record* (Kitchener), October 30, 1997, B2.
75 Adrian Humphreys and Bill Dunphy, "Crossing the Line: 41 Teachers Across Region Break Ranks," *Hamilton Spectator*, October 28, 1997, A1.

76 Pat Halpin, "Teachers, Supporters Attend Rally," *Record* (Kitchener), October 29, 1997, A5.
77 Ross Longbottom, "Teachers Gain Principal Allies: Few Students Attend Classes on First Day of Education Protest," *Hamilton Spectator*, October 28, 1997, N1.
78 Canadian Press, "Teacher-Teachers Support Strike," *Record* (Kitchener), November 1, 1997, A14.
79 Quoted in Casey Korstanje, "Catholic Bishops Say Strike Not Immoral: Concerns Also Raised About Bill 160 Centralizing Decision-Making," *Hamilton Spectator*, October 29, 1997, A3.
80 The Spectator, "Nelson Students Show Teacher Support," *Hamilton Spectator*, October 28, 1997, N2.
81 Ann Lukits, "Nurses Support Teachers," *Kingston Whig-Standard*, October 28, 1997, 2.
82 Doug Draper, "Kids, Parents Join Strike Rally: Hundreds of Teachers Flock to Park to Show Displeasure with Tories," *Standard* (St. Catharines), October 28, 1997, A1.
83 Draper, "Kids, Parents Join Strike Rally."
84 Ann Lukits, "Community Supports Teachers - with Food," *Kingston Whig-Standard*, October 31, 1997, 4.
85 Sharon Boase, "'Never Felt like a Scab Before:' Showdown in Education," *Hamilton Spectator*, October 28, 1997, A3.
86 Carolyn Abraham and Richard Brennan, "Unions Look for a Way Out," *Kingston Whig-Standard*, October 29, 1997, 11.
87 Bill Dunphy, "Courts Will Decide: Minister Promises Injunction Filed Today," *Hamilton Spectator*, October 29, 1997, A1.
88 Richard Mackie and Jennifer Lewington, "New Offer Infuriates Teachers," *Globe and Mail*, October 31, 1997, A1.
89 Steve Cannon, "More Support Teachers: Government Losing the Battle for Public Opinion, Record Poll Finds," *Record* (Kitchener), November 1, 1997, A1.
90 Richard Brennan, "Support for Teachers Rising, Poll Suggests," *Standard* (St. Catharines), November 1, 1997, A5.
91 Wilson-Smith and Janigan, "Harris Under Siege," 12.
92 Quoted in Brennan, "Support for Teachers Rising."
93 Bill Dunphy, "Injunction Won't Deter Teachers: Determination to Fight Bill 160 Will Be Strong despite Court Ruling," *Hamilton Spectator*, October 31, 1997, A11.
94 Agnes Bongers and Bill Dunphy, "Injunction Bid 'Too Soon': Judge Suggests Tories Should Have Waited 2 Weeks," *Hamilton Spectator*, November 1, 1997, A1.

95 Quoted in Valerie Pringle, "Judge's Decision Boosts Ontario Teachers' Morale [Transcript]," *Canada AM - CTV Television*, November 4, 1997, http://search.proquest.com.
96 Richard Brennan and Carolyn Abraham, "Next Move Unclear," *Standard* (St. Catharines), November 5, 1997, A1.
97 Quoted in Richard Brennan and Carolyn Abraham, "Teachers Considering End to Strike," *Record* (Kitchener), November 5, 1997, A1.
98 Richard Mackie and Jennifer Lewington, "Teachers May End Walkout," *Globe and Mail*, November 5, 1997, A1.
99 Caroline Bourque Wiley, "Jubilant Teachers March: Judge's Ruling Called 'Win' as 2,000 Claim Streets," *Standard* (St. Catharines), November 4, 1997, A1.
100 Craig Sumi, "Teachers Rally All About 'Keeping up the Struggle': Fight Will Continue, They Vow," *Hamilton Spectator*, November 6, 1997, N1.
101 Canadian Press, "Protests Continue: Not Everyone Ready to Go Back Monday," *Record* (Kitchener), November 8, 1997, A12.
102 Carolyn Abraham and Richard Brennan, "Three Unions Call Off Strike," *Kingston Whig-Standard*, November 7, 1997, 13; "Unions, Parents, Students And Community Activists Join Together in Support of Ontario Teachers," *Contact* 27, no. 39 (November 16, 1997).
103 Carolyn Abraham and Richard Brennan, "50,000 Expected at Queen's Park," *Standard* (St. Catharines), November 6, 1997, A3.
104 Adrian Humphreys, "Teachers 'Put Their Lives on Line': 10,000 at Queen's Park," *Hamilton Spectator*, November 7, 1997, A1.
105 Canadian Press, "Premier Says Strike Is Over: Harris Speaks at Dinner as 2,500 Protesters Surround Building," *Record* (Kitchener), November 7, 1997.
106 Lloyd Robertson, "Thousands of Ontario Teachers Head Back to Work [Transcript]," *CTV News - CTV Television*, November 6, 1997, http://search.proquest.com.
107 Richard Mackie and Jennifer Lewington, "3 Unions to Teach Monday," *Globe and Mail*, November 7, 1997, A1.
108 Dan Matheson and Leslie Jones, "Some of Ontario's Striking Teachers Break Ranks [Transcript]," *Canada AM - CTV Television*, November 7, 1997, http://search.proquest.com; Carolyn Abraham and Richard Brennan, "It's Back to School: Three of Five Unions Tell Teachers to Go Back to Schools," *Standard* (St. Catharines), November 7, 1997, A1.
109 Steve Arnold and Carolynne Wheeler, "'We Have Been Betrayed': Local Elementary Teachers Shocked at Union Decision," *Hamilton Spectator*, November 7, 1997.
110 Quoted in Tom Blackwell, "Teachers Bitter: Decision by Three Unions to End Walkout Met with Criticism," *Kingston Whig-Standard*, November 8, 1997, 17.

111 Blackwell, "Teachers Bitter," 17.
112 Arnold and Wheeler, "'We Have Been Betrayed.'"
113 Steve Arnold, "Many Teachers Think Unions Backed Down," *Hamilton Spectator*, November 8, 1997, A14.
114 Doug Draper, "Teachers Feel Angry, Betrayed: Many Say They Have Been Abandoned by Union Leadership," *Standard* (St. Catharines), November 8, 1997, A1.
115 Blackwell, "Teachers Bitter."
116 Nesbitt, "Days of Action," 317.
117 Quoted in Blackwell, "Teachers Bitter."
118 Quoted in Richard Mackie and Jennifer Lewington, "Strike Likely Over," *Globe and Mail*, November 8, 1997, A.1.
119 "Magnificent – the Rebellion of the Rank and File," *Socialist Worker* (Toronto), no. 273 (November 22, 1997): 7.

Chapter 11

1 Henry Hess, "OFL Picks 'Diplomat' as Leader," *Globe and Mail*, November 26, 1997, A12.
2 Virginia Galt, "Upshaw Beats Racism to Reach Top," *Globe and Mail*, May 4, 1991, A5.
3 Sharon Boase, "'A Dramatic Shift to the Right' for OFL," *Hamilton Spectator*, November 26, 1997, A1.
4 Quoted in Michael Hanlon, "Social Contract Haunts Race for Labour Leader: Top Contenders Face Accusations over Past Actions," *Toronto Star*, November 22, 1997, A5.
5 Canadian Press, "Conciliation vs. Militancy: Samuelson, Forder in Battle for Presidency of Labor Federation," *Record* (Kitchener), November 22, 1997, E7.
6 Paul Kellogg, "Strike Action Is the Key, Not Convention Politics," *PolEconJournal*, October 21, 1997, https://poleconjournal.com/strike-action-is-the-key/.
7 Hess, "OFL Picks 'Diplomat' as Leader."
8 Hanlon, "Social Contract Haunts Race."
9 John Ibbitson, "Unions Ponder General Strike," *Kingston Whig-Standard*, November 14, 1997, 14.
10 Hess, "OFL Picks 'Diplomat' as Leader."
11 Boase, "'A Dramatic Shift to the Right.'"
12 Quoted in Boase, "'A Dramatic Shift to the Right.'"
13 "OFL Convention Supports Days of Action," *Contact* 27, no. 41 (December 4, 1997).
14 Quoted in Reshef and Rastin, *Unions in the Time of Revolution*, 150–1.

15 Clarke, "Fight to Win," 386–87.
16 "Unanimous Support For Province Wide Strike," *Contact* 27, no. 42 (December 7, 1997).
17 "St. Catharines: The Next Day."
18 Quoted in "St. Catharines Day of Action: Taking on the Harris Agenda," *Contact* 28, no. 12 (April 4, 1998).
19 "St. Catharines Day of Action Office Opens," *Contact* 28, no. 13 (April 12, 1998).
20 Paul Forsyth and Melanie Seal, "Shutdown: Auto Plants First to Be Paralysed by Huge Labour Rally," *Standard* (St. Catharines), May 1, 1998, A1.
21 Colleen Turner, "Mixed Reaction to Day of Action," *Standard* (St. Catharines), May 2, 1998, B1.
22 Turner, "Mixed Reaction," B1; Janet Davison, "Another Shot at Harris - a Small One," *Record* (Kitchener), May 2, 1998, A3; Doug Herod, "Judging by the Crowds, Protest Fatigue Has Set In," *Standard* (St. Catharines), May 2, 1998, B1.
23 "St. Catharines' Day of Action," *Contact* 28, no. 16 (May 9, 1998).
24 Andrew Lundy, "Day of Action Hits City," *Canadian Press NewsWire*, May 1, 1998, http://search.proquest.com.
25 Herod, "Judging by the Crowds."
26 Canadian Press, "Protesters Shut Down City Hall," *Canadian Press NewsWire*, June 8, 1998, http://search.proquest.com; "Belleville: Kingston Gets Support for Day of Action," *Kingston Whig-Standard*, June 3, 1998, 1.
27 "Kingston Day of Action: June 8."
28 Ann Lukits, "Anxious Moments on Line," *Kingston Whig-Standard*, June 9, 1998.
29 Jeff Outhit, "Day of Action Hits City," *Kingston Whig-Standard*, June 9, 1998.
30 "Kingston Day of Action: Taking on the Harris Agenda," *Contact* 28, no. 21 (June 14, 1998).
31 Jeff Outhit, "City Workers Join Protest," *Kingston Whig-Standard*, June 9, 1998, 8.
32 Keith Gerein, "Pickets Deny Lawyers Access to Offices," *Kingston Whig-Standard*, June 9, 1998, 4.
33 Outhit, "Day of Action Hits City."
34 Apologies to Simon and Garfunkel. Simon & Garfunkel, "The Sound of Silence."
35 Mackie, "Pickets Put Aside."
36 Ian Urquhart, "Liberals Could Benefit in Labour's Anti-Harris War," *Toronto Star*, July 30, 1998, 1.
37 Bickerton, "Ontario Labour Leaders," 7.

38 This and all quotations in this section from Kellogg, "Heads of Unions Cancel General Strike."
39 Reshef and Rastin, *Unions in the Time of Revolution*, 151.
40 Quoted in Reshef and Rastin, *Unions in the Time of Revolution*, 151.
41 Mackie, "Pickets Put Aside."
42 Joel Ruimy, "Ontario PCs Talk Policy, Election," *Toronto Star*, October 17, 1998, 1.
43 Julie Devaney, "Students Take Action Against Education Cuts," *Socialist Worker* (Toronto), no. 295 (October 28, 1998): 10.

Conclusion

1 Hackett, "Pie in the Sky," 2–72; Bullen, "The Ontario Waffle," 188–215; Warnock, "The Waffle," 10–15.
2 Andrew Coyne, "Teachers Are the Big Losers in Ontario Strike," *Hamilton Spectator*, November 11, 1997, E1.
3 Nesbitt, "Days of Action," 350.
4 Kellogg, "Ontario Mass Strike Movement," October 10, 1996; Kellogg, "Ontario Mass Strike Movement," September 9, 1997.
5 UK, "Historical Coal Data."
6 Kristin Rushowy, "'Historic Show of Unity': 200,000 Teachers and School Staff from Four Major Unions Stage One-Day Strike Across the Province," *Toronto Star*, February 22, 2020.
7 McCartin, "Professional Air Traffic Controller," 1126; On Hormel, see Green, *On Strike at Hormel*; Kellogg, "Review. *On Strike at Hormel*," 297–383.
8 Panitch and Swartz, *From Consent to Coercion*, 237.
9 Savage, "Politics of Strategic Voting," 78.
10 Luxemburg, "The Russian Revolution," 301–2; Quoted in Kellogg, "Defeat of Stephen Harper," 593.
11 Kellogg, "Defeat of Stephen Harper," 592.
12 Reshef and Rastin, *Unions in the Time of Revolution*, 142.
13 Not all polling firms are equal, and these results need to be approached as approximations only. According to John Ibbitson, Environics – from which polling numbers appear on this chart – was a firm that tended to underemphasize Tory support, as opposed to Angus Reid, which tended to overemphasize it. John Ibbitson, "Duelling Pollsters Don't Jibe in Ontario," *Ottawa Citizen*, August 14, 1998, A6. In the first year of the Harris administration, for instance, it was an Environics poll that showed that a majority in Ontario were opposed to health care cuts and supported either keeping hospital funding the same or increasing it. Donovan Vincent, "Public Opposed to Health-Care Cuts, Poll Says One in 10 Would Give up

Tax Savings for Hospitals," *Toronto Star*, November 6, 1995, A10. However, also in 1995, it was an Environics poll that business groups turned to, a poll which suggested that 77 per cent of Ontario residents opposed the Days of Action plan announced by the OFL. "Ontario Labor Vows," 1–2. So, while the first might be treated as suspect, reflecting a polling company with an anti-Tory bias, a similar case could not be made out of the second. Regardless, the point here is the trend in support over time, and pulling from one database should, in theory, help identify that trend with fewer distortions than having some polls coming from Environics and others from Angus Reid. And the trend is clear – support for the Tories falling while mobilization against them intensifies, support rising when that mobilization slackens.

14 Tanguay, "'Not in Ontario!'" 22; John Ibbitson, "'The Very Best Is Yet to Come': Harris: Tories Win 2nd Majority," *National Post*, June 4, 1999, A1; Environics Research Group, "It's a Horse Race"; Environics Research Group, "Latest Focus Ontario Results"; Elections Ontario, "Election Results."
15 Prokaska, "A Year After the Marches."
16 Albo and Evans, *Divided Province*, xiii.
17 Albo and Evans, *Divided Province*, xiv.
18 McDowell, *Neoliberal Parliamentarism*, 154; Quoting Evans, "Treading Water."
19 Savage, "The Politics of Labour," 303.
20 Savage, "The Politics of Labour," 303.
21 Walchuk, "Changing Union-Party Relations," 38.
22 Walchuk, "Changing Union-Party Relations," 38.
23 Esselment, "Ontario Liberals in Power," 233.
24 Walchuk, "Changing Union-Party Relations," 39.
25 Anderson and Ben Jaafar, "Policy Narrative for Ontario," 89.
26 Esselment, "Ontario Liberals in Power," 233–4.
27 This section adapted from Kellogg, "'Backlash.'"
28 Richard Brennan and Tess Kalinowski, "Wynne Vows to Invest $29B in Transit, Roads over 10 Years," *Toronto Star*, April 15, 2014; Robert Benzie, Richard J. Brennan, and Rob Ferguson, "Liberals Selling Off 60% of Hydro One," *Hamilton Spectator*, April 16, 2015, A1.
29 CBC News, "Ontario Becomes 2nd Province to Go Ahead with $15 an Hour Minimum Wage," *CBC News*, May 30, 2017, https://www.cbc.ca/news/canada/toronto/ontario-minimum-wage-announcement-1.4137339.
30 Office of the Premier Ontario, "41st Parliament of Ontario."
31 CBC News, "Ontario Liberals Would Make Prescription Drugs Free for People 65 and Older," *CBC News*, March 20, 2018, https://www.cbc.ca/news/canada/toronto/ontario-premier-prescription-drugs-seniors-free-people-65-and-over-1.4584082.

32 Benzie et al., "Liberals Selling," A1.
33 Quoted in Tess Kalinowski, "Wynne Eyes Relief Line and Electric GO Trains: Both Are Priorities for Half of New $29B Transit Subsidy," *Toronto Star*, April 15, 2014, GT1.
34 Savage, "The Politics of Labour," 303.
35 Walchuk, "Changing Union-Party Relations," 37.
36 Walchuk, "Changing Union-Party Relations," 38.
37 Savage, "The Politics of Labour," 305.
38 Walchuk, "Changing Union-Party Relations," 39.
39 Department of Finance Canada, "Table 11: Major Transfers"; Statistics Canada, "Consumer Price Index"; Statistics Canada, "Population Estimates"; Statistics Canada, "Estimates of Population, by Age Group and Sex."
40 Kellogg, "Heads of Unions Cancel General Strike."
41 An examination of three generations of class formation in the former prison town, Vorkuta, in the former Soviet Union. Kellogg, *"Truth Behind Bars."*
42 Kellogg, *"Truth Behind Bars,"* 90; Quoting Thompson, *English Working Class*, 9; De Ste. Croix, *Class Struggle*, 32.

References

Newspapers, News Services, and Frequently Cited Sources

Canadian Press NewsWire
CanWest News
CBC News
CTV
Contact
Financial Post
Global News
National Post
North Bay Nugget
NOW Magazine (Toronto)
Ottawa Citizen
rabble.ca
PolEconJournal
Socialist Worker (Toronto)
Standard-Freeholder (Cornwall)
The Evening Guide (Port Hope)
The Gazette (Montreal)
The Globe and Mail
The Hamilton Spectator
The Kingston Whig-Standard
The Kitchener-Waterloo Record
The Record (Kitchener)
The Sault Star
The Standard (St. Catharines)
The Vancouver Sun
Times-Colonist (Victoria)
Toronto Star

TVO Today
Waterloo Region Record
Windsor Star
Xtra

All Others

Aikenhead, Sherri. "The End of an Accord." *Maclean's*, July 6, 1987. https://web.archive.org/web/20200929112310/https://archive.macleans.ca/article/1987/7/6/the-end-of-an-accord.

Albo, Gregory, and Bryan M. Evans, eds. *Divided Province: Ontario Politics in the Age of Neoliberalism*. McGill-Queen's University Press, 2018.

Anderson, Carol. *White Rage: The Unspoken Truth of Our Racial Divide*. Bloomsbury, 2016.

Anderson, Stephen E., and Sonia Ben Jaafar. "Policy Narrative for Ontario." In *The Evolution of Professionalism: Educational Policy in the Provinces and Territories of Canada*, edited by Adrienne Chan, Donald Fisher, and Kjell Rubenson. Centre for Policy Studies in Higher Education and Training, 2007.

Angus Reid. "Premiers' Performance: Wynne's Approval Rating Sinks to 12 per Cent – an All-Time Low." *Angus Reid Institute* (blog), March 23, 2017. http://angusreid.org/premier-approval-march2017/.

Bakan, Abigail, and Audrey Kobayashi. "Affirmative Action and Employment Equity: Policy, Ideology, and Backlash in Canadian Context." *Studies in Political Economy* 79, no. 1 (2007): 145–66.

Bakan, Abigail, and Audrey Kobayashi. "Ontario: Lessons of the Rise and Fall of Employment Equity Legislation from the Perspective of Rights Advocacy." In *Employment Equity Policy in Canada and the Politics of Regional Context: Case Study One*. Canadian Race Relations Foundation, 2003.

Bakan, Abigail B., and Paul Kellogg. "Sexism and the Left: Case Studies in an Epistemology of Ignorance." *Socialist Studies/Études Socialistes* 16, no. 1 (2022). https://doi.org/10.18740/ss27330.

Bickerton, Geoff. "Ontario Labour Leaders Stop Days of Action." *Canadian Dimension* 32, no. 5 (1998): 7.

Black Rose Books Editorial Collective, ed. *Quebec Labour: The Confederation of National Trade Unions Yesterday and Today*. Black Rose Books, 1972.

Bouie, Jamelle. "How Trump Happened." *Slate*, March 13, 2016. http://www.slate.com/articles/news_and_politics/cover_story/2016/03/how_donald_trump_happened_racism_against_barack_obama.html.

Bullen, John. "The Ontario Waffle and the Struggle for an Independent Socialist Canada: Conflict within the NDP." *Canadian Historical Review* 64, no. 2 (June 1, 1983): 188–215.

Camfield, David. "Assessing Resistance in Harris's Ontario, 1995–1999." In *Restructuring and Resistance: Canadian Public Policy in the Age of Global Capitalism*, edited by Mike Burke, Colin Peter Mooers, and John Shields. Fernwood, 2000.

Canadian Labour Congress. "The Largest Labour Protest in Canadian History," October 14, 2018. https://canadianlabour.ca/the-largest-labour-protest-in-canadian-history/.

Clarke, John. "Fight to Win. (Notebook/Carnet)." *Labour/Le Travail* 50 (Fall, 2002): 383–92.

Cole, David P., Greg Ioannou, and Margaret Gittens. *Report of the Commission on Systemic Racism in the Ontario Criminal Justice System: A Community Summary*. Commission on Systemic Racism in the Ontario Criminal Justice System, 1995.

Cranston-Reimer, Sharlee. "How Homophobia, Misogyny & Race Played a Role in the Ontario Election." *The Conversation*, June 6, 2018. https://theconversation.com/how-homophobia-misogyny-and-race-played-a-role-in-the-ontario-election-97767.

Crenshaw, Kimberlé. "Demarginalizing the Intersection of Race and Sex: A Black Feminist Critique of Antidiscrimination Doctrine, Feminist Theory and Antiracist Politics." *University of Chicago Legal Forum*, 1989 (1989): 139–67. https://chicagounbound.uchicago.edu/uclf/vol1989/iss1/8/.

Crenshaw, Kimberlé. "Mapping the Margins: Intersectionality, Identity Politics, and Violence Against Women of Color." *Stanford Law Review* 43, no. 6 (1990): 1241–99.

CURC. "Thunder Bay." *Congress of Union Retirees of Canada* (blog), 2013. https://web.archive.org/web/20140612223140/http://unionretiree.ca/affiliates/local-area-councils/thunder-bay/.

Dare, Bill. "Harris's First Year: Attacks and Resistance." In *Open for Business, Closed to People: Mike Harris's Ontario*, edited by Diana S. Ralph, André Régimbald, and Nérée St-Amand. Fernwood, 1997.

Department of Finance Canada. "Table 11: Major Transfers to Other Levels of Government." Fiscal Reference Tables. Ottawa, October 27, 2022. https://www.canada.ca/en/department-finance/services/publications/fiscal-reference-tables/2022.html.

Department of Finance Canada. "Table 45: Actual, Cyclically Adjusted and Primary-Cyclically Adjusted Budget Balances (Millions of Dollars)." Fiscal Reference Tables. Ottawa, September 29, 2008. https://web.archive.org/web/20130622011534/http://www.fin.gc.ca/frt-trf/2008/frt08_8-eng.asp.

Department of Labour Canada. "Table IX." In *Collective Bargaining Review.* March. Ottawa, 1996.

Department of Labour Canada. "Table IX." In *Collective Bargaining Review.* November. Ottawa, 1996.

Department of Labour Canada. "Table VI." In *Collective Bargaining Review.* July-August. Ottawa, 1996.

Department of Labour Canada. "Table VI." In *Collective Bargaining Review.* March. Ottawa, 1996.

Department of Labour Canada. "Table VII." In *Collective Bargaining Review.* January. Ottawa, 1996.

De Ste. Croix, G.E.M. *The Class Struggle in the Ancient Greek World: From the Archaic Age to the Arab Conquests.* Cornell University Press, 1981.

Donaldson, Walter K. "The Ontario Insurance Crisis – The Fight Against No-Fault/No-Tort Insurance, Law and Practice." *Defense Counsel Journal* 54, no. 3 (1987): 376–92.

Draper, Hal. "The Two Souls of Socialism." In *Socialism from Below,* edited by E. Haberkern. Humanities Press, 1992.

Duménil, Gérard, and Dominique Lévy. *Capital Resurgent: Roots of the Neoliberal Revolution.* Harvard University Press, 2004.

Dyck, Rand. "The Social and Economic Context of Ontario Politics." In *The Politics of Ontario,* edited by Jonathan Malloy and Cheryl N. Collier. University of Toronto Press, 2017.

Eaton, Jonathan. "Jockeying for Survival." *Our Times,* July-August, 1996, 10.

Elections Ontario. "Election Results," 2025. https://www.elections.on.ca/en/resource-centre/elections-results.html.

Employment and Social Development Canada. "Work Stoppages." Policies. Collective Bargaining Information, October 4, 2019. https://www.canada.ca/en/employment-social-development/services/collective-bargaining-data/work-stoppages.html.

Environics Research Group. "It's a Horse Race – Support up for Ontario Liberals, down for Tories." Focus Ontario, April 30, 1999. http://web.archive.org/web/20010420045713/http://erg.environics.net/news/default.asp?aID=382.

Environics Research Group. "Latest Focus Ontario Results: Conservatives Lead in Post-Election Survey." Focus Ontario, July 21, 1999. Internet Archive. http://web.archive.org/web/20010425045708/http://erg.environics.net/news/default.asp?aID=391.

Esselment, Anna. "An Inside Look at the Ontario Liberals in Power." In *The Politics of Ontario,* edited by Cheryl N. Collier and Jonathan Malloy. University of Toronto Press, 2017.

Evans, Bryan. "Treading Water: Four Years of Ontario's Liberals." The Bullet, September 23, 2007. https://socialistproject.ca/2007/09/b59/.

Flexer, Joe. "The Ontario Fightback Movement in Crisis: Days of Action or D.O.A?" *Canadian Dimension* 31, no. 5: (September-October 1997): 7–11.

Galabuzi, Grace-Edward. "Unequal Futures: Race and Class under Neoliberalism." In *Divided Province: Ontario Politics in the Age of*

Neoliberalism, edited by Gregory Albo and Bryan M. Evans. McGill-Queen's University Press, 2018.

Gindin, Sam. *The Canadian Auto Workers: The Birth and Transformation of a Union*. James Lorimer, 1995.

Gittens, Margaret, David P. Cole, Moy Tam, Toni Williams, Ed Ratushny, and Sri-Skanda-Rajah Sri-Guggan. *Racism Behind Bars: The Treatment of Black and Other Racial Minority Prisoners in Ontario Prisons: Interim Report*. Commission on Systemic Racism in the Ontario Criminal Justice System, 1994.

Graefe, Peter, and Carol-Anne Hudson. "Poverty and Policy in Ontario: You Can't Eat Good Intentions." In *Divided Province: Ontario Politics in the Age of Neoliberalism*, edited by Gregory Albo and Bryan M. Evans. McGill-Queen's University Press, 2018.

Green, Hardy. *On Strike at Hormel: The Struggle for a Democratic Labor Movement*. Temple University Press, 1990.

Ground Zero Productions. "London Calling." Working TV, 1996. http://www.workingtv.com/order/tapecat96.html.

Hackett, Robert. "Pie in the Sky: A History of the Ontario Waffle." *Canadian Dimension* 15, no. 1–2 (October–November 1980): 2–72.

Haglund, Rick. "CAW's Actions Could Cripple GM, Smith Says." *Flint Journal*, October 10, 1996, A12.

Hall, Stuart. "The Great Moving Right Show." *Marxism Today*, January, 1979, 14–20.

Hargrove, Buzz, and Wayne Skene. *Labour of Love: The Fight to Create a More Humane Canada*. Macfarlane Walter & Ross, 1998.

Harvey, David. *A Brief History of Neoliberalism*. Oxford University Press, 2007.

Heron, Craig. *The Workers' Revolt in Canada, 1917–1925*. University of Toronto Press, 1998.

Hyman, Richard. *Marxism and the Sociology of Trade Unionism*. Pluto Press, 1971.

Hyman, Richard. "The Politics of Workplace Trade Unionism: Recent Tendencies and Some Problems for Theory." *Capital & Class* 3, no. 2 (1979): 54–67.

Ibbitson, John. *Promised Land: Inside the Mike Harris Revolution*. Prentice-Hall Canada, 1997.

"Interview with Kam Rao: Beginnings of Embarrass Harris." *Ginger: Bulletin of Socialist Debate* 1, no. 1 (1996). http://web.archive.org/web/20090627105719/http://www.pance.ca/ginger/n01_kam_rao.html.

International Socialists. "Ontario Branches." Emergency IS Notes. Internal document, October 28, 1995. Paul Kellogg personal archive.

Kellogg, Paul. "Assessing the Ontario Mass Strike Movement." Internal document, International Socialists, October 10, 1996. Personal archive.

Kellogg, Paul. "Assessing the Ontario Mass Strike Movement." Internal document, International Socialists, September 9, 1997. Personal archive.

Kellogg, Paul. "'Backlash': comment l'ultra droite s'infiltre au sommet de l'État." *Nouveaux Cahiers du socialisme* 23 (Hiver 2020): 21–5.

Kellogg, Paul. *Escape from the Staple Trap: Canadian Political Economy After Left Nationalism.* University of Toronto Press, 2015.

Kellogg, Paul. "Labour Against Austerity: Lessons from the OPSEU and Hamilton Strikes of 1996." Presented at the Annual Conference, Canadian Association of Work and Labour Studies / Association Canadienne d'études du travail et du syndicalisme (CAWLS/ACETS), McGill University, June 2024.

Kellogg, Paul. "Ontario's Days of Action and the Politics of Numbers: An Application of Statistical Discourse Analysis." Presented at the Canadian Political Science Association / Association canadienne de science politique (CPSA/ACSP), York University, Toronto, May 31, 2023.

Kellogg, Paul. "Psychological Wage and the Trump Phenomenon." In *Challenging the Right, Augmenting the Left*, edited by Robert Latham, A. T. Kingsmith, Niko Block, and Julian von Bargen. Fernwood, 2020.

Kellogg, Paul. "Review. *On Strike at Hormel: The Struggle for a Democratic Labor Movement*, by Hardy Green. Temple University Press, 1991." *Labour / Le Travail* 34 (Fall/Automne 1994): 297–383. http://www.lltjournal.ca/index.php/llt/article/view/4951.

Kellogg, Paul. "Sitting-In and Speaking Out: Social Movement Electoralism and the Opposition to Mike Harris' 1996 'Bully Bill.'" Presented at the Canadian Political Science Association / Association canadienne de science politique (CPSA/ACSP), Virtual, June 2, 2022.

Kellogg, Paul. "Social Movements and Trade Unions in an Age of Austerity: Reflections on Ontario's 1995–1998 'Days of Action.'" Presented at the Arts and Science Research Speakers Series, Edmonton: Athabasca University, March 2012 and at the Weighs Like a Nightmare: Ninth Annual Historical Materialism Conference, London: School of Oriental and African Studies, November 2012.

Kellogg, Paul. "The Defeat of Stephen Harper: A Case Study in Social Movement Electoralism." *Journal of Canadian Studies/Revue d'études canadiennes* 52, no. 3 (Fall 2018): 591–623.

Kellogg, Paul. "The Lost Voice of Iulii Martov." In *World Bolshevism*, by Iulii Martov, translated by Paul Kellogg and Mariya Melentyeva. Athabasca University Press, 2022.

Kellogg, Paul. *"Truth Behind Bars": Reflections on the Fate of the Russian Revolution.* Athabasca University Press, 2021.

Kellogg, Paul. "Twenty-Five Years Since Ontario's Common Sense Revolution: Revisiting the Political Economy of Austerity." Presented at the Canadian Political Science Association / Association canadienne de science politique (CPSA/ACSP), Virtual, June 10, 2021.

Kellogg, Paul. "Workers Against Austerity: Lessons from Canada's 'Days of Action,' 1995–1998." Presented at the Annual meetings of the British Sociological Association (BSA), Work, Economy and Society stream, London School of Economics, April 2011.

Kellogg, Paul. "Workers Versus Austerity: The Origins of Ontario's 1995–1998 'Days of Action.'" *Socialist Studies / Études Socialistes* 7, no. 1–2 (Spring/Fall 2011): 116–40. https://doi.org/10.18740/S4GK5Z.

Kinsman, Gary. "Open Letter in Support of the Democratic Right to Self-Determination for Quebec." Hartford Web Publishing, January 16, 2000. https://web.archive.org/web/20120318034142/http://www.hartford-hwp.com/archives/44/159.html.

Kuitenbrouwer, Peter. "Days of Factions." *Canadian Forum* 75 (January/February 1997): 14–18.

La Botz, Dan. "Ontario's 'Days of Action' – A Citywide Political Strike Offers a Potential Example for Madison." *Labor Notes*, March 9, 2011. http://www.labornotes.org/2011/03/ontarios-days-action-citywide-political-strike-offers-potential-example-madison.

Lavigne, Brad. *Building the Orange Wave: The Inside Story Behind the Historic Rise of Jack Layton and the NDP.* Douglas and McIntyre, 2013.

LUFA. "LUFA's History." 2020. https://lufappul.ca/wp/?page_id=687.

Luxemburg, Rosa. "The Mass Strike, the Political Party and the Trade Unions." In *The Rosa Luxemburg Reader*, edited by Peter Hudis and Kevin Anderson, translated by Patrick Lavan. Monthly Review Press, 2004.

Luxemburg, Rosa. "The Russian Revolution." In *The Rosa Luxemburg Reader*, edited by Peter Hudis and Kevin Anderson, translated by Bertram D. Wolfe. Monthly Review Press, 2004.

MacDermid, Robert, and Greg Albo. "Divided Province, Growing Protests: Ontario Moves Right." In *The Provincial State in Canada: Politics in the Provinces and Territories*, by Keith Brownsey and Michael Howlett. . University of Toronto Press, 2001.

McCartin, Joseph A. "Professional Air Traffic Controller Organization Strike (1981)." In *Encyclopedia of U.S. Labor and Working-Class History*, edited by Eric Arnesen. Taylor & Francis, 2007.

McDowell, Tom. *Neoliberal Parliamentarism: The Decline of Parliament at the Ontario Legislature.* University of Toronto Press, 2021.

Miliband, Ralph. "Class War Conservatism." *New Society* 52, no. 918 (1980): 278–80.

Ministry of Labour Ontario. "Table VI." In *Ontario Collective Bargaining Review.* Ministry of Labour. July-August, 1996.

Morgan, Anthony. "Populism and Racism in Two Ontario Elections." *The Monitor*, May 1, 2018. https://www.policyalternatives.ca/news-research/the-monitor-may-june-2018/.

Morrison, Toni. "Mourning for Whiteness." *New Yorker*, November 21, 2016.

Munro, Marcella. "Ontario's 'Days of Action' and Strategic Choices for the Left in Canada." *Studies in Political Economy* 53, no. 1 (1997): 125–40.

NDP.ca. "Wayne Marston," April 30, 2006. https://web.archive.org/web/20060430021039/http://waynemarston.ndp.ca/mpbio.

Nesbitt, Douglas. "Days of Action: Ontario's Extra-Parliamentary Opposition to the Common Sense Revolution, 1995–1998." PhD diss., Queen's University, 2018.

Office of the Premier Ontario. "41st Parliament of Ontario Passed Landmark Legislation to Increase Care, Create Opportunity and Build Ontario Up." May 8, 2018. https://news.ontario.ca/opo/en/2018/05/41st-parliament-of-ontario-passed-landmark-legislation-to-increase-care-create-opportunity-and-build.html.

Oliver, Jonathan, Isabel Oakeshott, and David Smith. "UK Prepares 'Doomsday' Cuts Plan." *Sunday Times* (London, UK), July 5, 2009, 19.

Ontario. "Committee Transcript 1992-Aug–27." Labour Relations and Employment Statute Law Amendment Act, 1992. Legislative Assembly of Ontario. Standing Committee on General Government, August 27, 1992.

Ontario. "Committee Transcript 1997-Aug–12." Workers' Compensation Reform Act, 1996, Bill 99. Legislative Assembly of Ontario. Standing Committee on General Government, August 12, 1997.

Ontario. "Committee Transcripts." Bill 26, Savings and Restructuring Act, 1995. Legislative Assembly of Ontario. Standing Committee on General Government. 36th Parliament, 1st Session, December 14, 1995.

Ontario. "Committee Transcripts – 1996-Jan-8 [Windsor 1]." Bill 26, Savings and Restructuring Act, 1995. Legislative Assembly of Ontario. Standing Committee on General Government, January 8, 1996.

Ontario. "Committee Transcripts – 1996-Jan-22 [Debate]." Bill 26, Savings and Restructuring Act, 1995. Legislative Assembly of Ontario. Standing Committee on General Government. 36th Parliament, 1st Session, January 22, 1996.

Ontario. "Committee Transcripts – 1997-08-06." Bill 96, Tenant Protection Act, 1996. Legislative Assembly of Ontario. Standing Committee on General Government, August 6, 1997.

Ontario. Employment Equity Act, 1993, S.O. 1993, c. 35. https://www.ontario.ca/laws/statute/93e35.

Ontario Federation of Labour. "Political Action and Ontario Labour." OFL 2nd Biennial Convention, Toronto, November 22, 1993.

"Ontario Labor Vows to Fight Tories." *Plant: Canada's Industrial Newspaper* 54, no. 18 (December 1995): 1–2.

Pan, Evelina. "Judith Mongrain." Thunder Bay, 2016. https://web.archive.org/web/20160210162845/http://www.thunderbay.ca/City_Government

/City_Records_and_Archives/Web_Exhibits/Women_s_History_Month /Judith_Mongrain_profile.htm.

Panitch, Leo, and Donald Swartz. *From Consent to Coercion: The Assault on Trade Union Freedoms*. 3rd ed. Garamond Press, 2003.

Paolone, Victor J. "NDP-Labour Relations: Crises and Challenges in the 1990s." Master's thesis, Department of Political Science, University of Windsor, 1995.

Parliament of Canada. "Elections and Candidates." Parlinfo, October 11, 2021. https://lop.parl.ca/sites/ParlInfo/default/en_CA/ElectionsRidings /Elections.

Rachlis, Chuck, and David Wolfe. "An Insiders' View of the NDP Government of Ontario: The Politics of Permanent Opposition Meets the Economics of Permanent Recession." In *The Government and Politics of Ontario*, edited by Graham White. University of Toronto Press, 1997.

Ralph, Diana S., and André Régimbald, eds. *Open for Business, Closed to People: Mike Harris's Ontario*. Fernwood, 1997.

Rapaport, David. *No Justice, No Peace: The 1996 OPSEU Strike Against the Harris Government in Ontario*. McGill-Queen's Press, 1999.

Rayside, David M. *On the Fringe: Gays and Lesbians in Politics*. Cornell University Press, 2018.

Reshef, Yonatan, and Sandra Rastin. "Sins of Commission and Sins of Omission: The Ontario Days of Action and Missed Opportunities in Alberta." In *Unions in the Time of Revolution: Government Restructuring in Alberta and Ontario*. University of Toronto Press, 2003.

Reshef, Yonatan, and Sandra Rastin. *Unions in the Time of Revolution: Government Restructuring in Alberta and Ontario*. University of Toronto Press, 2003.

"Rethinking Our Mission in Ontario: A Discussion Paper for Union Leaders." August 1994 NDP renewal conference, November 1, 1993. https://www .rankandfile.ca/wp-content/uploads/2018/01/Rethinking-our-mission-in -Ontario-1993-aka-Pink-Paper.pdf.

Rosenthal, Ron. *Where Is CUPE Going? Lessons of the 1981 Ontario Hospital Strike*. Workers' Action Books, 1981.

Royal Commission on Labour. "Report on the Labour Question in Newfoundland and the Dominion of Canada." In *The Colonies and the Indian Empire*, Vol. 2, *Foreign Reports*. Her Majesty's Stationery Office, 1892. https://archive.org/details/royalcommissiono0042grea/page/76/mode /2up?q=Cornwall.

Ryan, Sid. *A Grander Vision: My Life in the Labour Movement*. Dundurn, 2019.

Savage, Larry. "Organized Labour and the Politics of Strategic Voting." In *Rethinking the Politics of Labour in Canada. Labour in Canada 1*, edited by Stephanie Ross and Larry Savage. Fernwood, 2012.

Savage, Larry. "The Politics of Labour and Labour Relations in Ontario." In *The Politics of Ontario*, edited by Cheryl N. Collier and Jonathan Malloy. University of Toronto Press, 2017.

Savage, Larry. *Socialist Cowboy*. Roseway Publishing, 2014

Schwarz, Salomon. *Lénine et le mouvement syndical*. Éditions "Nouveau Prométhée," 1935.

Scheinberg, Ellen. "The Tale of Tessie the Textile Worker: Female Textile Workers in Cornwall During World War II." *Labour/Le Travail* 33 (1994): 153–86.

Senate of Canada. "The Health of Canadians – The Federal Role: Volume One – The Story So Far." Standing Senate Committee on Social Affairs, Science and Technology (37th Parliament, 1st Session), March 2001. https://publications.gc.ca/Collection/YC17-371-1-01E.pdf.

Simon & Garfunkel. "The Sound of Silence," track 1 on *Sounds of Silence*. Vinyl. Columbia Studios, 1966.

Statistics Canada. "Table 510026: Estimates of Population, by Age Group and Sex, Canada, Provinces and Territories, Annually (Persons Unless Specified)." CANSIM (database). Using CHASS (distributor), February 19, 2000.

Statistics Canada. "Table 18100004: Consumer Price Index, monthly, not seasonally adjusted, monthly." CANSIM (database). Using CHASS (distributor), April 15, 2025.

Statistics Canada. "Table 1830002: Public Sector Employment, Wages and Salaries, Seasonally Unadjusted and Adjusted, Monthly." CANSIM (database). Using CHASS (distributor), May 30, 2012.

Statistics Canada. "Table 2820001 V2091177: Canada; Unemployment Rate (Rate); Both Sexes; 15 Years and over (Jan-1976 to Aug-2013, Data: 435)." CANSIM (database). Using CHASS (distributor), September 7, 2018.

Statistics Canada. "Table 2820087: Labour Force Survey Estimates (LFS), by Sex and Age Group, Seasonally Adjusted and Unadjusted, Monthly (Persons Unless Specified)." CANSIM (database). Using CHASS (distributor), June 10, 2016.

Statistics Canada. "Table 3260020: Consumer Price Index, Monthly (2002=100 Unless Specified)." CANSIM (database). Using CHASS (distributor), November 16, 2022.

Statistics Canada. "Table 14100284 – Person-Days Not Worked in Canada as a Result of Work Stoppages, by Industry, Monthly (Number)." CANSIM (database). Using CHASS (distributor), February 11, 2016.

Statistics Canada. "Table 17100005 – Population Estimates on July 1st, by Age and Sex, Annually." CANSIM (database). Using CHASS (distributor), September 28, 2022.

Statistics Canada. "Table 17100027 – Estimates of Population, Canada, Provinces and Territories, Annually (Persons)." CANSIM (database). Using CHASS (distributor), February 18, 2000.

Statistics Canada. "Table 17100029 – Estimates of Population, by Age Group and Sex, Canada, Provinces and Territories, Annually." CANSIM (database). Using CHASS (distributor), February 19, 2000.

Tanguay, A. Brian. "'Not in Ontario!' From the Social Contract to the Common Sense Revolution." In *Revolution at Queen's Park: Essays on Governing Ontario*, edited by Sid Noel. James Lorimer, 1997.

The Clash. *London Calling*. Vinyl. Columbia, 1979.

The Dream Academy. *Life in a Northern Town*. Vinyl. Warner Bros., 1985.

Thompson, E.P. *The Making of the English Working Class*. Penguin Books, 1963.

Tosstorff, Reiner. *The Red International of Labour Unions (RILU) 1920–1937*. Translated by Ben Fowkes. Brill, 2016.

"Toward the Renewal of Social Democracy in Canada." CLC/NDP review committee, Toronto, August 31, 1995.

Turk, James L. "Days of Action: Challenging the Harris Corporate Agenda." In *Open for Business, Closed to People: Mike Harris's Ontario*, edited by Diana S. Ralph, André Régimbald, and Nérée St-Amand. Fernwood, 1997.

UK. "Historical Coal Data: Coal Production, Availability and Consumption." Department for Business, Energy & Industrial Strategy, July 25, 2019. https://www.gov.uk/government/statistical-data-sets/historical-coal-data-coal-production-availability-and-consumption.

Walchuk, Bradley. "Changing Union-Party Relations in Canada: The Rise of the Working Families Coalition." *Labor Studies Journal* 35, no. 1 (2010): 27–50.

Walkom, Thomas. *Rae Days: The Rise and Follies of the NDP*. Key Porter Books, 2002.

Walkom, Thomas. "The Harris Government: Restoration or Revolution?" In *The Government and Politics of Ontario*, edited by Graham White. University of Toronto Press, 1997.

Warnock, John. "The Waffle: Lessons to Build On." *Briarpatch* 18, no. 7 (September 1989): 10–15.

Watson, Stephen. "Ontario Workers Take On the 'Common Sense Revolution.'" In *Open for Business, Closed to People: Mike Harris's Ontario*, edited by Diana S. Ralph, André Régimbald, and Nérée St-Amand. Fernwood, 1997.

White, Michael. "Taking an Axe to Public Spending the Canadian Way." *Guardian* (London, UK), July 8, 2009, 8.

Wilson-Smith, Anthony, and Mary Janigan. "Harris Under Siege: Teachers Lead a Labor Uprising in Ontario." *Maclean's* 110, no. 45 (November, 1997): 12.

York University. "F0225 – Reg Whitaker Fonds," May 15, 2003. http://archivesfa.library.yorku.ca/fonds/ON00370-f0000225.htm.

Ziedenberg, Jason. "A Great Day in Hamilton: A Personal Notebook." *Canadian Dimension* 30, no. 1 (May 1996): 17–20.

Ziedenberg, Jason. "Labour's Dirty Secret: They're Voting Conservative, and Hotly Oppose Affirmative Action." *This Magazine* 30, no. 3 (November-December 1996): 16–21.

Ziedenberg, Jason. "The Counter Revolution: Is Mike Harris Helping Regenerate the Ontario Left?" *Canadian Dimension* 30, no. 2 (April 1996): 6–8.

Ziedenberg, Jason. "The Metro Toronto Days of Action: The Hogtown Shutdown." *Canadian Dimension* 31, no. 1 (January-February 1997): 8–11.

Index